Botnet Detection
Countering the Largest Security Threat

Advances in Information Security

Sushil Jajodia
Consulting Editor
Center for Secure Information Systems
George Mason University
Fairfax, VA 22030-4444
email: jajodia@gmu.edu

The goals of the Springer International Series on ADVANCES IN INFORMATION SECURITY are, one, to establish the state of the art of, and set the course for future research in information security and, two, to serve as a central reference source for advanced and timely topics in information security research and development. The scope of this series includes all aspects of computer and network security and related areas such as fault tolerance and software assurance.

ADVANCES IN INFORMATION SECURITY aims to publish thorough and cohesive overviews of specific topics in information security, as well as works that are larger in scope or that contain more detailed background information than can be accommodated in shorter survey articles. The series also serves as a forum for topics that may not have reached a level of maturity to warrant a comprehensive textbook treatment.

Researchers, as well as developers, are encouraged to contact Professor Sushil Jajodia with ideas for books under this series.

Additional titles in the series:

PRIVACY-RESPECTING INTRUSION DETECTION by Ulrich Flegel; ISBN: 978-0-387-68254-9

SYNCHRONIZING INTERNET PROTOCOL SECURITY (SIPSec) by Charles A. Shoniregun; ISBN: 978-0-387-32724-2

SECURE DATA MANAGEMENT IN DECENTRALIZED SYSTEMS edited by Ting Yu and Sushil Jajodia; ISBN: 978-0-387-27694-6

NETWORK SECURITY POLICIES AND PROCEDURES by Douglas W. Frye; ISBN: 0-387-30937-3

DATA WAREHOUSING AND DATA MINING TECHNIQUES FOR CYBER SECURITY by Anoop Singhal; ISBN: 978-0-387-26409-7

SECURE LOCALIZATION AND TIME SYNCHRONIZATION FOR WIRELESS SENSOR AND AD HOC NETWORKS edited by Radha Poovendran, Cliff Wang, and Sumit Roy; ISBN: 0-387-32721-5

PRESERVING PRIVACY IN ON-LINE ANALYTICAL PROCESSING (OLAP) by Lingyu Wang, Sushil Jajodia and Duminda Wijesekera; ISBN: 978-0-387-46273-8

SECURITY FOR WIRELESS SENSOR NETWORKS by Donggang Liu and Peng Ning; ISBN: 978-0-387-32723-5

MALWARE DETECTION edited by Somesh Jha, Cliff Wang, Mihai Christodorescu, Dawn Song, and Douglas Maughan; ISBN: 978-0-387-32720-4

ELECTRONIC POSTAGE SYSTEMS: Technology, Security, Economics by Gerrit Bleumer; ISBN: 978-0-387-29313-2

Additional information about this series can be obtained from
http://www.springer.com

We wish to thank the generous financial support from the U.S. Army Research Office that made it possible to run the Botnet workshop and publish this book.

Atlanta, GA   *Wenke Lee*
Research Triangle Park, NC   *Cliff Wang*
August 2007   *David Dagon*

Contents

List of Contributors

John Bambenek
University of Illinois at Urbana-
Champaign
Urbana, IL 61801
bambenek@uiuc.edu

David Brumley
Carnegie Mellon University
5000 Forbes Avenue
Pittsburgh, PA 15213
dbrumley@cmu.edu

Yan Chen
Northwestern University
Evanston, IL 60208
ychen@cs.northwestern.edu

David Dagon
266 Ferst Drive
Georgia Institute of Technology
Atlanta, GA 30332
dagon@cc.gatech.edu

Nick Feamster
266 Ferst Drive
Georgia Institute of Technology
Atlanta, GA 30332
feamster@cc.gatech.edu

Jason Franklin
5000 Forbes Avenue
Carnegie Mellon University
Pittsburgh, PA 15213
jfrankli@cs.cmu.edu

Anup Goyal
Northwestern University
Evanston, IL 60208
gao210@cs.northwestern.edu

Guofei Gu
266 Ferst Drive
Georgia Institute of Technology
Atlanta, GA 30332
guofei@cc.gatech.edu

Cody Hartwig
Carnegie Mellon University
5000 Forbes Avenue
Pittsburgh, PA 15213
chartwig@cmu.edu

Agnes Klus
University of Illinois at Urbana-
Champaign
Urbana, IL 61801
aklus@uiuc.edu

David Lapsely
BBN Technologies
Cambridge, MA 02138
dlapsely@bbn.com

Christopher P. Lee
266 Ferst Drive
Georgia Institute of Technology
Atlanta, GA 30332
chrislee@gatech.edu

Zhichun Li
Northwestern University
Evanston, IL 60208
lizc@cs.northwestern.edu

Zhenkai Liang
Carnegie Mellon University
5000 Forbes Avenue
Pittsburgh, PA 15213
zliang@cmu.edu

Carl Livadas
Intel Research
Santa Clara, CA 95054
carlx.livadas@intel.com

Mark Luk
5000 Forbes Avenue
Carnegie Mellon University
Pittsburgh, PA 15213
mluk@cmu.edu

Jonathan M. McCune
5000 Forbes Avenue
Carnegie Mellon University
Pittsburgh, PA 15213
jonmccune@cmu.edu

John C. Mitchell
Stanford University
Stanford, CA 94305
mitchell@cs.stanford.edu

James Newsome
Carnegie Mellon University
5000 Forbes Avenue
Pittsburgh, PA 15213
jnewsome@cmu.edu

Adrian Perrig
5000 Forbes Avenue
Carnegie Mellon University
Pittsburgh, PA 15213
perrig@cmu.edu

Anirudh Ramachandran
266 Ferst Drive
Georgia Institute of Technology
Atlanta, GA 30332
avr@cc.gatech.edu

Arvind Seshadri
5000 Forbes Avenue
Carnegie Mellon University
Pittsburgh, PA 15213
arvinds@cs.cmu.edu

Dawn Song
Carnegie Mellon University
5000 Forbes Avenue
Pittsburgh, PA 15213
dawnsong@cmu.edu

Elizabeth Stinson
Stanford University
Stanford, CA 94305
stinson@cs.stanford.edu

W. Timothy Strayer
BBN Technologies
Cambridge, MA 02138
strayer@bbn.com

Leendert van Doorn
Advanced Micro Devices
Austin, TX 78741
Leendert.vanDoorn@amd.com

Robert Walsh
BBN Technologies
Cambridge, MA 02138
rwalsh@bbn.com

Heng Yin
Carnegie Mellon University
5000 Forbes Avenue
Pittsburgh, PA 15213
hyin@cmu.edu

Botnet Detection Based on Network Behavior

W. Timothy Strayer[1], David Lapsely[1], Robert Walsh[1], and Carl Livadas[2]

[1] BBN Technologies, Cambridge, MA 02138
   `strayer|dlapsely|rwalsh@bbn.com`
[2] Intel Research, Santa Clara, CA 95054
   `carlx.livadas@intel.com`

Current techniques for detecting botnets examine traffic content for IRC commands, monitor DNS for strange usage, or set up honeynets to capture live bots. Our botnet detection approach is to examine *flow characteristics* such as bandwidth, packet timing, and burst duration for evidence of botnet command and control activity. We have constructed an architecture that first eliminates traffic that is unlikely to be a part of a botnet, classifies the remaining traffic into a group that is likely to be part of a botnet, then correlates the likely traffic to find common communications patterns that would suggest the activity of a botnet. Our results show that botnet evidence can be extracted from a traffic trace containing over 1.3 million flows.

1 Introduction

Botnets are one of the most dangerous species of network-based attack today because they involve the use of very large, coordinated groups of hosts for both brute-force and subtle attacks. These large groups of hosts are assembled by turning vulnerable hosts into so-called *zombies*, or *bots*, after which they can be controlled from afar. A collection of bots, when controlled by a single command and control (C2) infrastructure, form what is called a *botnet*. Botnets obfuscate the attacking host by providing a level of indirection — the attack host is separated from its victim by the layer of zombie hosts, and the attack itself is separated from the assembly of the botnet by an arbitrary amount of time.

Botnets derive their power by scale, both in their cumulative bandwidth and in their reach. Botnets can cause severe network disruptions through massive distributed denial-of-service attacks, and the threat of this disruption can cost enterprises large sums in extortion fees. They are responsible for a vast majority of the spam on the Internet today. Botnets are also used to harvest personal, corporate, or government sensitive information for sale on a thriving organized crime market. They are a reusable and renewable resource.

Governments are taking the threat of botnets seriously. In August 2005, Britain's NISCC (National Infrastructure Security Coordination Centre, the UK equivalent to US-CERT) issued a warning about the increase in trojan activity targeting UK government networks, stating that "the attacker's aim appears to be covert gathering and transmitting of commercially or economically valuable information" [22]. In November 2005, the discovery of a botnet in US Department of Defense [32] caused the head of DoD networks to issue an "information assurance standdown," followed by a full sweep of all DoD networks [5].

Efforts are underway to quantify the botnet problem, detect the presence of botnets, and design defenses against attacks by botnets. In academia, for example, Ramachandran *et al.* have been studying the effectiveness of monitoring queries to DNS blackhole lists to find bot masters looking to see if their bots have been blacklisted [23]. Dagon *et al.* use diurnal models to compare the propagation rate for different botnets [4]. Karasaridis *et al.* use suspicious host activity reports (scanning ports, emailing spam and virus, generating DDoS traffic) as indicators of flows to analyze [14]. And Kandula *et al.* suggest ways for websites and other services to thwart bot and other mechanical agents by using Turing tests [13].

Non-profit and volunteer organizations are involved. The Honeynet Project [31], for example, has done extensive work on capturing live bots and characterizing botnet activities, and a group of white-hat vigilantes is scouring the Internet looking for evidence of botnets [21]. Industry and federally funded centers are also active: Symantec publishes a semi-annual *Internet Security Threat Report* [30] identifying trends in attack mechanisms, and CERT maintains a Vulnerability Notes Database [1] with information on botnet and other attack vectors.

Determining the source of a botnet-based attack is a particular challenge. First, there is a distinction between the attack and the attack mechanism. For single-flow [26] and "stepping stone" chained-flow [37] attacks, the flow is both the mechanism and the attack, but for botnets, the mechanism (the botnet) is constructed and maintained independently of how it is used. Second, there is a difference in what constitutes the "attack origin." Tracing flow-based attacks attempts to yield a single responsible host; with botnets, every zombie host is an attacker. Finally, most flow-based traceback systems adopt a reactive approach to attacks; the tracing of packets back to their origin hosts is triggered after an attack is detected. Botnets can exist in a benign state for an arbitrary amount of time before they are used for a specific attack, affording some opportunity to identify them prior to the attack.

We are interested in botnets with tight command and control infrastructures, as shown in Figure 1. IRC is the most common botnet C2 mechanism [10, 11, 16, 18, 19, 31] because it is scalable and easy to hide within. While instances of botnets with looser control structures, such as those that use peer-to-peer networks, are increasing, IRC-style C2 is still the most prevalent because it is scalable and provides instantaneous control over the bots.

In botnets that use the chat style of command and control, the attacker issues commands to the zombie hosts via a "rendezvous point," which is usually an IRC server. The rendezvous point may or may not be a compromised machine — there are many public IRC servers that host unmonitored channels. The attacker and the zombie hosts subscribe to the same IRC channel. The attacker issues commands and the bots respond through that channel.

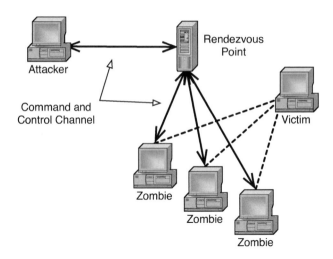

Fig. 1. Actors in IRC-Based Botnet Architecture

This chapter presents a system for detecting the presence of a botnet and identifying the rendezvous point using passive traffic analysis. (Some initial results were presented in [29].) Our goal is to determine if we can find evidence of botnet activity by only monitoring network traffic, and not by examining the traffic content, relying on port numbers (IRC's is 6667), or by watching DNS servers. We adopt a proactive approach by identifying hosts that are likely part of a botnet *before an attack* by extracting and analyzing flow characteristics that seem to match botnet C2 traffic.

Our technique employs a pipeline of increasingly more complex analyzers, filtering out unlikely flows along each step, so that the most computationally intensive analysis is done on a dramatically reduced traffic set. First, individual flows are subjected to a series of filters and classifiers to eliminate as many of the flows as possible, while being somewhat conservative so that botnet flows are not likely to be eliminated. Next, the flows are correlated with each other, looking for groups of flows that may be related by being part of the same botnet. Finally, the topological information in the correlated flows is examined for the presence of a common communication hub.

2 Approach

Since the vast majority of botnets are controlled using variations on IRC bots, many botnet detection systems begin by simply looking for chat sessions (TCP port 6667) [12], and then examining the content for botnet commands [2]. Like many client-server protocols, however, the use of a standard port number is largely just a suggestion. Also, relying on having access to the packet contents and, even with that access, being able to identify botnet commands, is an overly simplistic assumption.

Our system assumes only that the botnet command and control (C2) infrastructure is based loosely on IRC.

2.1 Characterization of IRC-based C2 Flows

IRC-based botnets currently dominate as the preferred deployment technique. This reflects the freely available bot-building source code, allowing attackers to focus on botnet applications rather than on architecting and coding "mere plumbing." IRC is implemented through text-based interactions. Strings are sent to the chat server, which replicates that data to each client. In the case of botnets, the clients are zombies, and botnet commands are special strings.

We use chat traffic as an initial proxy for botnet C2 traffic. By looking at example botnet commands [31], the important insight is that C2 messages are brief in addition to being text-based. In the absence of access to extensive botnet traces, we characterize chat flows to identify how we can separate the C2 channel from other Internet traffic.

Specifically, there are four notable points. First, identification of chat is a statistical problem. For each attribute of a flow, chat flows are spread across the spectrum of values. Instead of a deterministic decision, one is left with a probabilistic conclusion, complete with the risk of false positives and false negatives.

Second, identification of chat in the absence of well-known ports and access to the packet content is a difficult problem. Flows can be winnowed into likely chat and likely non-chat classifications, but the likely chat classification will certainly include a number of non-chat flows.

Third, consideration of attributes in isolation is a good start, but is not sufficient — it is equivalent to using independent probabilities to evaluate the traffic. Stronger techniques based upon interdependent conditional probabilities may be needed as well.

Finally, the resulting characterization is good for guiding the construction of efficient filters for data reduction. By reducing the data set, even if it contains some false positives, later steps can take advantage of more computationally intensive approaches.

2.2 The Processing Pipeline

Figure 2 shows our traffic-processing pipeline. Packet traces (in our case these are recorded traces, but there is no reason the input cannot be live) are fed into a series of quick reduction filters. With some *a priori* knowledge, one can also imagine a set of white lists and black lists based on known good sites (packets to or from eBay, for example, are very unlikely to be part of a botnet) and bad sites (those places on a watch list, for example). Other filters examine simple flow attributions such as duration or average packet size.

After the initial filters, the remaining flows are passed through a flow classification engine based on machine learning techniques. The classifiers attempt to group

Packet Traces

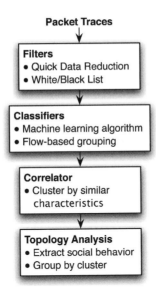

Fig. 2. Botnet Detection Processing Pipeline

flows into broadly defined categories. Those flows that appear to have chat-like characteristics are passed on to the correlator stage.

The correlator does a pairwise examination of the remaining flows looking for flows that are behaving in a similar manner, as one might expect of two flows generated by the same application. Botnets are so large that commands are issued to the whole group, or large subgroups, and not to individuals. Flows that are correlated are passed on to topological analysis, where "social topology" is applied to determine which flows share a common controller.

The result of this pipeline is a (hopefully) small set of flows that show a fair amount of evidence that they are related and are part of a botnet. The pipeline does not prove the flows are part of a botnet; rather, the flows that survive strongly suggest closer examination. This examination may be deep, if there is access to the hosts that are the flow endpoints, as may happen in an enterprise or campus, or the examination may be limited to listing the flows and the flow endpoints in a watch list for later use if a botnet-based attack occurs. Knowing the social structure of a group of hosts prior to an attack is better than trying to piece the structure together during the attack.

2.3 Source of Background Traffic

It would be too contrived to try to create a large dataset of both background and botnet traffic using a tightly controlled testbed. Instead, we incorporated a background traffic data set recorded from true Internet use. We chose packet traces collected on the Dartmouth campus under their CRAWDAD project [15]. The traces are a complete set of TCP/IP headers from the campus wireless, taken over a period of four months (November 1, 2003 to February 28, 2004) from a variety of campus locations. No payloads were included in the trace.

In all, the traces were 164 GBytes compressed, and approximately 3.8 times that amount when uncompressed. This large trace set means that we truly are looking for the needle (botnet C2 flows) in a haystack.

From this set of traces, we selected a subset of traces that corresponded to a particular building that we shall label "Building X." We believed the traces from Building X to be representative of "typical" Internet background traffic for our botnet scenario. We then selected a reference time point of Monday November 10, 14:30 EST, 2003 as the time at which we would attempt to detect our synthesized botnet (the needle) in the presence of this background traffic (the haystack). Our detection process examined all of the uni-directional flows of data between hosts from the start of the Building X traces on Monday November 1, 2003 at 23:12 EST until just after our reference time point on Monday November 10, 2003 at 14:30 EST. In total, 1.34 million uni-directional data flows were examined.

2.4 Source of Botnet Traces

In order to generate traffic that was representative of real botnet traffic, we implemented a benign bot based on the "Kaiten" bot, a widespread bot that has readily downloadable source code. The Kaiten bot was implemented in C using approximately 1000 lines of code. We reverse engineered the Kaiten code and then reimplemented it.

The original Kaiten bot had a repertoire of TCP- and UDP-based attacks. Our bot implementation does not implement these attacks. Like the Kaiten bot, our bot provides a number of remotely controlled features, including a mechanism to execute arbitrary commands on the bot client, HTTP download capability, a flexible multiprocess architecture, a highly configurable architecture and a rich command set.

In order to obtain traces of actual botnet traffic, we constructed a botnet testbed within BBN's production network. Our setup consisted of an IRC server (rendezvous point), a code server, 10 zombie hosts, and an attacker. Figure 3 shows the topology of our botnet testbed. The attacker, the rendezvous point, and one zombie host reside on an external network. Nine zombies and the victim were hosted within the BBN network. The code server was a large well known public Internet site.

We used this test facility to obtain actual traces of the communications between the various botnet entities while the botnet was in operation. Our experiments entailed using the IRC server to instruct the zombies to download attack code from the code server and to subsequently launch a coordinated TCP "attack" on the victim host. The traces collected involved *ssh* transmissions used for setting up and monitoring the experiments, IRC traffic between the bots and the IRC server, *http* traffic between the zombies and the code server (for downloading the attack code), and the TCP traffic involved in the coordinated TCP attack on the victim host. The setup and the launch of the attack were successively repeated in order to increase the amount of trace data collected.

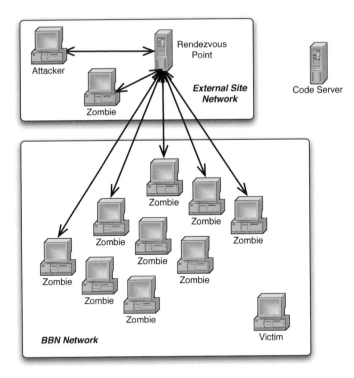

Fig. 3. Botnet Trace Collection Testbed

We collected 539 flows associated with our botnet using tcpdump at the IRC server. Forty two of these flows were C2 flows. We merged this botnet trace with the Dartmouth traffic data set in order to create a test data set that contained ground truth that could be verified after all of the data reduction filters and other analyzers have been applied. Our botnet was active on the order of hours, while the Dartmouth traces span four months, exacerbating the vast size difference between the needle and the haystack.

3 Filtering Stage

We recognize that the statistical nature of the problem creates a trade-off between keeping as many botnet C2 flows as possible and reduction of the data set to the meaningful subset of flows to speed later steps. The selection of the cutoff for quick filtering for data reduction requires both quantitative statistical information and human judgment. Even if the selection of the cutoff were phrased in terms of meeting a false positive or a false negative goal, that goal is based upon judgment. The filters and filter parameters we chose reflect this.

Packet Traces

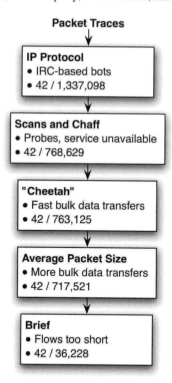

Fig. 4. Filtering Out Flows Not Likely Part of a Botnet

There were five distinct filters in this stage, as shown in Figure 4. The first filtered by IP protocol to select TCP-based flows, resulting in 1,337,098 flows. Since the bot was derived from an IRC-style TCP base, all of the ground-truth botnet C2 flows were TCP based. All of the C2 flows survived this filter.

The second filter removed the nuisance port-scanning chaff, reducing the data set to 786,629 flows. Flows containing only TCP packets with SYN or RST flags indicate that communication was never established, and so provide no information about chat or botnet C2 flows. No application-level data was transferred by these flows. Unfortunately for today's Internet, probes of system vulnerabilities are commonplace. While SYN-RST exchanges indicate suspicious activity that may be worth investigation, they do not assist with characterizing botnet C2 flows. About 43% of the flows are eliminated by this step. Again, all of the ground-truth botnet C2 flows survived the filter.

Since botnets do not sustain bulk data transfers, the next filter removed high bitrate flows. Peer-to-peer file sharing is a significant load on the Internet, and may take place on chat ports by coincidence (since the chat port is not reserved) or by intent (to avoid identification and filtering). Dropping bulk transfers (flow bandwidth greater than 8 Kb/s with at least 50 packets) also eliminates software updates and rich web page transfers. Yet, filtering the high bit-rate flows had a small effect. About

1% of the flows are dropped, leaving 763,125. From a flow perspective, this is a minor amount, but from a packet and forensic archive perspective this represents a worthwhile effort. Again, all of the bot C2 flows survived the filter.

Chat (and botnet C2 commands) generally generate small packets. Using a 300-byte packet size cutoff for the chat packets in the Dartmouth data set shows that about 0.25% of the chat traffic would be falsely rejected and 72% of the non-chat flows are eliminated. Since there are several orders of magnitude more non-chat flows than chat flows, filtering exclusively on average packet size would cut the amount of data to process in half; since this filter comes fourth, it has a relatively moderate effect. About 6% of the flows are dropped, leaving 717,521. All of the ground-truth botnet C2 flows survived the filter.

The fifth filter drops brief flows (less than 2 packets or 60 seconds) from consideration. Real chats and botnets are likely not well represented by excessively short duration flows. This filter has a significant effect, reducing the data by a factor of about 20, dominating even the elimination of the port-scanning activities. All of the ground-truth botnet C2 flows survived the filter.

Overall, the data set is reduced by a factor of about 37, from 1,337,098 TCP flows down to 36,228, while still preserving the ground-truth botnet C2 flows. This filtering stage avoided the use of TCP port numbers, and therefore is relevant to situations where applications may be masquerading on unexpected ports. Furthermore, this significant data reduction resulted without the use of white-listing services as trusted IP address and port number combinations.

4 Classifier Stage

Once the simple filters have reduced the data set, the next step is to process the data set using more sophisticated flow classification techniques. Several techniques have been developed to automatically identify (and often classify) various types of communication streams. Some use clues from the traffic content. Dewes *et al.* [6], for instance, proposed a scheme for identifying chat traffic that relies on a combination of discriminating criteria, including service port number, packet size distribution, and packet content. Sen *et al.* [25] used a signature-based scheme to discern traffic produced by several well-known P2P applications by identifying particular characteristics in the syntax of packet contents exchanged as part of the operation of the particular P2P applications.

Other flow classification approaches focus on the use of statistical techniques to characterize and classify traffic streams. Roughan *et al.* [24] used traffic classification for the purpose of identifying four major classes of service: interactive, bulk data transfer, streaming, and transactional. They investigated the effectiveness of using packet size and flow duration characteristics, and simple classification schemes were observed to produce very accurate traffic flow classification.

In a similar approach, Moore and Zuev [20] applied variants of the Naïve Bayesian classification scheme to classify flows into 10 distinct application groups. The authors also searched through the various traffic characteristics to identify those that are most effective at discriminating among the various traffic flow classes. By also identifying highly correlated traffic flow characteristics, this search was also effective in pruning the number of traffic flow characteristics used to discriminate among traffic flows. Highly correlated characteristics provide comparable and, often, redundant information about the traffic flows. Thus, in many cases it suffices to use only one of the correlated characteristics to discriminate among traffic flows.

Since IRC-type botnet C2 flows share many characteristics with normal IRC chat flows, we adopt and build upon the above statistical flow classification techniques to discriminate among IRC and non-IRC traffic (see Livadas *et al.* [17]). The focus on IRC traffic simplifies the training step because the default IRC port (namely, port 6667) can be used to accurately identify and label IRC traffic for training and ground truth.

We considered three machine learning classification algorithms, namely J48 decision trees (the WEKA [34] implementation of C4.5 decision trees [8]), Naïve Bayes, and Bayesian Networks, and evaluated the performance of each classifier using the false negative rate (FNR) and the false positive rate (FPR). The relative importance of each of these metrics depends on the ultimate use of the classification results. A low FNR attempts to minimize the fraction of the IRC flows will be discarded, while a low FPR attempts to minimize the amount of non-IRC flows included. We explored the effectiveness of these machine learning techniques along three dimensions: (1) the subset of characteristics/features used to describe the flows, (2) the classification scheme, and (3) the size of the training set size.

Table 1 summarizes the flow characteristics that we collected for each of the flows in the Dartmouth traces. The characteristics in the top of the table were not used for classification purposes — they either involve characteristics that seemed inconsequential in classifying flows, or are accumulated quantities, which are indirectly captured by the corresponding rates or percentages and the flow duration. Our experiments revealed that the following attributes have high discriminatory value: duration, role, average bytes per packet (Bpp), average bits per second (bps), and average packets per second (pps). Among these, the Bpp provided the most discriminatory power.

Figure 5 depicts the FNR vs. FPR scatter plot for several runs of J48, Naïve Bayes, and Bayesian Networks for the labeled Building X trace. Each data point corresponds to a different subset of the initial flow attribute set. The figure reveals clustering in the performance of each of three classification techniques. Naïve Bayes seems to have low FNR, but higher FPR. The Bayesian Networks technique seems to have low FPR, but higher FNR. J48 seems to strike a balance between FNR and FPR.

Only the Naïve Bayes classifiers were successful in achieving low FNR in the case of our botnet testbed IRC flows — notably, one of our Naïve Bayes classifiers accurately classified 41 out of the 42 botnet testbed IRC flows, thus achieving an FNR of 2.17%. In contrast, the J48 and the Bayesian Networks classifiers, possibly tuned too tightly to the training set, performed very poorly with FNRs of 28.26 and 19.57% respectively. However, while the Naïve Bayes classifiers had a low FNR, they also had a high FPR of 30.41%. Of the 36,136 non-botnet flows, 11,004 were

Table 1. Traffic Flow Characteristics

start/end	Flow start/end times
IP-proto	IP protocol of flow
TCP flags	Summary of TCP SYN/FIN/ACK flags
pkts	Total pkts exchanged in flow
Bytes	Total Bytes exchanged in flow
pushed pkts	Total packets pushed in flow
duration	Flow duration
maxwin	Maximum initial congestion window
role	Whether client or server initiated flow
Bpp	Average Bytes-per-packet for flow
bps	Average bits-per-second for flow
pps	Average packets-per-second for flow
PctPktsPushed	Percentage of packets pushed in flow
PctBppHistBin0–7	Percent of packets in one of eight packet size bins; these variables collectively form a histogram of packet size for flow
varIAT	Variance of packet inter-arrival time for flow
varBpp	Variance of Bytes-per-packet for flow

classified as belonging to the botnet. After training on the flows yielded from the earlier heuristic filtering stage, our best-performing classifiers achieved a 70% reduction in the number of candidate chat flows. Presuming that such performance would be routinely achievable in this stage, the 36K flows yielded from the heuristic filtering stage would be further reduced to 11K flows. In the case of the testbed flows, our best-performing classifiers retained 41 of the 42 chat flows.

Despite their promise, the training and performance of classifiers was quite sensitive to the flow attributes used, the training set, and the number of flows used for training. Thus, prior to their use in a deployable system we expect that further effort would be needed in order to identify the most beneficial flow characteristics and training set. For the processing of our testbed experiment, we bypassed the classification stage and proceeded directly from filtering to correlation.

5 Correlation Stage

The filters and classifiers have reduced the traffic data set from almost 1.34 million flows to about 36 thousand, but recall that these flows span a four-month period. Our next stage, correlation, looks for relationships between two or more flows that suggest that they are part of the same botnet. The question about whether one flow

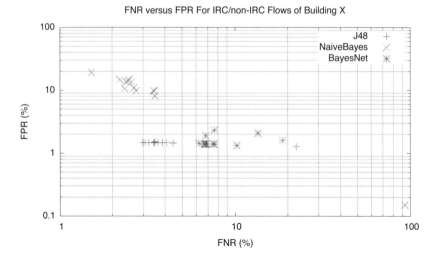

Fig. 5. FNR and FPR of J48, Naïve Bayes, and Bayesian Net Classification Schemes for IRC/non-IRC Flows of Building X

is correlated with another only makes sense if the two flows are active at the same time, so while we have four months of data, the correlation stage is run at a particular instance in time. The question is: Which flows are correlated at this moment?

We picked a time during the data when we knew the botnet was active. There were 95 post-filtered flows active at that time, where 20 of these flows were the ground-truth botnet C2 flows (a forward and a reverse flow from each of the 10 zombie hosts to the rendezvous point).

5.1 Flow Correlation

Two flows are said to be *correlated* when they exhibit one or more common properties. In general, there are three reasons that two flows exhibit common properties:

- They are the product of similar applications, such as those applications that transfer bulk data as quickly as possible
- There is a causal relationship, such as in remote logins or proxies, where an event on one flow causes an event to occur on another flow
- There is one transmitter and multiple receivers, such as in multicast, where one message is transmitted to many receivers

The first reason is a product of the nature of network protocols. TCP behaves the same no matter what application is driving it. If two applications present large files for transfer, there is little at the packet level to distinguish the traffic outside of the addressing information.

The second correlation reason speaks to the so-called stepping stone detection problem, where an attacker remotely logs into one host, then from there remotely logs into another host, repeating to form a chain of remote logins. The attacker sees the login shell of the last host, and anything typed in at the local keyboard cascades its way to the pseudo terminal at the last host. The cascading of the data is what provides the casual relationship among the flows in the chain.

The third reason for correlation happens because the same data is being sent to different receivers, so naturally the set of flows will show similar characteristics. Botnets that use IRC for the command and control channel essentially form multicast groups via a series of operations on unicast connections.

No matter the reason for correlation, any algorithm that sets out to determine which pairs of flow are correlated must begin with this question: What is a sufficient description scheme for flows so that the algorithm can determine if two flows are correlated under a particular meaning of correlation?

Flow Description

A flow is defined as a set of packets that belong to the same instance of communication between an application at a source host, and an application at a destination host. The most common way to identify a particular TCP or UDP flow is using a 5-tuple of values from the packets' layer 3 and 4 headers: the source and destination IP addresses, the source and destination port numbers, and the protocol identifier number. These five values definitively identify a particular instance of communication between a source host application and destination host application.

It is one thing to uniquely identify the flow; it is something all together different to uniquely describe a flow. Describing an object allows that object to be compared and contrasted with other objects. The same is true for flows. Choosing a certain set of characteristics and quantizing those characteristics provides one means of capturing describable aspects of the flow for comparison with other flows.

Certainly a flow can be completely described using a full packet trace, as one might get from a tool such as tcpdump. Such a trace lists when each packet event occurred, what was inside the packet's header, and what data each packet was carrying. Since a flow can be arbitrarily long, a packet trace can be arbitrarily long.

Packet trace files are a complete description, but they are not a compact one. It may be sufficient to extract and efficiently express a set of flow characteristics as a proxy for the full flow description.

Flow Characteristics

Flow characteristics fall into two categories: static characteristics that do not change over the lifetime of the flow, and dynamic characteristics that vary as the flow progresses through time. The immutable information kept in the IP and TCP/UDP headers of a packet is a good source of static characteristics. These include the values that form the flow identification 5-tuple — source and destination IP address, source and destination port numbers, and protocol. Flow start and stop times, and the flow's duration, are examples of static characteristics that are not carried in the packet.

Dynamic characteristics can also be drawn from the packet header and payload information, such as packet size values, flow control window settings, IPid values, protocol flag settings, and application data. Looking outside of the packet, dynamic characteristics include packet arrival and departure times. Further dynamic characteristics can be derived, such as throughput (amount of data transferred divided by the transfer duration), and burst times (groupings of packet arrivals or departures that are close in time).

Among the common dynamic flow characteristics that are easily expressed as a time series are:

- Packet event times
- Packet inter-arrival times
- Inter-burst times
- Bytes per packet
- Cumulative bytes per packet
- Bytes per burst
- Periodic throughput samples

Flow Correlation Algorithms

The most common flow correlation algorithms compare connections to see if they might be stepping stones — the causal relationship noted above. Our aim is to find correlations between flows based on a multicast relationship. We hypothesize that stepping stone correlation algorithms can be used to find botnets. Consequently, we will take a quick survey of stepping stone correlation algorithms looking for one that may be appropriate for our purposes.

Since traffic is often encrypted, flow correlation algorithms usually compare connections based on some characteristic other than packet content. Most correlation algorithms use only a single characteristic to describe packet flows. For example, an algorithm might describe a flow based on its packet inter-arrival times. Whatever the characteristic may be, it is chosen so that it can be used to identify related connections. These algorithms use the characteristic values as inputs into one or more functions that compare flows. The comparison function(s) create a metric used to decide if the flows are correlated. If the correlation between two flows is strong enough, one might decide that the flows are a stepping stone pair. Often, this decision is made by comparing the metric to a threshold.

Zhang and Paxon [37] describe a stepping stone detection method based on comparing the end times of "off periods," or idle times, in two data streams. The characteristics they focus on is the timing of the edge of bursts. Yoda and Etoh [35] describe an algorithm based on the difference between the average propagation delay and the minimum propagation delay between the two connections. Their flow characteristic is the round-trip time. Wang et al. [33] present a stepping stone identification scheme that uses similarity function over a vector of inter-packet delay measures (their flow characteristic) between two packet streams.

The aim of some approaches is to assert guaranteed false positive and negative rates under delay and chaff perturbations. Blum *et al.* [3] designed a stepping stone detection algorithm based on the deviation in the number of packets in each connection. Zhang *et al.* [36] propose three schemes that match packets from one flow to packets in a second flow to detect stepping stone connections. Both Blum and Zhang use packet counts as the flow characteristic. He and Tong [9] propose four packet counting (their flow characteristic) strategies — two algorithms based on bounded memory or bounded delay perturbation and chaff, and two algorithms that handle timing perturbation and chaff insertion simultaneously.

Strayer *et al.* [28] proposed a correlation algorithm that examines the causal relationship between packet events based on the assumption that, because networks attempt to operate efficiently, the likelihood of a transmission on one connection being a response to a prior receipt on another generally decreases as the elapsed time between them increases. Packet arrival time is the flow characteristic maintained here.

Donoho *et al.* [7] use character counts at different time scales, along with an assumption that there is a "maximum delay tolerance" to produce theoretical limits on the ability of attackers to disguise their traffic for sufficiently long connections.

Each of these techniques creates a time series of a certain flow characteristic and uses it to compare flow pairs. This implies a pairwise comparison over each value of the time series. It also means that the stepping stone detection algorithms rely heavily on the accuracy of series of one flow characteristic value.

Because of the one-to-many "multicasting" model of the C2 (and chat) architecture, we expect the communication flows between the botnet C2 host and the IRC server, and between the IRC server and the botnet members, to be temporally correlated. Since data sent to the chat server is promptly multicast to all chat members, the flows to (and from) all chat members should exhibit similar timing characteristics as well as contemporary fluctuations in bandwidth.

Any of the flow correlation algorithms based on temporal flow characteristics cited above could be applied to this stage, but they are each computationally expensive. These and most other current flow correlation algorithms examine each flow every time there is a new packet arrival, and every pairwise "correlation value" is updated. This implies $O(n^2)$ calculations for each packet, where n is the number of active flows. We prefer an algorithm that performs a calculation only once per packet arrival — to update that packet's flow value — delaying the $O(n^2)$ comparison until the time when flow correlation question was asked. We developed such an algorithm for use in stepping stone detection [27]. This algorithm uses multiple flow characteristics but remains efficient in per-flow correlation value updating.

5.2 Multi-Dimensional Flow Correlation

In constructing a new flow correlation algorithm, our first aim is to increase robustness by including more than one flow characteristic for comparison. Our second aim is to record the time series of the values of these characteristics more efficiently and eliminate the need for maintaining a full correlation matrix over all time. Let us look at the second aim first.

Time series are arbitrarily long time-value pairs that are not easy to manipulate. Statistical measures over the time series, however, attempt to describe the shape of the data in a finite space, and are much easier to manage. Taking the average, for example, describes an arbitrarily long series of values in one value, but at the loss of a lot of fidelity. Taking the second moment, the variance, gets some of that fidelity back by describing how different the values are from each other. Further moments describe the peakedness of the data (kurtosis) and the symmetry of the peaks (skew).

A nice aspect of using moments is that they can be estimated on the fly, and any new event causes the recalculation of the moments for that flow only. So a characteristic of a flow — say packet sizes — can be described by a small vector of statistical moments of that characteristic. This satisfies part of the second aim for efficient recording of the values for the flow characteristics.

If a single characteristic for a flow can be described using a small vector, then why not widen the vector to include statistical moments for other flow characteristics? Doing this would satisfy the first aim of including multiple characteristics in a flow correlation algorithm, but it does not suggest how to combine the multiple characteristics into a single comparison.

Our answer is to treat each flow's description vector as a point in n-space, where n is the cardinality of the vector, and apply a distance calculation as a measure of correlation, where nearness is more correlated. The distance does not have to be maintained for all flow pairs over all time, but calculated only when the correlation question is raised. This satisfies the second part of aim two.

Expressing a time series as a set of moments loses fidelity, which means that some unrelated flows with different time series of values over a particular characteristic might accidentally have the same moments over that time series. This is a matter of entropy; if there /indexentropy is not enough descriptive power in the vector, the flows cannot be adequately distinguished one flow from another, and false positives will occur. Our hypothesis is that, by adding more characteristics, the entropy is raised, mitigating the loss of fidelity of reducing any one characteristic to a vector of moments.

Determining the Characteristics

We have been abstractly discussing the use of multiple flow characteristics in a flow correlation algorithm, but determining which characteristics are most useful is the subject of studies and experiments. However, there are some useful features in a flow characteristic that might make one better suited than another.

First, the characteristic should be dynamic and expressed as a time series. Samples of the moments of a dynamic data set are themselves dynamic. Two flows that share this dynamic nature of the moments are likely to be correlated. If the moments remain static, then two uncorrelated flows with the same values will always show as a false positive.

Next, the characteristic should measure something about the flow that is imposed externally, not by the communications protocol. Since TCP/IP is probably the common transport, then characteristics imposed by TCP or IP will likely not discriminate between flows. Packet size is an example of a bad characteristic when the application gives TCP/IP a very large amount of data to send, but it is a good one when the application offers small amounts of data. Packet inter-arrival times and packet inter-burst times are similar.

Finally, for practical purposes, the characteristic should be easily measured. Throughput, for example, requires maintaining an amount of data seen over a window of time, while packet arrival times require no history.

Estimating the Moments

Since the time series values are arbitrarily long, and the are arriving in real time, we need to calculate the moments as a running estimate. The estimated weighted moving average (EWMA) is a nice way to estimate an average while weighting the influence of the past. The formula is: $newEWMA = \alpha(newValue) + (1-\alpha)(oldEWMA)$. We set α at 0.75 to emphasis new events while maintaining the smoothing effect of old events. The second moment, variance, is estimated in a similar fashion: $newVAR = \alpha(|newValue - EWMA|) + (1 - \alpha)(oldVAR)$. We do not use higher moments.

Calculating the Distance

We treat a flow's vector of characteristics as a point in n-space, and use a distance measure to determine correlation based on closeness. But values from different characteristics, and from different moments within each characteristic, have magnitudes that must be normalized before they can be used, otherwise characteristics with large values will artificially outweigh characteristics with smaller values. Further, some characteristics can have unbounded values.

Rather than normalize values and then use them to find the distance, it is better to normalize the difference. This way we maintain the natural meaning of the difference of v_1 and v_2, then fit that into a 0-to-1 scale.

One common normalizer is an exponential: $norm\_diff = 1^{e-\lambda}(|v_1 - v_2|)$, where λ is a weighting factor to determine how steeply the asymptote rises to 1. It makes sense that each characteristic would need a different λ, but if λ is set incorrectly, there will be too much or too little distinction between values of $v_1 - v_2$.

Instead, we use the following: $norm\_diff = (|v_1 - v_2|)/(v_1 + v_2)$. As v_2 approaches v_1 from below, the normalized difference drops off nearly linearly. As v_2 grows larger than v_1, the normalized difference grows asymptotically to 1. This normalizer is self-weighting and does not require special values such as λ.

The distance between two flows is calculated using the Euclidean formula of taking the square root of the sum of the squares of the differences:

$$distance = \sqrt{\sum_{i=1}^{n} (norm\_diff_i)^2}$$

where n is the number of values in the flow characteristics vector, and norm_diff$_i$ is the normalized difference of the ith value in the vector. Since each vector element difference is normalized to 1, the maximum distance is $\sqrt{n}$.

5.3 Correlation Results

Figures 6 and 7 display the results of pairwise distances between each of the 95 filtered flows. (Because the classification stage dropped some of the ground-truth botnet flows, we ran the correlation algorithm over the filtered, but not classified, flows.) Figure 6 clearly shows a horizontal band of flow pairs whose Euclidean distance is very small, separated by a band of white space up to distance of about 2. This indicates that a group of flows are clustered very near each other in n-space, and that there is a gap between that cluster and the next nearest flows.

Figure 7 also shows this gap in terms of a probability distribution of the distances. Note that there is a substantial spike near distance 0, then there is a flat area (no or few flow pairs) until distance 2. The spike is a cluster of flow pairs that are very close in distance. In fact, there are 9 flow pairs whose distance is less than 0.5, and it is this set that forms the cluster of interest.

The identification of clusters of correlated flows certainly suggest further investigation, which is the aim of the next stage, the topological analysis. This correlation stage does not prove the existence of a botnet — there is no test for maliciousness in the filtering, classifying, and clustering of flows — but given a cluster of flows, the natural next question is, What structure do these and other flows form, and does this structure identify a host that is acting like a botnet controller.

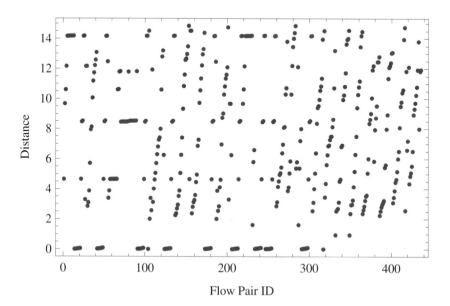

Fig. 6. Scatter Plot of Distances between Flow Pairs

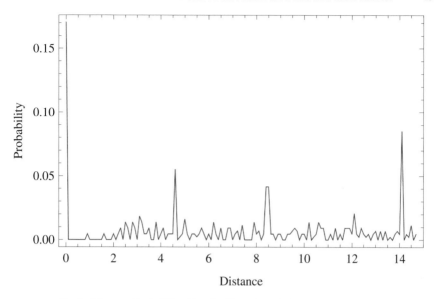

Fig. 7. Distance Probability Density Function of Flow Pair Distances

6 Topological Analysis Stage

The topological analysis starts by selecting only those flow pairs that are highly correlated. Figures 6 and 7 both show that there is a grouping of highly correlated flow pairs with distances close to 0. Our hypothesis is that these highly correlated flow pairs correspond to botnet C2 flows. We isolate these flow pairs by selecting only those flow pairs with a distance of less than 0.5. These flow pairs correspond to the top 17% most highly correlated flow pairs. On further investigation, we note that every one of these flow pairs corresponds to a C2 connection between a zombie host and the rendezvous point (IRC server), thus validating our hypothesis.

The next step in the topological analysis is to analyze the overall correlation structure of the correlated flow pairs. This process can be easily automated. Figure 8 shows a graph where each node corresponds to a unique flow pair identifier and each edge connects two highly correlated flow pairs. The graph shows a "perfect" or mesh clustering between the set of nine highly correlated flow pairs. This perfect clustering shows that each of the highly correlated flow pairs correlates with all of the other highly correlated flow pairs. In other words, the nine botnet C2 connections all correlate extremely well with each other. This again confirms our hypothesis.

The final step in the topological analysis is to determine the communication topology that corresponds to these highly correlated flow pairs and to identify which of the hosts, if any, is acting as a rendezvous point. This is a two part process that can be automated easily. First, we generate a graph that has as its edges the highly correlated flow pairs identified in the first step of the topological analysis and as its nodes the host IP addresses that correspond to the endpoints of these flow pairs. Second, we look for the node with the highest in-degree or out-degree and select that as

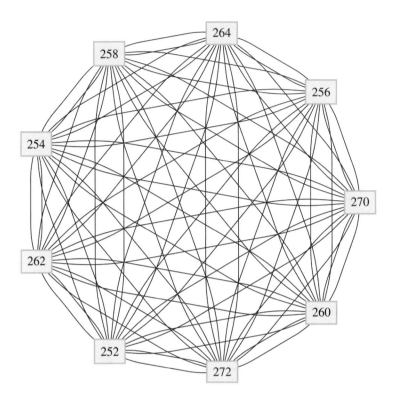

Fig. 8. Flow Pair Clustering

a candidate rendezvous point (IRC Server). Figure 9 shows a directed graph generated using the first part of this procedure (in this figure, IP addresses have been replaced by labels to identify the roles of the hosts). The communication structure of the botnet is immediately obvious from the figure and it is very easy to identify the rendezvous point as the node having the highest in-degree.

The topological analysis is able to identify nine out of the ten zombie hosts in our botnet. The nine zombies identified correspond to "local" zombies that are all located on machines in the same building at BBN (see Figure 3). The one zombie host not identified corresponds to a "remote" bot running on an offsite host. This result is perfectly understandable: we would not expect flows from a remote bot to correlate that well with flows from local bots as the difference in communication paths would almost always result in significant differences in flow characteristics.

In summary, the topological analysis stage examines the structure of highly correlated flow pairs. By constructing graphs of these correlated flow pairs, graphs of the corresponding node pairs and then looking for nodes with high in-degree, it is

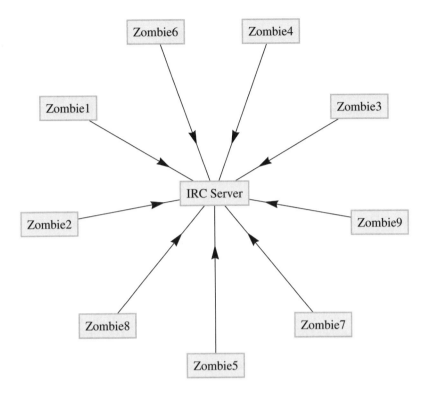

Fig. 9. Host-based Clustering

possible to identify the communication structure of our botnet, the rendezvous point and nine out of ten zombies. The results from topological analysis stage clearly supported our hypothesis that C2 botnet flows are highly correlated.

7 Discussion

While it has been suggested that botnet controllers will migrate from IRC as their preferred C2 infrastructure [25], the abstract model of tight central control represented by IRC is very efficient and will likely survive for quite some time. It is important, therefore, to consider a system that detects very large, high volume data sets for evidence of tight botnet C2 activity.

Our system performs gross, simple filtering to reduce the amount of data that will be subjected to more computationally intensive algorithms. Once the data has been filtered, the flows are classified using machine learning techniques, then the flows that are in the "chat" class are correlated to find clusters of flows that share similar timing and packet size characteristics. The cluster is then analyzed to try to identify the botnet controller host.

Our experiment with Dartmouth campus data, starting with nearly 9 million flows augmented with traffic traces from a benign botnet, shows that the ground truth botnet C2 flows can indeed survive the data reduction and correlation to be identified as a cluster. These results show that the method is promising.

This method is also nicely suited for real-time analysis of traffic data. The filtering stage requires very simple logic to cull the data set down by a factor of 37. While we may not be able to expect that degree of reduction in all cases, there was nothing particularly special about the Dartmouth data that contributed to the reduction factor. The culling of the data, especially when done in real time, allows much more time for more complex algorithms later in the pipe, namely the machine learning classifiers and the correlation.

An important lesson learned from our classification stage is the importance of both legitimate and malicious training traffic and an accurate manner to label it. Given such representative training traffic, machine learning-based classifiers can perform well and be very effective. The trick is to get a good training set.

Our experience with the new correlation algorithm showed that the algorithm holds promise. The algorithm we used is designed to reduce the computational complexity of comparing n flows in a pairwise manner. The resulting cluster, while not a complete set of flows from the ground truth botnet, was certainly enough to allow the topological analysis of the flow endpoints, and the rest of the ground-truth botnet traffic was easily extracted.

Detecting botnet activity is presently labor intensive and largely *ad hoc*. Our pipelined botnet C2 detection system shows that it is possible to comb through packet traces, even in real time, to extract evidence of tight command and control activity and, from that evidence, discover the botnet controller.

Acknowledgments

This work was sponsored by the U.S. Army Research Office under contract No. W911NF-05-C-0066. The content of the information does not necessarily reflect the position or the policy of the U.S. Government, and no official endorsement should be inferred.

The authors wish to thank Doug Maughan and Cliff Wang for their support, and Mark Allman for his valuable insights. We also thank David Kotz and gratefully acknowledge the use of wireless data from the CRAWDAD archive at Dartmouth College. We also wish to acknowledge the support and contributions of our colleagues at BBN Technologies: Christine Jones, Beverly Schwartz, Sarah Edwards, Walter Milliken, and Alden Jackson.

References

1. US-CERT Vulnerability Notes Database. http://www.kb.cert.org/vuls/.

2. Paul Barford and Vinod Yegneswaran. An inside look at botnets (to appear in series: Advances in information security, springer), 2006.
3. A. Blum, D. Song, and S. Venkataraman. Detection of interactive stepping stones: Algorithms and confidence bounds. In *Proceedings of the 7th International Symposium on Recent Advances in Intrusion Detection (RAID '04)*, September 2004.
4. David Dagon, Cliff Zou, and Wenke Lee. Modeling botnet propagation using time zones. In *Proceedings of the 13th Annual Network and Distributed System Security Symposium (NDSS '06)*, February 2006.
5. Defense Security Service. Memorandum for facility security officers: Foreign-based threat to defense contractor unclassified networks, October 18, 2005.
6. Christian Dewes, Arne Wichmann, and Anja Feldmann. An analysis of internet chat systems. In *IMC '03: Proceedings of the 3rd ACM SIGCOMM conference on Internet measurement*, pages 51–64, New York, NY, USA, 2003. ACM Press.
7. David L. Donoho, Ana Georgina Flesia, Umesh Shankar, Vern Paxson, Jason Coit, and Stuart Staniford. Multiscale stepping-stone detection: Detecting pairs of jittered interactive streams by exploiting maximum tolerable delay. In *Proc. International Symposium on Recent Advances in Intrusion Detection*, pages 17–35, October 2002.
8. Richard O. Duda, Peter E. Hart, and David G. Stork. *Pattern Classification*. John Wiley & Sons, Inc., 2 edition, 2001.
9. T. He and L. Tong. Detecting encrypted stepping-stone connections. *IEEE Transactions on Signal Processing*, 2007.
10. Thorsten Holz. A Short Visit to the Bot Zoo. *IEEE Security & Privacy*, 3(3):76–79, May 2005.
11. Kevin J. Houle and George M. Weaver. Trends in denial of service technology. CERT Coordination Center, October 2001.
12. A. Householder, Art Manion, Linda Pesante, George M. Weaver, and Rob Thomas. Managing the threat of denial-of-service attacks. CERT Coordination Center, October 2001.
13. S. Kandula, D. Katabi, M. Jacob, and A. Berger. Botz-4-sale: Surviving organized ddos attacks that mimic flash crowds. In *Proceedings of the 2nd Symposium on Networked Systems Design and Implementation*, May 2005.
14. Anestis Karasaridis, Brian Rexroad, and David Hoeflin. Wide-scale botnet detection and characterization. In *Proceedings of the First Workshop on Hot Topics in Understanding Botnets*, April 2007.
15. David Kotz and Tristan Henderson. CRAWDAD: A Community Resource for Archiving Wireless Data at Dartmouth. *IEEE Pervasive Computing*, 4(4), oct-dec 2006.
16. Elias Levy. The Making of a Spam Zombie Army. *IEEE Security & Privacy*, 1(4):58–59, July 2003.
17. Carl Livadas, Robert Walsh, David Lapsley, and W. Timothy Strayer. Using Machine Learning Techniques to Identify Botnet Traffic. In *Proceedings of the 2nd IEEE LCN Workshop on Network Security*, 2006.
18. Bill McCarty. Automated Identity Theft. *IEEE Security & Privacy*, 1(5):89–92, September 2003.
19. Bill McCarty. Botnets: Big and Bigger. *IEEE Security & Privacy*, 1(4):87–90, July 2003.
20. Andrew W. Moore and Denis Zuev. Internet traffic classification using bayesian analysis techniques. In *SIGMETRICS '05: Proceedings of the 2005 ACM SIGMETRICS international conference on Measurement and modeling of computer systems*, pages 50–60, New York, NY, USA, 2005. ACM Press.
21. R. Naraine. Botnet hunters search for 'command and control' servers. *eWeek*, June 17, 2005.

22. National Infrastructure Security Coordination Center. Targeted trojan email attacks. NISCC Briefing 08/2005, June 16, 2005.

23. Anirudh Ramachandran, Nick Feamster, and David Dagon. Revealing botnet membership using DNSBL counter-intelligence. In *Proceedings of the 2nd Workshop on Steps to Reducing Unwanted Traffic on the Internet (SRUTI)*, 2006.

24. Matthew Roughan, Subhabrata Sen, Oliver Spatscheck, and Nick Duffield. Class-of-service mapping for qos: a statistical signature-based approach to ip traffic classification. In *IMC '04: Proceedings of the 4th ACM SIGCOMM conference on Internet measurement*, pages 135–148, New York, NY, USA, 2004. ACM Press.

25. Subhabrata Sen, Oliver Spatscheck, and Dongmei Wang. Accurate, scalable in-network identification of p2p traffic using application signatures. In *WWW '04: Proceedings of the 13th international conference on World Wide Web*, pages 512–521, New York, NY, USA, 2004. ACM Press.

26. Alex C. Snoeren, Craig Partridge, Luis A. Sanchez, Christine E. Jones, Fabrice Tchakountio, Beverly Schwartz, Stephen T. Kent, and W. Timothy Strayer. Single-packet IP traceback. *ACM/IEEE Trans. on Networking*, December 2002.

27. W. Timothy Strayer, Christine Jones, Beverley Schwartz, Sarah Edwards, Walter Milliken, and Alden Jackson. Efficient multi-dimensional flow correlation. In *Proceedings of the 32st IEEE Conference on Local Computer Networks (LCN'07)*, November 2007. Submitted for publication.

28. W. Timothy Strayer, Christine Jones, Beverly Schwartz, Joanne Mikkelson, and Carl Livadas. Architecture for Multi-Stage Network Attack Traceback. In *Proceedings of the IEEE LCN Workshop on Network Security (WoNS 2005)*, Sydney, Australia, November 2005.

29. W. Timothy Strayer, Robert Walsh, Carl Livadas, and David Lapsley. Detecting Botnets with Tight Command and Control. In *Proceedings of the 31st IEEE Conference on Local Computer Networks (LCN'06)*, November 2006.

30. Symantec. Symantec Internet Security Threat Report. Trends for July – December 06, March 2007.

31. The Honeynet Project. *Know Your Enemy : Learning about Security Threats*. Addison-Wesley Professional; 2 edition (May 17, 2004), March 2004.

32. Rob Thormeyer. Hacker arrested for breaching dod systems with 'botnets'. *Government Computer News*, November 4, 2005.

33. Xinyuan Wang, Douglas S. Reeves, and S. Felix Wu. Inter-packet delay based correlation for tracing encrypted connections through stepping stones. In *Proc. European Symposium on Research in Computer Security*, pages 244–263, October 2002.

34. Ian H. Witten and Eibe Frank. *Data Mining: Practical Machine Learning Tools and Techniques (2nd Edition)*. Morgan Kaufmann, San Francisco, CA, 2005.

35. Kunikazu Yoda and Hiroaki Etoh. Finding a connection chain for tracing intruders. In *Proc. European Symposium on Research in Computer Security*, pages 191–205, October 2000.

36. L. Zhang, A. G. Persaud, A. Johnson, and Y. Guan. Detection of stepping stone attacks under delay and chaff perturbations. In *Proceedings of the 25th IEEE International Performance Computing and Communications Conference*, April 2006.

37. Yin Zhang and Vern Paxson. Detecting stepping stones. In *Proc. USENIX Security Symposium '00*, pages 171–184, August 2000.

Honeynet-based Botnet Scan Traffic Analysis

Zhichun Li, Anup Goyal, and Yan Chen

Northwestern University, Evanston, IL 60208
{lizc,ago210,ychen}@cs.northwestern.edu

1 Introduction

With the increasing importance of Internet in everyone's daily life, Internet security poses a serious problem. Nowadays, botnets are the major tool to launch Internet-scale attacks. A "botnet" is a network of compromised machines that is remotely controlled by an attacker. In contrast of the earlier hacking activities (mainly used to show off the attackers' technique skills), botnets are better organized and mainly used for the profit-centered endeavors. For example, the attacker can make profit through Email spam [16], click fraud [6], game accounts and credit card numbers harvest, and extortion through DoS attacks.

Although thorough understanding and prevention of botnets are very important. Currently, the research community gains only limited insight into botnets.

Several approaches can help to understand the botnet phenomena:

Source code study is to examine the botnets' source code, given that the most famous bot sources are under GPL. This can give us an insight about all the malicious activities that can be achieved by the botnet. However, there are different versions of botnets and major versions have different variants. It is hard to study all their source codes, given many of them might not be obtained in the first place. Another problem is that this approach only gives us the static features of botnets, but not the dynamic features, such as the size of botnets, the geological distribution of the bots, *etc.*. However this study can give us some insight into their current functionalities and how they achieve that.

Command and Control study is the study of IRC traffic or other communication protocols that botnets use for communication. Potentially, this approach can be used to observe the global view, if the traffic of IRC command and control channel can be sniffed. However, the trend has moved towards using private IRC servers or other communication protocols, such as WEB or P2P. Moreover, a more fundamental problem is that botnets may encrypt their command and control channels. The covert channel detection could be extremely difficult.

Controlling botnet is to gain the control of the botnet, so that we can have a global view and study its behavior. Usually, researchers limited their approach to either set up or buy a botnet. Another way is to hijack the botnets' DDNS entries [5]. However, this is dependent on whether the DDNS vendors are willing to cooperate and whether the DDNS names can be detected.

Behavior study is the study of the botnet by observing their behaviors. For example, botnet scanning, botnet based DoS attack, botnet based spam, botnet based click fraud *etc.*. This study usually can capture dynamic features and measurements become easier.

We are interested in developing a general technique which has a minimum monitoring overhead for observing botnet behavior, and hard to evade by botnets. Therefore, people from any corner around the world can easily adopt it to measure the characteristics of the botnet behavior. If we could aggregate the measurements, potentially we can get a more accurate global picture of the botnets. After carefully analyzing the above behavioral list, we found that the botnet scanning behavior is ingrained to the botnet because this is the most effective way for them to recruit new bots. Therefore, we believe in near future, the botmaster will not give up scanning. Moreover, monitoring scanning is relatively easy. With a honeynet installed people can easily get the botnet scanning traffic.

With this motivation, we designed a general paradigm to extract botnet related scanning events and analyzing methods. We further analyzed one year honeynet traffic from a large research institution to demonstrate the methods.

In [15], three types of scanning strategies of botnets have been introduced: localized scanning, targeted scanning and uniform scanning. Localized scanning is that each bot chose the scanning range based their own IP prefixes. Targeted scanning is that the botmaster specified a particular IP prefix for bots to scan. The uniform scanning is the botnet scanning the whole Internet. Here, we call the targeted scanning and the uniform scanning as global scanning, since usually it is hard to determine the scanning range of a botnet. In the honeynet, the global scanning events can be easily identified since it usually related to large number of sources. However, the localized scanning is quite hard to identify. It is hard to differentiate whether it is a single scanner or it is part of a large botnet.

In this chapter, we mainly studied the botnet scanning behaviors, and use its scanning behavior to infer the general properties of botnets. Scanning is the major tool for recruiting new bots. In our study we found out that 75% of the successful botnet scanning events followed by the malicious payloads. Understanding the botnet scanning behavior is very important since it will help us to understand how to detect/prevent botnet propagation. Moreover, we can gain insight into the general properties of botnets through this study. Because of the prevalence of botnet scan activities, we believe that scan based botnet property inference is also very general.

In this book chapter we mainly wanted to answer the following questions.

- How to use botnet scan behavior to infer the general properties of the botnets?
- How to extract the botnet scan events?
- How are the network level behavior of the botnets?

- What are the different scan strategies used by the botnets and how these related to dynamic behavior of the bots?

In this book chapter, we demonstrated that the botnet scan traffic can be very useful in terms of inferring the general properties of the botnets. We developed a general paradigm for botnet scan event extraction. Based on it we analyzed one year honeynet traffic. In our study, we found that the bot population is highly diverse. Although, 41% of bots come form top 20 ASes, but the total population is from 2860 ASes. But the bot population is pretty concentrated in certain IP ranges, which confirmed the conclusion from botnet spamming study [16]. The IP range distributions have high variance from botnets to botnets. This implies the IP blacklist might not always be effective for different botnets. In most cases, the scan arrival follows a Poisson process and the inter arrival time follow an exponential distribution. This suggested that the bots scan randomly and the scan range is much larger than the sensor size. We found there are two clear modes for bots to arrive. They either arrive mostly at the very beginning or they are pretty evenly distributed in the whole scan event duration. This might due to different scan strategies the botmasters used. We also found some very complex scan strategies used by the botmasters.

The rest of this book chapter is organized as follows. We discussed the related work in Section 2. Section 3 described the design of the general botnet scan event extraction paradigms. Section 5 discussed our findings of analyzing botnet scan events extracted from one year honeynet traffic from a large research institution. Finally, Section 6 stated the conclusions.

2 Related Work

Currently, most botnet studies leverage on two approaches: IRC channel monitoring [3, 15] and DNS hijacking [5, 16]. If the botnet uses an IRC based command and control mechanism and does not encrypt the channel, potentially a faked bot can be inserted into the channel to monitor the botnet behavior. To be really useful, this further requires the botnet IRC channel allows message broadcasting, so that a bot can hear the information of other bots. Obviously, this approach can get the botnet behavior from a "insider's perspective". However, given the trend of botnet command and control mechanisms are changing towards WEB [14] or P2P [7] based approach. This approach might bias the study towards the characteristics of IRC based botnets.

If we can know the domain name of a botnet's command and control server, and we can convince the domain name service provider to redirect the domain name to another system, potentially we can hijack the botnet and control it by ourselves. In this way, we can fully control the botnet and study its behavior. However, usually to find the domain name and convince the DNS service provider to redirect the domain name for us is not always easy, especially when the botnet use a DNS service provider in a foreign country.

Botnets have been used for cyber-crimes for quite some time, but studies on botnet detection are sparse. Known techniques for botnet detection includes honeynets and IDS system with signature detection. Honeynets [12] or darknets can be proved useful in studying botnet behavior, but cannot track the actual infected host. Signature matching and behavior of existing botnet can be used for detection. An open-source system like Snort [8] can be used for detection of known botnets. Signature matching has its own disadvantage that it can be easily fooled by smart bots and also fails for new botnets. [2] has suggested an anomaly-based detection method, which combine an IRC mesh detection component with a TCP scan detection heuristic for detecting botnet attacks. However, this system suffers from false positive and could be evaded by simple encoding of IRC channel. Another interesting work for finding botnet membership is by using DNSBL Counter-Intelligence [17]. This method is limited to the detection of spamming botnets and it is computationally expensive and memory intensive.

As [3] firstly suggested that botnet propagation and attack behavior can be another way to study the botnets. We mainly studied the scan behavior of botnets and through it we inferred the general properties of botnets. We argue this also is a very important angle, since most botnets leverage on scanning and exploiting the vulnerable hosts to recruit new bots. Therefore, it is a very common behavior of the botnets. Understand it better will help us improve the botnet detection/prevention. Since the botnet scanning activities are prevalence, it is also a general way to infer the properties of botnets. In [19], they mainly infer the difference between the botnet scanning event with worm propagation and misconfigurations. Here, we focused on using the scanning events to understand the botnet scan behavior and botnet proprieties in general.

Most general honeynet [1, 13, 20] and honeyfarm [4, 18] approach can be used to monitor the botnet scanning behavior. A large continuous IP space is good for monitoring the botnet global scan, *i.e.*, scan a given IP prefix which is different from the bots' IP prefix. A distributed honeynet/honeyfarm can be better in terms of monitoring local scan activities in which case each bot scan their local prefixes.

3 Botnet Scanning Event Identification

Figure 1 shows the botnet event extraction and analysis paradigm. To understand the botnet scanning behavior, we first extract coordinated scanning events from the honeynet traffic. A botnet scan event is a large scale coordinated scanning event which normally has to employ large number of bots. We use the large number of unique sources contacting the honeynet as an indicator of the botnet scanning. Then, we separate the misconfiguration and worm cases from botnet cases. We focus on the analysis of botnet events

3.1 Honeynet and Data Collection

Traffic sent to unused Internet addresses ("darknets") can reflect a variety of activity. We cannot determine the nature of the activity by simply watching it passively as probes arrive because the specifics of most forms of activity only manifest after the

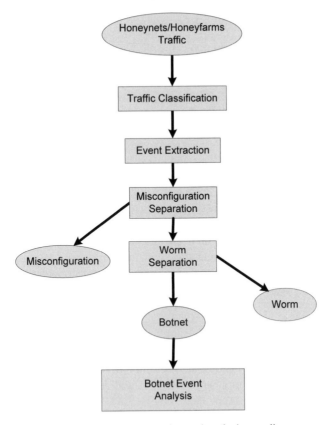

Fig. 1. Botnet event extraction and analysis paradigm

source establishes a connection (or, sometimes, a whole set of connections comprising a *session*) with the destination. As a general approach, we can take traffic sent to unresponsive darknets and channel it to a *honeypot* system that will respond in some fashion. Such a combination is often referred to as a *honeynet*. Honeynet systems can employ low- or medium-interaction honeypots [1, 13], which provide fake responses of varying detail, and thus can elicit a range of possible activity from the sender. Going further, one can employ high-interaction honeypots (full, infectible systems, often running inside virtual machines), which when coupled with a honeynet is termed as a *honeyfarm* [4, 18].

Our analysis is based on one year (2006) honeynet data from a large research institution. The honeynet has ten continuous class C networks. The half of the sensor is dark which means no response to any incoming packets and the second half accompanied with Honeyd responder which simulate most popular protocols and respond the SYN/ACK packets to the unknown protocols. The configuration is similar to the ones used in [10, 19]. We also adapt the source-destination filtering [10].

3.2 Traffic Classification

Some attack traffic can have complex session structures involving multiple application protocols. For example, the attacker can send an exploit to TCP port 139 which, if successful, results in opening a shell and issuing a http download command. In general, the application protocol contacted first is the protocol being exploited, so we label the entire session with the first protocol used. This also provides consistent labeling for those connection attempts in which the honeynet did not respond and we observe only the initial SYN packet. We aggregate the connections to sessions using an approach similar to the first step algorithm by Kannan et al [9]. We consider all those connections within T_{aggreg} of each other as part of the same session for a given pair of hosts. We used the same threshold, $T_{aggreg} = 100$ seconds, as Kannan et al [9], and found that this grouped the majority of connections between any given pair of hosts.

For application protocols which are not commonly used, the average background radiation noise is low and thus port numbers are used to separate event traffic. However, noise is usually quite strong for more popular protocols, thus requiring further differentiation. Assuming that we observe at least one successful session from each sender, we can use the payload analysis of that session to separate it from other traffic. We use a similar approach for the *Radiation-analy* summaries proposed in [19], which further classify the traffic within one application protocol or one application protocol family by rich semantic analysis. We analyzed the semantics of 20 common and backdoor protocols based on Bro's application semantic analysis [11], and generated a session summary for each session (e.g., 445/tcp/[exploit] (NAMED_PIPE:"\\<dst-IP>\IPC$ \wkssvc"; RPC request (4280 bytes))). Based on the session summary we can further classify the traffic within one protocol family.

3.3 Event Extraction

We found for the traffic of all the port number or protocol semantics, the traffic consists of a steady background noise with some large spikes. The large spikes usually are corresponding to the botnet scanning events. We found to extract the big spikes is similar to the traditional signal detection problem. Signal strength S is defined as the peak of unique source count arrival, and the typical unique source count when there are no events is defined as noise strength N. Noise strength is calculated as the median of unique source counts of every time interval for T_N days before the event. If the event occurrence time is less than $T_N/2$, then noise strength is the median of the time window T_N. We define the signal to noise ratio as $SNR = \frac{S}{N}$, and examine only those events with large SNR. We use $T_N = 30$ (30 days) since we never see an event last more than two days. The thresholds we use are $SNR \geq 50$.

We calculate the unique source count of every pre-defined time interval for a given protocol. Event extraction is done using time series analysis. While many general statistical signal detection approaches might be applied here, we currently extract the events semi-manually. We first automatically extract potential events using the following algorithm: for any given time interval, we calculate the median of the previous T_N intervals and the SNR. For those spikes which exceed our SNR threshold, we extend the range until $S \leq \omega N$ where ω is a tunable parameter controlling the amount of the signal tail to include in the event.

After an event is extracted, we might refine the event by re-scaling it into smaller time intervals and recalculating the unique source counts. We use manual analysis and visualization techniques at this point, since re-scaling might make the shape of events more complex.

3.4 Misconfiguration and Worm Separation

Events with a large number of sources are usually misconfigurations, botnets and worms [19]. We separate misconfigurations from worms or botnets based on the observation that botnet scans and worms contact a significant range of the IP addresses in the sensor, whereas events with few hotspots target are caused by misconfigurations. We use two metrics to separate misconfiguations from other events. The address hit ratio, N_E/N_D, where N_E is the number of destination addresses involved in the event and N_D is the number of destination addresses in the honeynet, should be much smaller for misconfigurations than for botnet sweeps or worms. Secondly, the average number of sources per destination address should be much larger for misconfigurations. If the first metric is below given threshold while the second crosses a given threshold, we consider the event to be a misconfiguration; otherwise it is classified as a worm or botnet event.

Worm behavior and botnet probes are quite similar: both scan and send exploits to the address range in a similar manner. However, usually the number of sources for worms grows much more quickly than botnets, and events also last longer for worms. But if botnets scans the entire Internet, with new infected bots continuing to join the scan activity, then there is no observable difference from worms. Hence it is difficult to define a strict distinction between botnet sweeps and worms. In this paper, we treat all events with an exponential growing trend in the number of sources as worms [22], and the other events as botnet sweeps. We use the Kalman filter based exponential trend detection proposed in [22] to differentiate botnet and worm events.

4 Botnet Scanning Event Analysis

In our one year honeynet traffic, we found 43 botnet global scan events. We first analyzed the overall sender (bot) characteristics of the all the senders. Then, we analyzed each event individually and compare the characteristics among different events.

In this book chapter, we focused on the following characteristics of botnet scanning behavior.

- Bot IP distribution and AS distribution
- Bot operating system characteristics
- Botnet scan arrival behavior
- Bot arrival and departure process observed in the scanning events

- Bot observed local scan rate behavior
- Botnet scanning source and destination relationship

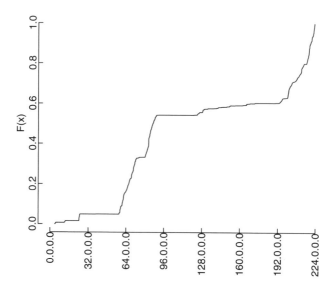

Fig. 2. The number of all unique source IP addresses, as a function of IP address space. On the x-axis, IP address space is binned by /24.

4.1 Source Characteristics of Bots

We observed thousands of senders in most of the events. In 43 events, we totally observed 63,851 unique senders. Figure 2 shows the number of senders (bots) observed over all the events, as a function of IP address space. The overall trend is very similar to the spamming IP distribution in [16]. From the figure we knew, most bots are from 60.* – 90.* and 193.* – 222.* and some are from 24.* (cable modem provider). The figure illustrated that the bots mostly come from quite concentrated IP ranges. This result confirmed the result from the bot spamming behavior study [16].

We also analyzed the IP space distribution for every event. We found for most events we got the similar IP space distribution as figure 2. However, there are some events whose IP space distributions are far from the total distribution. Figure 3 and Figure 4 shows a few such examples. Since different events might be corresponding to different botnets, this implies the IP space distributions of different botnets can be quite different. Therefore, the coarse grain IP range based botnet filtering or detect might not work well in practice.

In our study, we found most bots are from a relative small number of ASes. More than 22% of bots are from the five ASes, and 41% of the bots from 20 ASes. In

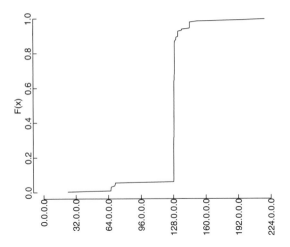

Fig. 3. The number of all unique source IP addresses for the event on TCP port 2967 on 2006-11-26, as a function of IP address space. On the x-axis, IP address space is binned by /24.

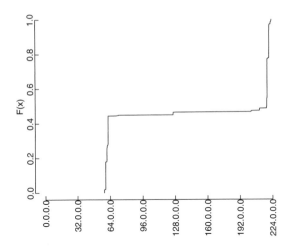

Fig. 4. The number of all unique source IP addresses for the event on TCP port 5000 on 2006-8-24, as a function of IP address space. On the x-axis, IP address space is binned by /24.

Table 1, we showed the top 20 ASes and the corresponding number of bots for each AS. From the analysis of the top 20 ASes, we found about 21% of the bots are Asia, mainly from China, Korea and Taiwan. Europe and North America (Unite States and Canada) have similar amount of bots 9.5% and 9% respectively. Surprisingly there are also about 2% bots coming from Brazil. The bot population is from 2860 ASes in total. Although our honeynet detection sensor is in Unite States but the bots indeed

AS number	#Source	AS Name	Primary Country
4134	4449	CHINANET-BACKBONE	China
9318	2988	Hanaro Telecom Inc	Korea
3462	2712	Data Communication Business Group	Taiwan
4837	2091	CHINA169-BACKBONE	China
5617	1849	Polish Telecom's commercial IP network	Poland
7132	1660	SBC Internet Services	United States
6327	1545	Shaw Communications Inc.	Canada
19262	1441	Verizon Internet Serv	United States
3320	1060	Deutsche Telekom AG	Germany
3352	855	Internet Access Network of TDE	Spain
7738	744	Telecomunicacoes da Bahia S.A	Brazil
20961	675	Autonomous System	Poland
577	619	Bell Canada	Canada
3269	609	Telecom ITALIA	Italy
9394	541	CHINA RAILWAY Internet(CRNET)	China
12322	533	PROXAD AS for Proxad/Free ISP	France
8167	498	Telecomunicacoes de Santa Catarina SA	Brazil
3356	493	Level 3 Communications	United States
25310	469	Cable and Wireless Access LTD	United Kingdom
4766	429	Korea Telcom	Korea

Table 1. Amount of scan received from botnet scanning in the top 20 ASes.

come from all over the world. The overall result are similar to the result from [16]. The difference between our result and the result from [16] is mainly that we observed more hosts from Europe than them.

4.2 Operating Systems of Bots

We also investigated the prevalence of operating system among the bots. We used p0f [21] tool to identified the operating system versions. P0f is a passive OS fingerprinting tool which mainly uses the TCP options within the TCP SYN packets to identify the operating system versions. For each bot, we might observe multiple SYN packets. Sometimes, the different SYN packets from a bot might be given different OS results by p0f. We used the following priorities to solve the potential conflict. We think the other OS types have higher priority than Windows, and Windows has higher priority than Unknown. The rule is to favorite the non-Windows operating systems

Operating System	Clients
Windows	58797 (92%)
-Windows 2000 or XP	58028 (90.8%)
-Windows 98	404 (0.63%)
-Windows NT	329 (0.51%)
-Windows 2003	25 (<.1%)
-Windows 95	11 (<.1%)
Linux	9 (<.1%)
Novell	23 (<.1%)
HP-UX	1 (<.1%)
Unidentified	5021 (7.8%)
Total	63851

Table 2. The operating system distribution for unique senders of received scan, as determined by passive OS fingerprinting.

and to try to avoid assigning Unknown. Table 2 shows the operating system distribution we found. We found 92% of the bots are identified as Windows machines by p0f [21]. And among the Windows machines, 90.8% of the bots are Windows 2000 or XP. This result supported the conventional wisdom that botnet army are mainly comprised Windows machines.

We also did the similar analysis at per event level. We found for all the 43 events the dominated operating system are Windows. We did not observe any events which mainly consist of other types of machines. Although, there are some rumors that some botnets are Linux or Unix based, based on our finding, we believe the percentage of non-Windows based botnets in the botnet population are really low.

4.3 Scan Arrival Characteristics

For all the botnet events, we analyzed how the scan sessions arrive in time. We found for most events the very beginning and the very end of the events have complex arrival behavior. However, for most events in the middle part, the scan arrival speeds are quite constant, and the more than half of the events' inter-arrival time follows exponential distributions. This suggested that the scan arrivals follow a Poisson distribution. One plausible explanation for this is based on the law of rare events. Usually the botnet scans a large IP scope, and the sensor is only a tiny portion of it. If the botnet uses random scanning, for each scan session there is a small probability p to arrive the honeynet detection sensor. According the law of rare events, the observed scan sessions in a given time interval will follow a Poisson distribution and the inter arrival time will follow an exponential distribution. Among the 43 events,

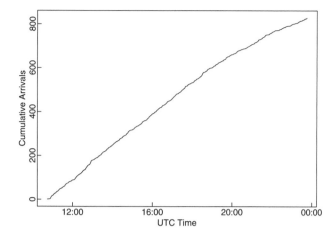

Fig. 5. The cumulative scan session arrival process of the event on TCP port 8888 on 2006-02-06, which corresponding to a backdoor shell.

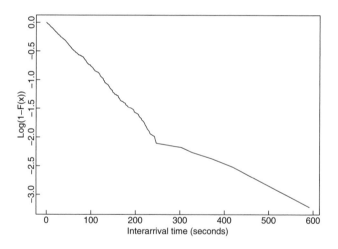

Fig. 6. The inter-arrival time log scale CDF of the event on TCP port 8888 on 2006-02-06, which corresponding to a backdoor shell.

about 25 (58%) events the inter-arrival time follows an exponential distribution. This suggested most botnets indeed use a random scan strategy. An example of the scan arrival and scan inter arrival time is shown in Figure 5 and Figure 6 respectively.

4.4 Source Arrival and Departure

We also investigated for each event when the bots are observed. We defined, for a given bot, the time it begins to scan as its true source arrival time, and the time it

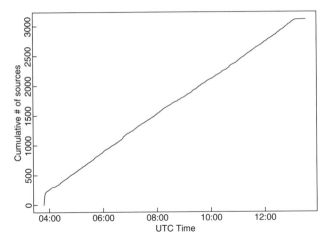

Fig. 7. The arrival process of the event on TCP port 1433 on 2006-01-22 (from 2006-01-22 21:00 to 2006-01-23 07:00), which corresponding to a MS SQL Server vulnerability.

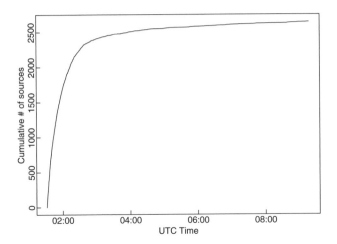

Fig. 8. The arrival process of the event on TCP port 1433 on 2006-08-24, which corresponding to a MS SQL Server vulnerability.

stops to scan as its true source departure time. We cannot measure the true arrival time and departure time of the bots, since the botnet might scan a large range and the honeynet sensor can only observe a small sample of the scans. Instead, we defined the time of the first scan we seen from a given bot as its observed arrival time, and the time of the last scan we seen from the same bot as its observed departure time. For random scanning, we can assume the scans we observed are a random sampling from the total scan population. Certainly the sampling errors will influence the results. The number of scan between the first scan sent out by a bot and the first scan we observed from that given bot follows a geometry distribution. If we assume the scan speed is close to constant, the time difference of the first scan sent out by a bot and the first scan we observed from that bot will also follow a geometry distribution. We can make the similar argument to the true departure time of the bot and the departure time we observed. For the long lived events usually we can use the observed arrival and departure time as good approximation of the true arrival and departure time. For the short lived event the observed arrival and departure time might not be able to present true arrival and departure time.

For the long lived events, we found there are two types of source arrival processes. In some events, most bots arrived at the beginning part of the events, but on some other events bots arrivals distributed over the whole period of the event duration. Figure 7 and Figure 8 showed such two representative cases respectively.

In Figure 7, most bots arrived at the beginning part of the events. This might correspond to the case that after the botmaster typed the scan command in the command and control channel, immediately the bots in the channel received the scan command and began to scan. The true source arrival times of bots are same, so the observed source arrival time follows a geometry distribution.

In Figure 8, the bot arrive uniformly in the event duration, which indicate the true source arrival time of different bots are different and also should be uniformly distributed in time. There are two possibilities to make this happen. One possibility is that every bot defer to execute the scan command by random seconds uniformly. The other possibility is that the scan command is the default channel topic [15]. Therefore, after a bot join the channel, it will get the scan command and start scanning. From the data we cannot separate these two cases.

In the departure process, we found, in all the long-lived events, many bots depart before the events end.

For the events most bots arrived at the beginning part of the events, we observed at the end of event, the bot departure rate increased sharply. We analyzed several botnet source code genres and found in most case the botmaster asks the bot to scan a fixed amount of time. If that is the case, it makes sense that at the end of the time specified by the botmaster all the remaining bots end the scanning.

There is one event different from other events, in which the bots arrived in groups, but the total scan arrivals are still linear in time. In Figure 9 we can see there are four major groups of bots arrived in batch. But in Figure 10 the number of scan arrivals is still linear in time. Through further analysis we found, after the first group of bots departed, the second group of bots arrived immediately. This is also true for other consecutive groups of bots. Obviously, the botmaster intentionally divide the bots in four groups to do the scanning one after another.

We also studied the observed bot scan duration, *i.e.*, the time between the first scan observed from a given bot and the last scan observed from the given bot. An example CDF of the scan duration is shown in Figure 11. However, we found the scan duration varies from events to events. There is no clear pattern can be found.

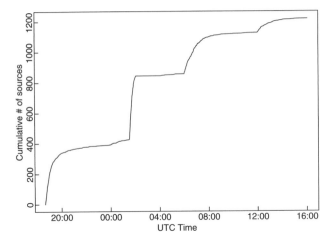

Fig. 9. The bot arrival process of event on TCP port 139 from 2006-08-24 13:40 to 2006-08-25 11:04, which corresponding to a Netbios-SSN scan.

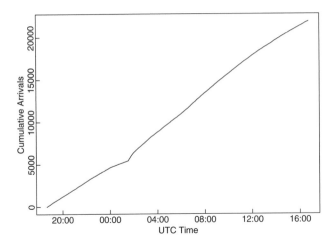

Fig. 10. The scan arrival of event on TCP port 139 from 2006-08-24 13:40 to 2006-08-25 11:04, which corresponding to a Netbios-SSN scan.

4.5 Observed Local Scan Rate

We calculated the local scan rate of a given bot as the number of scans we observed minus one over its observed scan duration. The idea behind is that we can think after the first scan arrives we started the timer, and in the observed scan duration we will observed the scans except the first one. We will not define the local scan rate for the senders from which only one scan is observed.

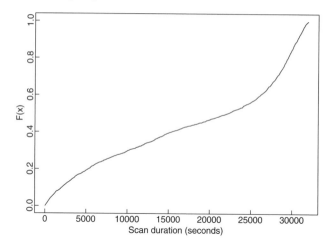

Fig. 11. The CDF of observed scan duration of bots of event on TCP port 1433 on 2006-08-24, which corresponding to a MS SQL Server vulnerability.

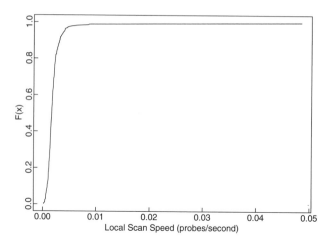

Fig. 12. The CDF of local scan rate distribution of the event on TCP port 5900 on 2006-09-26, which corresponding to a VNC vulnerabilty.

We first looked at the CDF of local scan rate of different events. In four cases, the numbers of bots which send more than one scans are very small, so the CDF is not very representative. For the remaining cases, we found most bots have similar local scan rate with a few bot with very high local scan rate. We further analyzed the bots with very high local scan rate, and find they are not necessarily the bots which send most scans. Many of such cases are due to they have very short observed scan duration. Figure 12 shows an example of such a CDF distribution.

We further investigated whether the local scan speed have any correlation with the bot arrival and departure time. We did not find any obvious trend. We believe in most case, the bot arrival and departure time might not have strong correlation with their local scan speed. However they might have certain weak correlation and which can be buried into the random noises in the data. Figure 13 and Figure 14 show an example of this analysis.

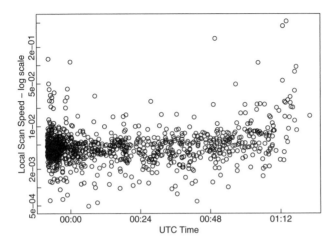

Fig. 13. The scatter plot of the source observed arrival times and their corresponding observed scan rate of the event on TCP port 1025 on 2006-09-19.

4.6 Scan Source Destination Relationship

We also analyzed source destination relationships. We mainly studied two distributions: how many sources target a destination address in the honeynet sensor, and how many destinations are contacted by a source.

We found in all the events, the distribution of how many sources a destination contacts is close to the binomial distribution with only very few exceptions. This implies that the source usually choose the destination uniform randomly. Figure 15 is such an example.

The distribution of how many destinations a source targets is more complex. Sometimes it has multiple modes. The conjecture is that it can be explained as a multiplex of multiple binomial distributions, due to different bots might have different scan speeds and durations. In Figure 16 we showed an example which clearly has this pattern.

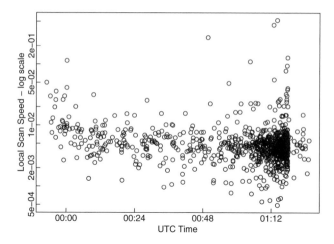

Fig. 14. The scatter plot of the source observed departure times and their corresponding observed scan rates of the event on TCP port 1025 on 2006-09-19.

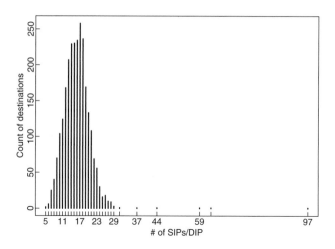

Fig. 15. The distribution of number of sources a destination contacted of the event on TCP port 1433 on 2006-08-24, which corresponding to a MS SQL Server vulnerability.

5 Conclusion

Botnets have become the most serious threats to the Internet security. Many cyber-crimes are botnet related. Measuring and understanding the botnet will help us gain more insight to the botnet phenomenon, and further help us design better detection and prevention systems.

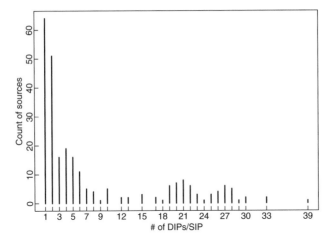

Fig. 16. The distribution of number of destinations a source touched of the event on TCP port 2967 on 2006-11-27, which corresponding to a backdoor shell.

In this book chapter, we proposed a general framework to extract botnet global scanning events. Based on one year honeynet traffic from a large research institution we studied the six different botnet scanning characteristics. We found botnets although mainly from a small number of ASes but indeed spread out all over the world from totally 2860 ASes. There are two different botnet arrival/departure patterns: all together and gradually. We conjecture this is related to different scan strategies. We also found the scan arrivals are linear in time and inter-arrival time follows a exponential distribution, which might imply the scans are random scanning and the scan range is much larger than the detection sensor.

References

1. M. Bailey et al. The Internet motion sensor: A distributed blackhole monitoring system. In *Proc. of NDSS*, 2005.
2. James Binkley and Suresh Singh. An algorithm for anomaly-based botnet detection. In *Proceedings of Steps to Reducing Unwanted Traffic on the Internet Workshop (SRUTI '06)*, 2006.
3. E. Cooke, F. Jahanian, and D. McPherson. The zombie roundup: Understanding, detecting, and disrupting botnets. In *Proceedings of USENIX Workshop on Steps to Reducing Unwanted Traffic on the Internet*, July 2005.
4. W. Cui et al. GQ: Realizing a system to catch worms in a quarter million places. Technical Report TR-06-004, ICSI, 2006.
5. D. Dagon, C. Zou, and W. Lee. Modeling botnet propagation using time zones. In *Proceedings of the 13th Network and Distributed System Security Symposium (NDSS'06)*, 2006.

6. Neil Daswani, Michael Stoppelman, the Google Click Quality, and Inc Security Teams, Google. The anatomy of Clickbot.A. In *USENIX First Workshop on Hot Topics in Understanding Botnets (HotBots)*, 2007.
7. Julian Grizzard, Vikram Sharma, Chris Nunnery, Brent ByungHoon Kang, and David Dagon. Peer-to-peer botnets: Overview and case study. In *USENIX First Workshop on Hot Topics in Understanding Botnets (HotBots)*, 2007.
8. Christopher W. Hanna. Using snort to detect rogue irc bot programs, Oct 2004. http://www.giac.org/certified_professionals/practicals/gsec/4095.php.
9. J. Kannan et al. Semi-automated discovery of application session structure. In *Proc. of ACM IMC*, 2006.
10. R. Pang et al. Characteristics of Internet background radiation. In *Proc. of ACM IMC*, 2004.
11. V. Paxson. Bro: A system for detecting network intruders in real-time. *Computer Networks*, 31, 1999.
12. The Honeynet Project and Research Alliance. Know your enemy: Tracking botnets. http://honeynet.org/papers/bots, March 2005.
13. N. Provos. A virtual honeypot framework. In *Proc. of USENIX Security*, 2004.
14. Niels Provos, Dean McNamee, Panayiotis Mavrommatis, Ke Wang, and Nagendra Modadugu. The ghost in the browser: Analysis of web-based malware. In *USENIX First Workshop on Hot Topics in Understanding Botnets (HotBots)*, 2007.
15. Moheeb A. Rajab, Jay Zarfoss, Fabian Monrose, and Andreas Terzis. A multifaceted approach to understanding the botnet phenomenon. In *Proc. of ACM/USENIX IMC*, 2006.
16. Anirudh Ramachandran and Nick Feamster. Understanding the network-level behavior of spammers. In *Proceedings of ACM SIGCOMM '06*, September 2006.
17. Anirudh Ramachandran, Nick Feamster, and David Dagon. Revealing botnet membership using DNSBL counter-intelligence. In *Proceedings of Steps to Reducing Unwanted Traffic on the Internet Workshop (SRUTI '06)*, 2006.
18. M. Vrable et al. Scalability, fidelity, and containment in the potemkin virtual honeyfarm. In *Proc. of SOSP*, 2005.
19. V. Yegneswaran, Paul Barford, and Vern Paxson. Using honeynets for Internet situational awareness. In *In Proc. of ACM Hotnets IV*, 2005.
20. V. Yegneswaran et al. On the design and use of Internet sinks for network abuse monitoring. In *Proc. of RAID*, 2004.
21. Michal Zalewski. the new p0f. http://lcamtuf.coredump.cx/p0f.shtml.
22. Cliff C. Zou et al. Monitoring and early warning for Internet worms. In *Prof. of ACM CCS*, 2003.

Characterizing Bots' Remote Control Behavior

Elizabeth Stinson and John C. Mitchell

Department of Computer Science, Stanford University, Stanford, CA 94305
{stinson,mitchell}@cs.stanford.edu

Summary. A botnet is a collection of bots, each generally running on a compromised system and responding to commands over a "command-and-control" overlay network. We investigate observable differences in the behavior of bots and benign programs, focusing on the way that bots respond to data received over the network. Our experimental platform monitors execution of an arbitrary Win32 binary, considering data received over the network to be tainted, applying library-call-level taint propagation, and checking for tainted arguments to selected system calls. As a way of further distinguishing locally-initiated from remotely-initiated actions, we capture and propagate "cleanliness" of local user input (as received via the keyboard or mouse). Testing indicates behavioral separation of major bot families (ago, DSNX, evil, G-SyS, sd, Spy) from benign programs with low error rate.

Key words: host-based, behavior-based, detection, taint, interposition, system call

1 Introduction

Botnets have been instrumental in distributed denial of service attacks, click fraud, phishing, malware distribution, manipulation of online polls and games, and identity theft [2, 17, 18, 24, 27, 30]. As much as 70% of all spam may be transmitted through botnets [4] and as many as $\frac{1}{4}$ of all computers may be participants in a botnet [34]. A bot master (or "botherder") directs the activities of a botnet by issuing commands that are transmitted over a command-and-control (C&C) overlay network. Some previous network-based botnet detection efforts have attempted to exploit this ongoing C&C behavior or its side effects [3, 6, 24]. Our work investigates the potential for host-based behavioral bot detection. In particular, we test the hypothesis that the behavior of installed bots can be characterized in a way that distinguishes malicious bots from innocuous processes. We are not aware of any prior studies of this topic.

Each participating bot independently executes each command received over the C&C network. A bot command takes some number of parameters (possibly zero) – each of a particular type – in some fixed order. For example, many bots provide a web-download command, which commonly takes two parameters; the first is a URL that identifies a remote resource (typically a file) that should be downloaded, and the second is the file path on the host system at which to store the downloaded data. A botnet constitutes a *remotely programmable platform* with the set of commands it supports forming its API.

Many parameterized bot commands are implemented by invoking operating system services on the host system. For example, the web-download command connects to a target over the network, requests some data from that target, and creates a file on the host system; all of these actions (connect, network send and receive, and file creation) are performed via execution of system calls. Typically, a command's parameters provide information used in the system call invocation. For example, the `connect` system call takes an IP address argument, which identifies the target host with which a connection should be established. Implementations of the web-download command obtain that target host IP from the given URL parameter. Thus, execution of many parameterized commands causes system call invocations on arguments obtained from those parameters.

In this chapter, we test the experimental hypothesis that the remote control of bots through parameterized commands separates bot behavior from normal execution of innocuous programs. We postulate that a process exhibits external or remote control when it uses data received from the network (an untrusted source) in a system call argument (a trusted sink). We test our hypothesis via a prototype implementation, BotSwat, designed for the environment in which the vast majority of bots operate: home users' PCs running Windows XP or 2000 [24]. BotSwat can monitor execution of an arbitrary Win32 binary and interposes on the run-time library calls (including system calls) made by a process. We consider data received over the network to be tainted and track tainted data as it propagates via dynamic library calls to other memory regions. We identify execution of parameterized bot commands when tainted arguments are supplied to select *gate functions*, which are system calls used in malicious bot activity.

Our experimental results suggest that the presence of network packet contents in selected system call arguments is an effective indicator for malicious Win32 bots, including tested variants of agobot, DSNXbot, evilbot, G-SySbot, sdbot, and Spybot. Bots from these families constitute 98.2% of malicious bots seen in the wild [17]. While these bots may implement commands in significantly different ways, similarities in the way they respond to external control allow a single approach to identify them. Additionally, the thousands of variants of each such family generally differ in ways that will not affect our ability to detect them; this is in contrast to traditional anti-malware signature scanners which may require a distinct signature for each variant [35]. Moreover, our generic approach does not rely on a particular C&C communication protocol (e.g., Internet Relay Chat (IRC)) or botnet topology (e.g., centralized).

Since our prototype implementation only has visibility into memory-copying calls made via a Dynamically Linked Library (DLL), we introduce strategies to counteract the effects of *out-of-band* memory copies – those which occur outside of the interposition mechanism. In particular, we perform *content-based tainting*, which considers a memory region tainted if its contents are identical to a known tainted string. We also introduce *substring-based tainting*, whereby a region will be considered tainted if its contents are a substring of any data received by the monitored process over the network. These strategies are applied upon calls by a monitored process into *taint propagation functions*, which are DLL functions used to copy or convert the contents of memory. Applying these strategies allows us to effectively identify bot behavior even when all of the bot's calls to memory-copying functions are out-of-band, which may occur if the bot statically links in C library functions.

Since BotSwat uses library-call-level taint propagation, bots could apply out-of-band encryption functions (e.g., XOR) to network data and consequently defeat detection by the prototype implementation. This is a limitation of our current testing platform rather than a deficiency in the characterization of bot remote-control behavior. Our testing of versions of agobot, which encrypt C&C communications via dynamic calls to the OpenSSL library, indicates that remote control behavior can still be identified (even when communications are encrypted), given visibility into the cryptographic function calls. Current botnet C&C communications tend to be unencrypted [18].

While both bots and benign programs may create files, interact with the network, and execute programs, we are able to separate bot behavior from that of benign programs by distinguishing between remotely-initiated and locally-initiated actions. We tested applications typical to the target environment (home-user PCs) which exhibit extensive network interaction. Early testing revealed that a benign program may use some tainted value in a system call argument as a result of local user input. For example, when a user downloads a webpage via a browser then clicks on a hypertext link therein, the browser will consequently request the content stored at the linked URL. In so doing, the browser will invoke system calls (e.g., `connect`, `send`) on tainted arguments (the URL). If user input were not tracked, this sequence of events would look similar to bot execution of the web download command. To account for this phenomenon in our experimental assessment, we designed and implemented a user-input module that identifies data values resulting from local user input as received via the keyboard or mouse. These *clean strings* are used to identify instances of local control. Our testing of eight benign programs over a variety of activities common to those applications resulted in eight total flagged behaviors (five different) whereas testing six bots resulted in a total of 202 flagged behaviors (18 different).

In Sect. 2, we provide background information on bots. Section 3 describes our experimental method, and Sect. 4 details our prototype implementation. Our experimental results are given in Sect. 5. We discuss the potential for and challenges to applying our findings for real-time host-based bot detection in Sect. 6. Section 7 describes related work and Sect. 8 provides concluding remarks.

2 Bots and Botnets

2.1 Bot Families and Variants

The Honeynet Project identifies four main Win32 bot families: (1) agobot – the most well known; (2) sdbot – the most common; (3) DSNXbot; and (4) mIRC-based bots [24]. A family is "a new, distinct sample of malicious code," whereas a variant is "a new iteration of the same family, one that has minor differences but that is still based on the original" [33]. Variants may be created by augmenting the functionality of a bot (e.g., adding a new exploit for use in spreading) or by applying "packing transformations" (such as compression and encryption) to a bot binary [33, 35]. We tested at least one variant from each of the first three major Win32 bot families (agobot, sdbot, and DSNXbot) as well as evilbot and Spybot. Data from McAfee suggests that bots from these tested families collectively constitute 98.2% of known variants (as of June 2005) [17]. Since bots in the wild may link in C library functions statically or dynamically, we tested bots under both conditions.

Fig. 1. Bot capabilities

capability	ago	DSNX	evil	G-SyS	sd	Spy
change C&C server	√	√		√	√	√
create/manage clone		√		√	√	
clone attacks		√				
create spy				√	√	
kill process	√			√		√
open/execute file	√	√		√	√	√
keylogging		√				√
create directory						√
delete file/directory		√				√
list directory		√				√
move file/directory						√
DCC send file		√				√
act as http server						√
create port redirect	√	√		√	√	√
other proxy	√					
download file	√	√		√	√	√
DNS resolution	√			√	√	
UDP/ping floods	√		√	√	√	
other DDoS floods	√			√		√
scan/spread	√	√		√	√	√
spam	√					
visit URL	√			√	√	

2.2 Bot Capabilities and Commands

Figure 1 provides a summary of some of the functionality exported by the tested bots. The shaded cells represent activities that are detected by BotSwat as described in Sect. 5. Note that, of the 22 different bot activities listed, 21 are implemented as parameterized commands by each of the bots that provides that capability. The exception is keylogging, which – for both of the bots that perform it – logs the captured keystrokes to a file whose name is statically configured. This chart reflects the bot versions we tested; different variants from each of these families may export more or less functionality.

Candidate Commands

Since our characterization of bot behavior exploits the fact that command parameters are often used in system call arguments, we identify a bot's *candidate commands* as those which take at least one parameter that is subsequently used (in whole or in part) in an argument to a critical system function. Our method considers *non-candidate commands*, those which take no parameters or parameters with only "local meaning" to the bot, out-of-scope.

Any bot execution of a received command is an instance in which that bot is being remotely controlled. The remote control behavior associated with a particular command consists of all the actions taken by the bot as a direct consequence of receipt of that command. Not all commands result in an equal amount of remote control behavior; e.g., a command that asks a bot to return its ID (some statically-configured value) to the bot controller entails fewer actions than the described web-download command. We approximate a command's remote control behavior by identifying the number of distinct system calls invoked during a successful execution of that command; these values were obtained through bot source code inspection. A bot's *total potential remote control behavior*, then, is the sum of the remote-control behavior of each of that bot's commands (Table 1, Row 1). Our coverage of that potential can be measured by summing the remote-control behavior of each of a bot's candidate commands (Table 1, Row 2). The complete list of system calls used in the tallies can be found in [44]. The number of system calls invoked by a bot's candidate commands accounts for around 64 to 79% of the system calls invoked over all of the bot's commands. Interestingly enough, the non-candidate commands that cause the highest number of system call invocations generally perform beneficial tasks (from the perspective of the compromised host); specific examples of this can be found in [44].

Table 1. The number of system calls invoked during successful execution of commands

	ago	DSNX	evil	GSyS	sd	Spy
# syscalls invoked over all cmds	591	145	5	187	173	202
# syscalls invoked over candidate cmds	417	114	5	122	110	145

3 Experimental Method

We developed a host-based method that identifies instances of external control, whereby a process uses data it received from an untrusted source in a system call argument without having received intervening (local) user input implicitly or explicitly agreeing to this use.

Tainting Component This component identifies when untrusted data is received by the system (taint instantiation) and tracks that data as it propagates to other memory regions (taint propagation). For our method, taint instantiation occurs upon network receive, and taint propagation keeps track of memory regions to which tainted data is written. This component exports an interface that enables querying whether a particular memory region is considered tainted.

User Input Component This purpose of this component is to identify actions that are initiated by the local application user. A primary challenge in designing this component is to identify the data values corresponding to mouse input events where this mapping (from event to value) is heavily application-dependent and not typically exposed (i.e., available via a library call). This component exports an interface that enables learning whether a data value or memory region is considered clean or whether a syscall invocation is likely the result of user input.

Behavior-Check Procedure Triggered by invocation of selected system calls, this procedure queries the tainting and user-input components to determine whether to flag the invocation as exhibiting external control. Invocations on arguments that contain more bytes of tainted than clean data are flagged.

4 Implementation

This section describes the interposition approach and the tainting, user-input, and behavior-check instrumentation used to evaluate our hypothesis.

4.1 Library and System Call Interposition

We use the `detours` library provided by Microsoft Research for library- and system-call interposition [9]. Our platform consists of a set of functions that we want to interpose upon, a replacement function for each, and a mechanism for performing interposition. The replacement functions contain the tainting, user-input, and behavior-check instrumentation. This platform is packaged as a DLL that can be injected into a target process upon its creation. Our implementation consists of approximately 70,000 lines of C++ code and, for the purpose of conducting thorough experiments, may intercept up to 2,200 API functions.

4.2 Tainting Module

Our tainting module operates dynamically at the library-call level and considers data received over the network to be tainted; consequently, network receive functions (e.g., `recv`, `WSARecv`) are instrumented as taint instantiators. Taint propagation functions include those which copy memory from a source to a destination buffer (e.g., `memcpy`), convert a buffer's contents to a numeric value (e.g., `atoi`), or convert one numeric value to another (e.g., `htons`). Taintedness can be a property of memory addresses, strings, or numeric values. A total of 172 different functions (enumerated in [44]) were instrumented as taint propagators.

As a result of out-of-band memory copies, our mechanism may possess one of two flawed views regarding a particular memory region. If a destination region D is written to with tainted data via an out-of-band operation, we will not know that D should be considered tainted. Our belief that D does not contain tainted data is a *false negative*. Similarly, a tainted region T may be written to via an out-of-band operation with untainted data; in this case, our belief that T is tainted is a *false positive*. We perform content-matching to reduce false positives and content-based and substring-based tainting to reduce false negatives.

To reduce false positives, we perform *content-matching*: for a believed-to-be-tainted memory region M, before taking any action on the basis of M's supposed taintedness (where actions include propagating taint or flagging a syscall invocation), we confirm that M's contents match the relevant portion of the network receive buffer N from which M allegedly descended. The information needed to perform such a comparison (an identifier of N, the offset into N from which this tainted data descended, the number of bytes of tainted data, etc.) is stored in the data structure describing a tainted memory region.

There are three conditions under which a region may be considered tainted: address-based, content-based, and substring-based. Under *address-based tainting*, a memory region is considered tainted if its address range overlaps with that of a known tainted region. With *content-based tainting*, a memory region is considered tainted if its contents are identical to a known tainted string. Under *substring-based tainting* , a memory region is considered tainted if its contents are a substring of any data received over the network by this process.

The tainting module may run in one of two modes, which differ in the conditions used to determine taintedness. Under *cause-and-effect propagation* (C&E), a memory region is considered tainted if the address-based or content-based conditions hold. Under *correlative propagation* (CORR), a memory region will be considered if any of the three conditions holds. Consequently, these modes differ in the amount of resilience provided against out-of-band copies. Cause-and-effect propagation was designed for the case where the majority of memory-copies made by a monitored process are visible to the interposition mechanism. We refer to this as cause-and-effect propagation since, in applying it, there is a tight causal relationship between receipt of some data over the network and use of that data in a system call argument. That is, we can point to a sequence of memory copies from a network receive buffer to a system call argument buffer. Correlative propagation, on the other hand, was designed for the case where most or all memory copies occur out of band – as occurs when a bot statically links in C library functions. This mode is referred to as correlative propagation since, in applying it, we are ultimately identifying when data received over the network correlates to that used in syscall arguments.

Upon a call to a taint propagation function f, that function's relevant arguments are checked for taintedness via applying the appropriate conditions, given the mode, and performing content-matching. Given a tainted source argument, taint propagation proceeds in the following way. For source buffers, we ensure that the tainted portion of that buffer is a known tainted string and its address range is a known tainted region. If f copies some portion of this source buffer to a destination buffer, the corresponding portion of the destination region is transitively marked tainted. If, on the other hand, f converts the source buffer to a numeric value, we add the numeric result to our collection of tainted numbers. Finally, if the tainted source argument is a number which f converts to another number, we add the destination value to our set of tainted numbers.

4.3 User Input Module

Our implementation tracks local user input as received via the keyboard or mouse and considers subsequent use of such clean data, such as in a system call argument, innocuous. Obtaining the data value corresponding to a keystroke is generally straightforward as the system generates a message in response to keyboard input for the target application identifying the key or character. Our implementation monitors such messages and creates, for each line of keyboard input, a clean string consisting of the previously input characters.

Obtaining the data value corresponding to a mouse input event is more challenging as the system generates, upon receipt of such an event, a message which merely identifies the target window, type of event (e.g. left button down), and coordinate pair within that window at which the event occurred. The actual data value corresponding to such an event is application-defined and not available via a library call. Our implementation addresses this opacity via exploiting locality of reference; in particular, our goal was to identify when an application was executing code to handle a user-input event. We posited that any data values referenced during execution of such code could be considered clean and that in this way we could infer a set of data values corresponding to a user input event. For a Windows user input event E, an application calls `DispatchMessage` in order to invoke that application's predefined handler for E. The handler must process E prior to returning from `DispatchMessage` [32] and may invoke system calls in its processing. Thus, upon entry to `DispatchMessage` and until return from it, we add any string referenced by any interposed-upon function to our collection of clean strings.

4.4 Behavior-Check Procedure

Our ability to identify bot behavior relies in part on our selection of appropriate system calls and their arguments to check for taintedness and cleanliness. The collection of bot capabilities (Fig. 1) informed our selection of system calls (gates) and their particular arguments (sinks); these are described below. The algorithm is as follows. If the sink type is numeric, if the argument value is tainted, we flag the invocation; otherwise, we pass control to the system call. While a numeric value will either be considered tainted or not, buffer arguments may contain some number of bytes of tainted and/or clean data. If the sink type is a data buffer which contains no tainted data, control is passed to the system call. Otherwise, we query the user-input module to determine whether that buffer also contains clean data. If not, the invocation is flagged; if so, this procedure will flag the invocation only if the argument contains more bytes of tainted than clean data.

A *behavior* is a general description of an action that may be detected via checking particular arguments for one or more system calls. The same gate function may be instrumented to detect multiple different behaviors. Conversely, multiple library functions may be instrumented to check for a single behavior. Table 2 contains the complete list of behaviors and associated gate functions. In general, we favored instrumenting lower-level API functions as gates; e.g., instrumenting `NtOpenFile` as a gate enables us to detect all behaviors that entail listing a directory, deleting a file, or replacing a file since the higher-level API functions for these tasks ultimately call into `NtOpenFile`.

Two behaviors (tainted send and derived send) require a bit more explanation. *Tainted send* occurs when data received over one connection (or socket) is sent out on another; e.g., when a bot is acting as a proxy, it echoes out on a second socket the data heard on the first. Since an application may commonly receive and send certain fixed strings over a variety of connections, we do not perform content-based or substring-based tainting for such strings. The set of such strings is small, application-specific, and generally consists of protocol header fields; e.g., a browser's set includes `HTTP/1.1` and `Accept-Range`. Consequently, the tainted send behavior is not flagged for transmission of routine messages that do not otherwise contain tainted data. *Derived send* occurs when a system call is invoked on some tainted input to obtain a result that is then sent on the network. Various data leaking commands match derived send, including one which takes a registry key name and returns its value.

5 Experimental Evaluation

This section provides the results of testing our experimental hypothesis – that the remote control behavior of bots can be detected via checking selected system calls for tainted arguments – on bots and benign programs. To determine the utility of our behavioral characterization, we compare the effects of detected commands to those of all commands.

5.1 Bot Experiment Setup

We edited the source code of each bot by altering its C&C parameters such that, when executed, that bot would connect to a C&C server under our control. We then built two versions of each bot: one which dynamically linked in C library functions (DYN) and a second which statically linked these in (STAT). We then executed each bot binary, injecting our DLL into the newly-spawned bot process so as to intercept its API calls (as described in 4.1). We were then able to exercise each bot over its set of commands and monitor the effects of each such command.

Table 2. Detected behaviors and the gate functions for each behavior

	Behavior	**gate function**
B1	tainted open file	NtOpenFile
B2	tainted create file	NtCreateFile
B3	tainted program execution	CreateProcess{A,W}
B4	tainted process termination	NtTerminateProcess
B5	bind tainted IP	NtDeviceIoControlFile
B6	bind tainted port	NtDeviceIoControlFile
B7	connect to tainted IP	connect; WSAConnect
B8	connect to tainted port	connect; WSAConnect
B9	tainted send	NtDeviceIoControlFile; SSL_write
B10	derived send	NtDeviceIoControlFile; SSL_write
B11	sendto tainted IP	sendto; WSASendTo
B12	sendto tainted port	sendto; WSASendTo
B13	tainted set registry key	NtSetValueKey
B14	tainted delete registry key	NtDeleteValueKey
B15	tainted create service	CreateService{A,W}
B16	tainted delete service	OpenService{A,W}
B17	tainted HttpSendRequest	HttpSendRequest{A,W}
B18	tainted IcmpSendEcho	IcmpSendEcho{A,W}

5.2 Terminology

When BotSwat *flags* a system call invocation, we say that a behavior is *detected*. If flagging this invocation is incorrect, we refer to this as a *false positive*. Any behavior flagged for a benign program is considered a false positive. If BotSwat fails to flag a system call invocation on an argument that contains data received over the network (most likely because BotSwat does not know that this argument should be considered tainted), we say a behavior is *exhibited* but not detected and refer to this as a *false negative*. We say that a command is detected when BotSwat correctly flags at least one behavior exhibited by that command; thus, commands which exhibit more than one behavior may have a false negative but still be detected.

5.3 Bot Results

In summary, we found that the external or remote control behavior of bots can be measured by identifying system call invocations which use tainted parameters. Moreover, the effects of a bot's detected commands account for the majority of the effects of all of a bot's commands (where effects are measured via number of system call invocations). Bots in general exhibit a great volume and diversity of behaviors. Table 3 provides a summary of our test results. Row 1 identifies the total number of commands provided by each of the tested bots. The number of those commands that take at least one parameter that is subsequently used (in whole or in part) in a critical system function is provided in row 2. The 3rd row gives the number of candidate commands that were detected using cause-and-effect propagation (C&E) for bots built with C library functions dynamically linked in (DYN). The last row shows the number of candidate commands detected using correlative propagation (CORR) on bots built with statically linked in C library functions (STAT). We did not have a version of evilbot which dynamically linked in C library functions.

Table 3. Summary of bot command detection

	ago	DSNX	evil	GSyS	sd	Spy
# cmds	88	28	5	56	50	36
# candidate cmds	36	14	5	26	20	15
# detected cmds (DYN, C&E)	33	14	N/A	26	20	15
# detected cmds (STAT, CORR)	31	10	5	12	12	15

Detection of Commands on Dynamically-Linked Bots

The best detection occurs under cause-and-effect propagation on dynamically-linked bots, since these conditions provide the best visibility into the bot's use of data received over the network. Only three total candidate commands were not detected in this mode: agobot's `harvest.registry` and scanning commands. Agobot's scanning commands use a transformation of a received parameter in a system call argument. Taintedness was not propagated across this transformation operation; thus, `scan.start` and `scan.startall` were not detected. Also, the same set of commands was detected (and the same behaviors flagged for each command) for agobot whether that bot encrypted C&C messages via dynamic calls to the OpenSSL library or not. Thus, detection of remote control is resilient to command encryption, given visibility into the cryptographic function calls.

Detection of Commands on Statically-Linked Bots

Since all tested bots either primarily or exclusively use C library functions for memory copying, static linking severely hinders visibility into a bot's use of received data. We were still, however, able to detect execution of many of the bots' candidate commands by correlating received network data to system call arguments. We explore below the effects of detected vs. undetected commands and provide some evidence that these undetected commands are significantly less harmful than are the detected commands. Many of the undetected commands rely on the previous execution of a command this *is* detected under these conditions. In particular, three of DSNX's four undetected commands (75%), seven of sdbot's eight (87.5%), and seven of G-SySbot's fourteen (50%) perform clone management; this functionality only makes sense when a clone exists to be managed. The command that creates a clone – for each of these three bots – was detected under STAT, CORR. There were three false positives under this mode; in all cases, the incorrectly flagged behavior was in fact malicious but not an example of external control.

The candidate commands that were not detected under STAT, CORR share a common property that could be used to produce even better detection results. Specifically, 24 of the 28 undetected commands use `sprintf` to format the argument buffers passed to system calls. Calls to this buffer-formatting function were not visible to BotSwat (under STAT), thus it was not able to infer that the resulting argument buffers contained (among other data) strings received over the network. Statistical tests that measure how similar a buffer's contents are to data received over the network may provide significant gains.

The Effects of Detected Commands Relative to All Commands

As discussed in Sect. 2.2, not all commands result in an equal amount of remote control behavior. We find that the commands we are able to detect for each bot – even under STAT, CORR – account for the majority of that bot's total potential remote control behavior. For Spybot, e.g., under STAT, CORR, the number of system calls invoked during execution of detected commands is 145 (Table 4) and during execution of all commands is 202 (Table 1). The same pattern held for all tested bots and is a consequence of the relative severity of commands we are able to detect even under these conditions.

Table 4. The number of system calls invoked during successful execution of candidate and detected commands

	ago	DSNX	evil	GSyS	sd	Spy
# syscalls invoked by candidate cmds	417	114	5	122	110	145
# syscalls ... detected cmds (DYN, C&E)	393	114	N/A	122	110	145
# syscalls ... detected cmds (STAT, CORR)	386	110	5	99	99	145

Bots Exhibit Volume and Diversity of Behaviors

For each bot command, we counted the number of distinct behaviors correctly detected in a successful execution of that command. Then we tallied these values across commands, giving us the number of times each behavior was detected for each bot (Fig. 2). It is not uncommon for execution of a single command to result in detection of multiple behaviors. Executing a port redirect command, e.g., generally results in four detected behaviors: binding a tainted port (B6), connecting to a tainted IP (B7), connecting to a tainted port (B8), and tainted send (B9). Note that in practice the raw number of detected bot behaviors might be much larger since execution of certain commands may cause the same behavior to be repeatedly flagged. Such is the case with denial-of-service (DoS) commands, which often cause a particular behavior to be flagged with transmission of each DoS packet. We note that the distribution of detected behaviors across bot families is not uniform; e.g., behavior B11 (sendto tainted IP) is frequently flagged in agobot but never in DSNXbot and only rarely in G-SyS, sd, and Spybots. Such differences may be leveraged to perform classification of an encountered bot as more likely to be a variant of a particular family.

Fig. 2. The number of times each behavior was detected, over all of a bot's commands

	B1	B2	B3	B4	B5	B6	B7	B8	B9	B10	B11	B12	B13	B14	B15	B16	B17	B18
ago	5	6	7	2	1	5	14	2	14	1	7	3	1	1	1	1	0	0
DSNX	4	4	2	0	0	1	6	4	8	0	0	0	0	0	0	0	0	0
evil	0	0	5	0	0	0	0	0	0	0	0	0	0	0	0	0	0	0
G-SyS	1	1	8	0	0	1	8	4	10	1	1	1	0	0	0	0	3	1
sd	1	1	2	0	0	1	8	4	10	1	1	1	0	0	0	0	3	1
Spy	4	5	1	1	0	2	4	3	1	0	1	1	0	0	0	0	0	0
Total	15	17	25	3	1	10	40	17	43	3	10	6	1	1	1	1	6	2

5.4 Benign Program Results

We tested eight benign applications that exhibit extensive network interaction across a variety of activities typical to these programs. False positives in this context are any instances in which a system call invocation is flagged. This could arise from imperfections in our user-input module implementation, which may not be able to infer that a system call invocation is the result of local user input. Alternatively, a benign program may genuinely exhibit external or remote control. There were eight false positives: two for the browser, three for the email client, two for the IRC client, and one for the IRC server. The programs, activities across which their behavior was traced, and results are described below.

Benign Program Testing

We tested a browser (firefox), email client (Eudora), IRC client (mIRC), ssh client (putty), FTP clients (WS_FP and SecureFX), anti-virus (AV) signature updater

(Symantec's LuComServer_3_0.exe), and IRC server (Unreal IRCd). Since the majority of systems infected with bots are those of home users (who do not typically run server programs) [29], we tested against only one server program. We note, however, that server programs may, at an abstract level, be designed to respond to certain types of external control (that exerted by the client).

We used the browser to visit a variety of sites, some containing linked-in images. Once at a site, we clicked on hypertext links, downloaded files specified by links, saved the web page's contents to a file, executed downloaded programs from within the browser, etc. With the email client, we received, composed, replied to, forwarded, and sent email, including and excluding attachments, and including and excluding HTML. We also saved and executed received attachments from within the email client. We exercised the IRC client over a range of its capabilities: connecting to a server and channel, messaging, DCC file transfer, etc. We used the ssh client to connect to and execute commands on a remote host. Using FTP clients, we connected to and browsed various FTP sites, navigated across directories (alternatively using the mouse and keyboard), and downloaded files. We tested the AV signature updater via establishing a base state with stale virus definitions files then instructing the updater to get the latest AV signatures. Finally, the IRC server was networked to other servers and serviced clients.

Benign Program Results

We present the results of running under correlative propagation (which has the most relaxed requirements for taintedness) with the user-input module enabled. Four of the eight false positives occur as a result of the automatic downloading of linked-in images performed in rendering an HTML document. Two of these were exhibited by the browser and two by the email client, both upon receipt of an HTML document containing an <IMG SRC="..."> element. Receipt of such an element causes the application to request the content specified in the SRC URL. Also, when the user receives an email with an attachment, Eudora automatically creates a file of the same name (as the received file), which causes the tainted open file behavior (B1).

The mIRC client generated two false positives as a result of performing Direct Client Protocol (DCC) file receipt. These false positives reveal limitations in our user-input module implementation. In preparation for DCC file transfer, the file sender provides an IP and port to the recipient via a network message. The recipient then creates a TCP connection to the sender using the specified IP and port. Therefore, behaviors B7 (connecting to a tainted IP) and B8 (connecting to a tainted port) were flagged. Prior to the chat client creating such a connection, however, the client asks the user whether he wishes to perform this operation and will only proceed if the user responds affirmatively. Our user-input module was not able to infer the connection between the user input agreeing to this behavior (via a dialog box) and the values used to create the network connection.

The IRC server repeatedly exhibited the tainted send behavior (B9) – which identifies when data heard over one socket is sent out on another. Clearly this behavior is expected, since the overriding purpose of an IRC server is to participate in a chat network, which entails receiving messages and sharing those with its clients and/or other servers.

Benign Results Discussion

We find it interesting that most of the detected behaviors of benign programs may be known to carry a risk and thus our flagging of these behaviors may not be totally inappropriate. In particular, [45] recommends disabling DCC file receipt so as to avoid malware infection (2 behaviors); the automatic downloading of linked-in images performed by the email client and browser may be exploited to perform DoS attacks [43] (4 behaviors); and email attachments are a known malware propagation vector (1 behavior).

Table 5 summarizes the detection of behaviors across all tested programs. Note that a single run of any such program may exhibit fewer behaviors depending upon the inputs to that particular run-time instance. In general, bots exhibit high volume (202 across all bots and all commands, as in Fig. 2) and great diversity (18 different) of behaviors. By contrast, only eight behaviors total (five different) were flagged over execution of all benign programs even when testing under the most liberal taint propagation mode, correlative. We discuss how one might handle these false positives in Sect. 6. Finally, we acknowledge the limitations of black-box dynamic testing; that is, there may be other inputs to these benign programs that would result in flagging additional behaviors. Similarly, it may be the case that higher fidelity taint propagation (e.g., assembly-code-level tainting) reveals additional behaviors. That said, all programs (malicious and benign) were tested using the same system, and the demonstrated behavioral gap between bots and benign applications under these conditions is dramatic.

5.5 Performance Results

Function interception via the `detours` library imposes an overhead of fewer than 400 nanoseconds per invocation [9]. We measured the overall performance impact of BotSwat's instrumentation via scripting a bot to receive then execute various commands; the bot's performance was measured natively and under each of the two propagation modes. The overall measured performance overhead is 2.81% when using C&E propagation and 3.87% under CORR.

6 Potential for Host-Based, Behavioral Bot Detection

Signature-based anti-malware mechanisms suffer from several critical limitations, including the inability to detect novel malware instances or obfuscated variants and the need to continuously update their signature sets [31, 35]. A recent study found that even the most effective anti-virus vendor failed to detect a significant percentage of malware samples found in the wild [38]. Behavior-based approaches to malware

Table 5. For each tested program, the number of distinct behaviors detected

	# distinct behaviors	which behaviors
agobot	16	B1 - B16
GSySbot	12	B1 - B3, B6 - B12, B17, B18
sdbot	12	B1 - B3, B6 - B12, B17, B18
Spybot	10	B1 - B4, B6 - B9, B11, B12
DSNXbot	7	B1 - B3, B6 - B9
evilbot	1	B3
Eudora	3	B1, B7, B17
Firefox	2	B7, B9
mIRC	2	B7, B8
Unreal IRCd	1	B9
putty	0	N/A
SecureFX	0	N/A
Symantec AV updater	0	N/A
WS_FTP	0	N/A

detection provide a powerful alternative: the ability to detect entire classes of malware including previously unseen instances. The primary challenge is to identify a useful behavioral characterization: one which identifies behavior fundamental to a class of malware but which is not generally exhibited by innocuous programs. The data presents a compelling argument that our characterization meets these criteria; the very behavior that makes bots most useful to their installers (their programmability) provides the basis for detection.

Our prototype implementation was designed to test the effectiveness of our behavioral characterization; a secure implementation of our method must be able to detect and differentiate such remote control behavior in a way that is difficult for malware to adaptively evade and subvert. Designing such a system is a research problem unto itself. We highlight some fundamental challenges and tradeoffs in building a bot detection mechanism based on our findings.

Process Monitoring Mechanism The mechanism that enables visibility into a process's actions may also be referred to as a *sandbox*. There are two primary design considerations: *visibility*, which refers to the type and granularity of events visible to the sandbox, and *isolation*, which refers to the difficulty of a monitored process to evade or subvert the sandbox. The (user-space) in-line function hooks [9] used in the prototype implementation provide high visibility (as the interposition code runs in the same address space as the monitored application) but very weak isolation [8, 10]. Kernel-space system call interposition and Virtual Machine Introspection [23] are additional possibilities.

Tainting Challenges and Tradeoffs Since a malicious bot may evade detection via performing data movement (or data transformation) operations out-of-band, coverage is a critical aspect of the system's security. There appears at present to be a fundamental tradeoff in dynamic tainting modules between coverage and performance; i.e., tainting implementations that provide thorough coverage (as in [12]) exact significant performance penalties. Also, if there are operations across which taintedness is not propagated (e.g., writes to persistent storage or pipes), surely such avenues will be used to launder tainted data. Propagating taint more thoroughly may result in more flagged behaviors and false positives.

User Input Module Challenges There are two types of attacks specific to this component: spoofing user input events and genuinely obtaining user input. Exposure to user-input-spoofing attacks may be minimized by incorporating a kernel-level component that identifies receipt of user input events. The latter attack, however, highlights the fundamental challenge in designing this module: since the meaning of user input events is inherently application-defined, a user-input module must rely on the application that received a user-input event to implicitly or explicitly identify the semantics of that input. Consequently, if a malicious process is able to legitimately obtain *any* local user input, that process may be able to arbitrarily assign meaning to that input.

System Inputs and Outputs An interesting question is which processes to monitor using the detection mechanism. A reasonable decision may be to not monitor known benign programs. Such a decision would inevitably cause attackers to explore ways in which such known benign programs could be coopted to do the attackers' bidding (as in [43]). Either way, a general decision must be made about when to label something a bot. A reasonable tradeoff may be to require some volume and diversity of behaviors; then a lower threshold more narrowly constrains the attacker's arena but may also result in more false positives. Additionally, one could whitelist certain behaviors known to be generated by particular applications during their legitimate operation (as in Sect. 5.4). A final option may be to identify and flag execution of commands – sequences of correlated behaviors – rather than individual behaviors.

7 Related Work

Tainting has been applied statically, dynamically, at a language level, via an interpreter, an emulator, compiler extensions, etc. [1, 11, 12, 14, 15, 19, 25].

Much previous run-time, host-based, anti-malware research has focused on identifying when a host program (generally assumed to be non-malicious) has been exploited [5, 12, 13, 20, 26]. While a bot may be spread via leveraging such exploits, monitoring execution of an installed bot using one of these mechanisms will generally not result in the bot being identified as malicious since no exploit of a local host program is entailed in normal bot execution. Other behavior-based research has been done to identify rootkits and spyware [7, 22, 28, 42].

Host-based approaches to bot detection include scanning the contents of files and memory for certain byte sequences as well as content-based filtering, which identifies receipt of packets containing known bot-command keywords. Network-based approaches to botnet detection include those which: (a) detect secondary effects of botnets [3, 6]; (b) set up honeypots to obtain bot binaries then infiltrate those botnets [24, 36, 37]; (c) mitigate the effects of a botnet at a DDoS victim [21]; (d) apply content-based Network Intrusion Detection System (NIDS) signatures [16]; (e) identify IRC NICK messages likely to have been generated by bots [40]; (f) track and correlate various types of NIDS alarms to identify *bot-infection sequences* [39]; (g) perform analysis of flow data to identify suspected bots then likely conversations between such suspected bots and their C&C servers [41].

8 Conclusions

Botnets present a serious and increasing threat, as launching points for attacks including spam, distributed denial of service, sniffing, keylogging, and malware distribution. Our work explores whether the execution of malicious bots can be distinguished from that of innocuous programs. We provided a characterization of the remote control behavior of bots, identified the fraction of current bot remote-control behavior covered by this characterization, built a prototype implementation, and evaluated our hypothesis against six bots from five different families and a variety of benign applications typical to the target environment. We introduce techniques, such as content-based and substring-based tainting, that enable us to effectively identify a bot's remote control behavior even when visibility into the memory-copying calls made by a bot is severely limited.

Experimental evaluation suggests that the external or remote control behavior of bots can be detected by identifying system call invocations which use tainted parameters. We see that the effects of a bot's candidate commands (as measured via number of system call invocations) constitute the vast majority of the effects of all of a bot's commands. We also see that bots in general exhibit a great volume and diversity of behaviors. Finally, we note that, when we track local user input and sanitize subsequent uses of it, benign programs relatively rarely exhibit the external control behavior that we're measuring. Significant challenges remain in the problem of building a secure and robust bot detection system based on these observed behavioral differences.

Acknowledgements. We are grateful to Galen Hunt, David Dagon, Andrew Sakai, Adam Barth, Tal Garfinkel, Wenke Lee, and Christian Kreibich.

References

1. Turoff, A.: Defensive CGI Programming with Taint Mode and CGI::UNTAINT
2. Schneier, B.: How Bot Those Nets? In Wired Magazine, July 27, 2006.
3. Dagon, D.: Botnet Detection and Response: The Network Is the Infection. In Operations, Analysis, and Research Center Workshop, July 2005.
4. Ilett, D.: Most spam generated by botnets, says expert. ZDNet, Sept. 22, 2004.

5. Wagner, D., Dean, D.: Intrusion Detection via Static Analysis. In IEEE Symposium on Security and Privacy, May 2001.
6. Cooke, E., Jahanian, F., McPherson, D.: The Zombie Roundup: Understanding, Detecting, and Disrupting Botnets. In Steps to Reducing Unwanted Traffic on the Internet, July 2005.
7. Kirda, E., Kruegel, C., Banks, G., Vigna, G., Kemmerer, R.: Behavior-based Spyware Detection. In Proc. 15th USENIX Security Symposium, August 2006.
8. Hoglund, G., Butler, J.: Rootkits: Subverting the Windows Kernel. First Edition, Addison-Wesley, Upper Saddle River, NJ, 2006.
9. Hunt, G., Brubacher, B.: Detours: Binary Interception of Win32 Functions. In 3rd USENIX Windows NT Symposium, July 1999.
10. Butler, J.: Bypassing 3rd Party Windows Buffer Overflow Protection. In phrack Volume 0x0b, Issue 0x3e, Phile #0x0, 7/13/2004.
11. Chow, J., Pfaff, B., Garfinkel, T., Christopher, K., Rosenblum, M.: Understanding Data Lifetime via Whole System Simulation. In Proc. of the USENIX 13th Security Symposium, August 2004.
12. Newsome, J., Song, D.: Dynamic Taint Analysis for Automatic Detection, Analysis, and Signature Generation of Exploits on Commodity Software. In Network and Distributed Systems Symposium, February 2005.
13. Rabek, J., Khazan, R., Lewandowski, S., Cunningham, R.: Detection of Injected, Dynamically Generated, and Obfuscated Malicious Code. In Proc. of the ACM Workshop on Rapid Malcode, October 2003.
14. Ashcraft, K., Engler, D.: Using programmer-written compiler extensions to catch security holes. In IEEE Symposium on Security and Privacy, May 2002.
15. Locking Ruby in the Safe http://www.rubycentral.com/book/taint.html
16. LURHQ. Phatbot Trojan Analysis. http://www.lurhq.com/phatbot.html
17. Overton, M.: Bots and Botnets: Risks, Issues, and Prevention. In Virus Bulletin Conference, Dublin, Ireland, October 2005.
18. Ianelli, N., Hackworth, A.: Botnets as a Vehicle for Online Crime. CERT Coordination Center, December 2005.
19. perlsec http://perldoc.perl.org/perlsec.html
20. Forrest, S., Hofmeyr, S., Somayaji, A., Longstaff, T.: A Sense of Self for Unix Processes. In IEEE Symposium on Security and Privacy, May 1996.
21. Kandula, S., Katabi, D., Jacob, M., Berger, A.: Botz-4-Sale: Surviving Organized DDoS Attacks That Mimic Flash Crowds. In Network and Distributed System Security Symposium, May 2005.
22. Strider GhostBuster Rootkit Detection http://research.microsoft.com/rootkit/
23. Garfinkel, T., Rosenblum, M.: A Virtual Machine Introspection Based Architecture for Intrusion Detection. In Network & Distributed Systems Security, Feb. 2003.
24. Honeynet Project & Research Alliance. Know your Enemy: Tracking Botnets.
25. Shankar, U., Talwar, K., Foster, J., Wagner, D.: Detecting format string vulnerabilities with type qualifiers. In Proc. 10th USENIX Security Symp., Aug. 2001.
26. Kiriansky, V., Bruening, D., Amarasinghe, S.: Secure execution via program shepherding. In Proc. 11th USENIX Security Symposium, August 2002.
27. Naraine, R. Money Bots: Hackers Cash In on Hijacked PCs. eWeek, Sept. 2006.
28. Cui, W., Katz, R., Tan, W.: BINDER: An Extrusion-based Break-in Detector for Personal Computers. In Proc. of the 21st Annual Computer Security Applications Conference, December 2005.
29. Martin, K.: Stop the bots. In The Register, April, 2006.

30. Keizer, G.: Bot Networks Behind Big Boost In Phishing Attacks. TechWeb, Nov. 2004.
31. Christodorescu, M., Jha, S.: Testing Malware Detectors. In Proc. of the International Symposium on Software Testing and Analysis, July 2004.
32. MSDN Library. Using Messages and Message Queues.
33. Symantec Internet Security Threat Report, Trends for July 05-December 05. Volume IX, Published March 2006.
34. Sturgeon, W.: Net pioneer predicts overwhelming botnet surge. ZDNet News, January 29, 2007.
35. Symantec Internet Security Threat Report, Trends for January 06-June 06, Volume X. Published September 2006.
36. Freiling, F., Holz, T., Wicherski, G.: Botnet Tracking: Exploring a Root-Cause Methodology to Prevent Distributed Denial-of-Service Attacks. In European Symposium On Research In Computer Security, September 2006.
37. Rajab, M., Zarfoss, J., Monrose, F., Terzis, A.: A Multifaceted Approach to Understanding the Botnet Phenomenon. In Proc. of ACM SIGCOMM/USENIX Internet Measurement Conference, October 2006.
38. Jevans, D.: The Latest Trends in Phishing, Crimeware and Cash-Out Schemes. Private correspondence.
39. Gu, G., Porras, P., Yegneswaran, V., Fong, M., Lee, W.: BotHunter: Detecting Malware Infection Through IDS-Driven Dialog Correlation. Manuscript.
40. Goebel, J., Holz, T.: Rishi: Identify Bot-Contaminated Hosts by IRC Nickname Evaluation. 1st Workshop on Hot Topics in Understanding Botnets, April 2007.
41. Karasaridis, A., Rexroad, B., Hoeflin, D.: Wide-Scale Botnet Detection and Characterization. 1st Workshop on Hot Topics in Understanding Botnets, April 2007.
42. Wang, Y., Beck, D., Vo, B., Roussev, R., Verbowski, C.: Detecting Stealth Software with Strider GhostBuster. Microsoft Technical Report MSR-TR-2005-25.
43. Lam, V., Antonatos, S., Akritidis, P., Anagnostakis, K.: Puppetnets: Misusing Web Browsers as a Distributed Attack Infrastructure. In the 13th ACM Conference on Computer and Communications Security, October 2006.
44. Stinson, E., Mitchell, J.: Characterizing the Remote Control Behavior of Bots. Manuscript.   `http://www.stanford.edu/\~{}stinson/pub/botswat\_long.pdf`
45. mIRC Help, Viruses, Trojans, and Worms.

Automatically Identifying Trigger-based Behavior in Malware

David Brumley, Cody Hartwig, Zhenkai Liang, James Newsome, Dawn Song, and
Heng Yin

Carnegie Mellon University, 5000 Forbes Avenue, Pittsburgh, PA 15213
{dbrumley,chartwig,zliang,jnewsome,dawnsong,hyin}@cmu.edu

Summary. Malware often contains hidden behavior which is only activated when properly
triggered. Well known examples include: the MyDoom worm which DDoS's on particular
dates, keyloggers which only log keystrokes for particular sites, and DDoS zombies which are
only activated when given the proper command. We call such behavior *trigger-based behavior*.

Currently, trigger-based behavior analysis is often performed in a tedious, manual fashion.
Providing even a small amount of assistance would greatly assist and speed-up the analysis. In
this chapter, we propose that automatic analysis of trigger-based behavior in malware is possible. In particular, we design an approach for automatic trigger-based behavior detection and
analysis using dynamic binary instrumentation and mixed concrete and symbolic execution.
Our approach shows that in many cases we can:

(1) detect the existence of trigger-based behavior, (2) find the conditions that trigger
such hidden behavior, and (3) find inputs that satisfy those conditions, allowing us to observe the triggered malicious behavior in a controlled environment. We have implemented
MineSweeper, a system utilizing this approach. In our experiments, MineSweeper has successfully identified trigger-based behavior in real-world malware. Although there are many
challenges presented by automatic trigger-based behavior detection, MineSweeper shows us
that such automatic analysis is possible and encourages future work in this area.

1 Introduction

In many malware programs, certain code paths implementing malicious behaviors
will only be executed when certain *trigger conditions* are met [15, 18, 23, 24]. We
call such behavior *trigger-based behavior*. Trigger-based behavior may be set off
by many different *trigger types*, such as time, system events, and network inputs.
For example, many viruses attack their host systems on specific dates, such as Fri-
day the 13th or April Fool's Day [18, 24]; worms may launch attacks at specific
times [13], some keyloggers only record keystrokes to files when the application
window name contains certain keywords [15]; some browser-helper-object-based
spyware only logs information if the URL contains a certain keyword [23]; some
distributed denial-of-service tools only start launching attacks when receiving certain network commands [3]. Thus, trigger-based behavior is a real problem, causing

millions of dollars of damage [15, 18, 23–27], and detecting trigger-based behavior is important for understanding the malware's malicious behavior and for effective malware defense.

Currently, trigger-based behavior is often analyzed in a tedious, manual process. To the best of our knowledge, there is no previous work on automating trigger-based behavior analysis. Given a piece of potentially malicious code, a typical manual analysis scenario is as follows: a) the analyst runs the malware in a virtual machine and may observe nothing since the trigger condition may not be met, b) he may then perform some disassembly and build up a mental model of the program execution, c) he may then guess which parts of the input or system setup to change and rerun the malware and hope to observe something new. This process is repeated until the analyst runs out of time, patience, or gets lucky and uncovers the trigger-based behavior. Such a manual process is slow, labor intensive, and does not scale.

These problems apply directly to botnets. From an analyst's point of view, a bot is a malicious binary containing many hidden behaviors. Using the framework we describe an analyst can find the behavior a certain bot exhibits including actions it takes and commands it responds to. We have specifically researched this application in our most recent work [4].

Our Approach. In this chapter, we propose that *automatically* identifying and reasoning about trigger-based behavior in malware is possible, and design a system as a first step towards this goal. In particular, we show how to design and integrate techniques from formal verification, symbolic execution, binary analysis, and whole-system emulation and dynamic instrumentation to enable automatic identification and analysis of trigger-based behaviors in malware. Automatic trigger-based behavior detection is an extremely challenging task. For example, completely automatic analysis of trigger-based behavior for all programs is undecidable (Section 5). However, we show that our approach can provide great value in many cases. Our system, *MineSweeper,* is able to automatically identify the trigger-based behaviors in several real-world malware examples. Even when complete automatic analysis is not possible, we design our system so that it still provides valuable information about potential trigger-based code paths which a human would otherwise have to discover manually.

To design an approach for automatic trigger-based behavior analysis, we first observe that at a high level, triggers in a program are implemented as conditional jumps depending on inputs from the trigger types of interest such as time, keyboard, or network inputs. The malicious code is triggered when the conditional jumps evaluate to the desired directions, e.g., the current time is equal to the trigger time. Therefore, given trigger types of interest, one key to uncovering trigger-based behavior is to construct values for trigger inputs (i.e., inputs from trigger types of interest) that makes the conditional jumps evaluate in the desired direction, activating the trigger-dependent code. We call the condition that the trigger inputs need to satisfy in order for the code execution to go down a path uncovering the trigger-based behavior the *trigger condition*, and the values of the trigger inputs satisfying the trigger condition the *trigger values*. Second, we observe that trigger-based behavior could be embedded at any point in the program. Thus, we need to be able to explore many different program paths which could depend on trigger inputs.

From these observations, we design an approach as a first step towards automatic trigger-based behavior analysis in malware. Our approach takes as inputs the binary program of the malware to be analyzed and a set of trigger types. In order to automatically explore trigger-based behavior in the program based on the given trigger types, we employ *mixed concrete and symbolic execution* to automatically and iteratively explore different code paths which could depend on trigger inputs. In particular, trigger inputs are represented symbolically, and instructions that depend upon the trigger inputs operate on symbolic values, and are executed symbolically. Conversely, instructions that do not depend on trigger inputs operate on concrete values, and are concretely (natively) evaluated (for efficiency). Thus, symbolic execution builds up symbolic formulas over the symbolic inputs (which are in turn based on the trigger types). Note that the ability to mix concrete and symbolic execution is important to reduce the formula size. As our experiments indicate, almost all instructions can be concretely executed.

For any path to be explored, the mixed concrete and symbolic execution automatically generates formulas representing the conditions that the trigger inputs need to satisfy for the program execution to go down the path. We then ask a solver (such as a decision procedure) whether the formula can be true, i.e., whether there are trigger input values which will satisfy the formula. An unsatisfiable formula indicates the path just explored is not actually feasible, and we continue to explore other paths. A satisfiable formula means we have discovered a new path which depends on trigger inputs, and the formula generated represents a trigger condition. In this case, the solver also constructs the trigger values, i.e., values for the trigger inputs necessary to execute the path of interest. We can then execute the program in a controlled environment, provide it with the discovered trigger values, and observe the trigger-based behavior. By iterating this process, we automatically explore different code paths to uncover trigger-based behaviors in the program.

In some cases the solver may not be able to return an answer to the formula within a reasonable amount of time. In this case, we simply set a timeout and go on to explore other paths. Therefore, we try to explore different branches and paths as much as possible, but do not guarantee to explore all branches or paths. As our experiments demonstrate, despite this technical difficulty in certain cases, this approach offers great practical value for automatic analysis of trigger-based behavior in real malware, and in any case, is a big step forward compared to the current manual process.

An additional technical challenge for malware analysis is that often we do not have the luxury of access to source code. Even worse, malware is often packed or obfuscated. Code packing is a technique where binary code is statically compressed to save space, and only decompressed at runtime. Obfuscation is a technique which is designed to make static analysis difficult. In either case, the code will be difficult, if not impossible, to disassemble. Thus, we need to make our approach work with only access to the binary program, and moreover, deal with binary programs which may dynamically generate code and are potentially difficult to statically analyze. To this end, we employ whole-system emulation and dynamic binary instrumentation to enable mixed concrete and symbolic execution on *binaries*. To the best of our knowledge, our system is the first to enable mixed concrete and symbolic execution on binaries (see Section 6).

We have implemented our approach in a system called *MineSweeper*. In our experiments, we show that our system is successful at automatically analyzing trigger-based behavior in several real world malware examples, some of which are widely spread, and some of which are packed. The total time for MineSweeper to perform the analysis is usually less than 30 minutes, which otherwise might have taken a manual process days to uncover.

Contributions. This chapter proposes that automatic analysis of trigger-based behavior is possible, and designs the first holistic approach for automatically identifying trigger-based behavior in binary programs.

- We demonstrate that automatic analysis of trigger-based behavior in malware is possible. Previous analysis was completely manual, thus any automated assistance is of great value.
- We develop techniques for mixed execution of binaries and apply them to analyzing trigger-based behavior. Previous work on mixed execution required source code [6, 14]. The ability to perform mixed execution on binaries may be of independent interest to other applications as well.
- We implement our ideas in a tool called *MineSweeper*. In particular, MineSweeper automatically: a) Detects the existence of trigger-based behavior for specified trigger types, b) Finds the trigger condition, c) Finds input values that satisfy the trigger condition, when the trigger condition can be solved, and d) Feeds the trigger values to the program, causing it to exhibit the trigger behavior, so that it may be analyzed in a controlled environment. In our experiments, the end-to-end time to perform all steps to analyze the trigger-based behavior automatically is usually less than 30 minutes.
- Minesweeper *does not need source code*, and works on unmodified binary programs. The ability to analyze binaries is absolutely necessary to be a realistic approach for malware analysis. Since we dynamically instrument code to perform mixed execution on the fly, we are also able to handle obfuscated and packed code, as demonstrated by our experiments. Also, our framework is extensible to accommodate many different trigger types.

2 Problem Statement and Approach Overview

In this section, we describe the overall problem of automatic trigger-based behavior analysis, and give an overview of our approach. We begin by introducing the running example we use throughout the chapter. We then introduce our terminology, and the automatic trigger-based behavior analysis problem. We then describe our approach.

Motivating Example. In Figure 1, we show the disassembly and source code for a typical malware worm similar to MyDoom. In this example, the ddos action will only be activated if the call from GetLocalTime returns 10:06 11/9. Thus, the ddos action is a trigger-based behavior which will only be triggered at this specific time.

Note that although we have provided the source code for illustrative purposes, this is not typically available to the analyst. Also, we have provided the complete disassembly, though malware is often obfuscated to prevent disassembly so such information would also not be available to the analyst. Thus, in a typical scenario, the analyst would only know the assembly instructions for runs actually executed. In addition, we have shown a relatively small example: real code is often much more complex, may contain more trigger-based branches, and often other functionality that makes it difficult to even recognize where trigger-based behavior might potentially be in the program. This raises the question: how do we reason about potential trigger-based behavior in a program automatically?

```
4012b1: call    401810 <_GetLocalTime@4>
4012b6: add     $0xc,%esp
4012b9: cmpw    $0x9,0xfffffffee(%ebp)
4012be: jne     40132d <_main+0xad>
4012c0: cmpw    $0xa,0xfffffff0(%ebp)
4012c5: jne     40132d <_main+0xad>
4012c7: cmpw    $0xb,0xffffffea(%ebp)
4012cc: jne     40132d <_main+0xad>
4012ce: cmpw    $0x6,0xfffffff2(%ebp)
4012d3: jne     40132d <_main+0xad>
4012d5: sub     $0xc,%esp
4012d8: push    $0x404000
4012dd: call    4017a0 <ddos>
4012e2: add     $0x10,%esp
4012e5: jmp     40132d <_main+0xad>
...
40132d: ret
```

```
SYSTEMTIME systime;
GetLocalTime(&systime);
site = ``www.usenix.org'';
if (9 == systime.wDay){
   if (10 == systime.wHour){
      if (11 == systime.wMonth){
         if (6 == systime.wMinute){
            ddos(site);
         }
      }
   }
}
```

Fig. 1. Our running example.

2.1 The Automatic Trigger-based Analysis Problem

In our problem setting, we focus on automatic discovery of trigger-based behavior when given a piece of potentially malicious code and a list of *trigger-types* of interest. Typical trigger types include the system time, system events, network and keyboard inputs, and return values from library or system calls. We call inputs from trigger-types of interest *trigger inputs*. In our running example, we assume the trigger type of interest is `GetLocalTime`, thus, the returned `systime` is the trigger input.

The program execution may take different paths depending on the values of trigger inputs. Thus, certain code paths performing malicious behaviors may only be executed if the values of trigger inputs make the program execution go down a particular path. Behaviors of such code paths are called *trigger-based behavior*. The condition that the trigger inputs need to satisfy to lead the program execution to go down a path to the trigger-based code is called the *trigger condition* for the trigger-based behavior, and the values of the trigger inputs which satisfy the trigger condition are called the *trigger values*. If we supply the trigger values as the trigger inputs, the program execution will satisfy the trigger condition and activate the trigger-based behavior which enables us to observe the trigger-based behavior in a controlled environment. Note that the trigger condition is a succinct form representing trigger values which will activate the trigger-based behavior.

In our running example, the trigger condition (from the source code) is when all 4 `if` statements are true:

$$\text{systime.wDay} == 9 \wedge \text{systime.wHour} == 10 \wedge \text{systime.wMonth} == 11 \wedge \text{systime.wMinute} == 6$$

And the trigger value is a compound statement where the `systime` structure's `wDay` field is 9, the `wHour` field is 10, the `wMonth` field is 11, and the `wMinute` field is 6.

Problem Statement. Thus the problem of automatic trigger-based behavior analysis is when given a piece of potentially malicious code and a list of trigger types of interest, we automatically explore as many different code paths as possible to: (1) discover code paths whose execution depends on trigger inputs, (2) identify the trigger condition, (3) when possible, derive trigger values which will satisfy the trigger condition, and (4) execute the program with the trigger values to observe the trigger-based behavior in a controlled environment.

2.2 Our Approach and System Overview

Our Approach. Since trigger-based behavior could be embedded anywhere in the program, automatically identifying trigger-based behavior requires us to automatically explore as many different execution paths that depend on trigger inputs as possible. One naïve solution would be to simply do random testing, where we could set random values to the trigger inputs and hope they will lead the program execution down different paths. However, such an approach would be hopelessly inefficient

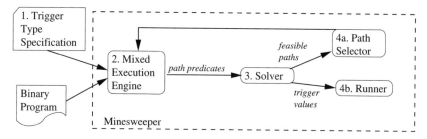

Fig. 2. Steps performed by MineSweeper.

and impractical since the probability of guessing the right values to satisfy the trigger conditions would be extremely slim in most cases.

Instead, we employ an iterative approach with mixed symbolic and concrete execution, as shown in Figure 2. The steps are:

- Step 1: When given a malicious program, the user first selects trigger types of interest. A trigger type can be time, system events, network inputs, or any library or system call. We supply a list of trigger types that are commonly used by malware. The user can choose from the supplied list as well as define their own trigger type of interest.
- Step 2: Given the trigger types of interest, our approach then iteratively conducts mixed concrete and symbolic execution to explore the different execution paths that depend on trigger inputs and observes the trigger-based behavior. In particular, trigger inputs will be represented symbolically, and the mixed concrete and symbolic execution builds up symbolic expressions and constraints as it goes down a path. When it hits the next conditional jump depending on symbolic inputs, it will generate two *path predicates*: one for the current path continuing with the true branch, and one for the current path continuing with the false branch. The path predicate is therefore the condition on trigger inputs which make the program execution go down that path.
- Step 3: The two path predicates will then be given to a solver to see whether each formula can be satisfied, indicating whether the path is feasible. Each feasible branch will then indicate a new feasible path to be further explored. The feasible path(s) are then added to the set of paths to be further explored. For each feasible path, the solver also returns the assignment to the trigger inputs to make the formula true, i.e., the trigger values.
- Step 4.a: Our approach then selects the next path from the set of feasible paths to be further explored. The process then goes back to Step 2 to continue mixed concrete and symbolic execution along the chosen path. Execution will continue until it hits the next conditional jump that depends on trigger inputs as described in Step 2. In this manner we can force the program execution down any feasible path and thus be able to iteratively explore different execution paths depending on trigger inputs.

- Step 4.b: Our approach then executes the program concretely using the trigger values returned by the solver in Step 3, to observe the trigger-based behavior in a controlled environment.

System Overview. We have designed and implemented a system, *MineSweeper*, to realize the above approach. At a high level, MineSweeper takes as inputs the binary program to be analyzed and the trigger type specifications. MineSweeper provides a default list of trigger types commonly used in malware for the user to choose from, and also allows the user to define their own trigger types of interest. If the user does not know what trigger type the malware may use, MineSweeper can offer further assistance by monitoring for any possible inputs to the program, e.g., system calls and library calls, and then prompting the user whether the input source should be further considered as a trigger type of interest (Section 3.1).

MineSweeper has four components which implement the aforementioned process: the *Mixed Execution Engine,* the *Solver,* the *Path Selector,* and the *Runner,* as shown in Figure 2. The Mixed Execution Engine performs mixed concrete and symbolic execution and creates the path predicates. The Solver solves the path predicates to see whether they can be satisfied, and thus are feasible. For feasible paths, the Solver constructs an assignment to the input variables from the trigger types which will make the path predicates to be true. The newly discovered feasible path(s) are added to the set of paths to be further explored. The Path Selector decides which path among the set of feasible paths should be explored next. The Mixed Execution Engine then continues the mixed concrete and symbolic execution along the selected path. The constructed assignments (the trigger values) are then used as inputs to the Runner which feeds these assignments as inputs to the original program and executes the original program, thus allowing us to observe the trigger-based behavior in a controlled environment.

Note that for most malware the source code is not available. Therefore, we need to perform mixed concrete and symbolic execution on the binary directly.

Previous work on mixed concrete and symbolic execution only applies to source code [6, 14]. To the best of our knowledge, no previous work could enable mixed concrete and symbolic execution directly on binaries. Even though the underlying principles between mixed execution on source code and binaries may have some parallels, mixed execution of binaries is significantly more challenging to deal with, and the actual techniques and engineering required are substantially different.

At a high level, previous work on mixed execution with source code statically rewrites the program itself to perform the mixed execution. To enable mixed concrete and symbolic execution on binaries, even those that may be obfuscated or packed, we employ whole-system emulation and dynamic binary instrumentation so that we can perform mixed concrete and symbolic execution on the fly.

3 MineSweeper Design

In this section, we describe the detailed design and implementation of the components in MineSweeper, including the trigger type specification, the Mixed Execution Engine, the Solver, the Path Selector, and the Runner.

3.1 Trigger Type Specification

The user begins analysis by specifying one or more trigger types of interest. Allowing multiple trigger types is necessary because trigger-based behavior may depend on multiple trigger types. For instance, malware may be triggered by a combination of the system time and a keyword in keyboard inputs.

By default, MineSweeper provides a list of typical trigger types commonly used in malware, including keyboard inputs, network inputs, the system clock, and other library and system calls used commonly in malware as triggers. In addition, MineSweeper is designed to be easily extensible and allows the user to add additional trigger types. For example, the user can specify any function call or system call as a trigger type.

For each trigger type that the user defines, he needs to specify where in memory the trigger inputs will be stored so that the Mixed Execution Engine can properly assign symbolic variables during mixed execution. For example, if the user specifies the return values of a new function call as a trigger type, he needs to specify where the return values are stored, e.g., in which registers, or the return memory structure of the call or call-by-reference pointers. In our running example, the specification would include that `GetLocalTime` is a trigger type. The specification would also include that `GetLocalTime` stores its results in a 16-byte structure pointed to by a stack value when `GetLocalTime` is called. During mixed execution, this information is used so that a call to `GetLocalTime` will result in a fresh symbolic variable for each byte returned. Such information is usually readily available in API documentation.

If the user does not know what trigger type the malware may use, they can configure MineSweeper to offer additional assistance. In this case, MineSweeper will monitor the program execution for possible inputs to the program, e.g., system calls and library calls. When a new input source is detected, MineSweeper prompts the user whether the input source should be considered a trigger type of interest.

3.2 The Mixed Execution Engine

Given the specified trigger types and the program, the Mixed Execution Engine performs mixed concrete and symbolic execution. In particular, trigger inputs are represented as symbolic variables, and the mixed execution builds up symbolic expressions and constraints on trigger inputs as it executes. When the mixed execution encounters the next conditional jump which depends on symbolic values, it generates two path predicates representing the constraints on the trigger inputs for two new paths: one is the current path continuing with the true branch, and the other is the current path continuing with the false branch. The Mixed Execution Engine then gives both path predicates to the Solver to decide whether either one is feasible. Feasible paths are then added to the set of paths to be further explored, and the Path Selector decides which path to explore next.

In this section, we first describe how we enable mixed execution on binaries by using whole-system emulation and dynamic binary instrumentation, and then describe how we create new symbolic variables for trigger inputs. Since x86 instruction set is very complex, we convert x86 instructions to be symbolically executed to a simpler Intermediate Representation (IR) that we design, and we perform symbolic execution on the IR. Since mixed execution can be viewed at high level as achieving the same results as plain symbolic execution, but with performance enhancements, for ease of explanation, we explain first plain symbolic execution and how we generate path predicates in Section 3.2, and then explain how we enhance the performance by using mixed execution in Section 3.2.

Whole system emulation and dynamic binary instrumentation. Since for most malware we do not have access to source code, we need to perform mixed symbolic and concrete execution with only access to the program binary. Static binary instrumentation is in general considered an unsolved problem, not to mention that malware routinely use code packing and obfuscation which makes static binary instrumentation look even more hopeless. Thus, we take the approach of dynamic binary instrumentation. In particular, we build our Mixed Execution Engine on top of a whole system emulator (in our implementation, we use QEMU [2], Section 4.1) and perform dynamic binary instrumentation on-the-fly. By adding hooks to the emulator, our system is notified for each instruction to be executed in the original program, at which time we insert code to perform the mixed execution.

To perform mixed execution, for each instruction to be executed in the original program, we need to insert code to do two things: (1) check whether the instruction will read any trigger inputs, and if yes, we need to create new symbolic variables to represent the trigger inputs; (2) depending on the instruction, executes the instruction concretely (if all operands are concrete) or symbolically (if at least one operand is symbolic). We describe how we accomplish these two things in more detail below.

Creating New Symbolic Variables for Trigger Inputs

For each instruction to be executed in the original program, the Mixed Execution Engine first checks whether the instruction reads any inputs from the trigger types, such as I/O reads including keyboard and network inputs or returns from a function call of a trigger type. If so, the Mixed Execution Engine then assigns the locations (e.g., return registers, stack variables, etc.) from the specification fresh symbolic variables.

In the case where a function call is declared as a trigger type, when the entry point of the function call is executed, Mixed Execution Engine identifies the return address. Then, when the function call returns the Mixed Execution Engine sets the specified buffers on the stack or the registers returning values as fresh symbolic variables. Note that this is why we require the user to provide the information about which buffer on the stack or which register contains inputs from the trigger types when the user defines a particular function as a trigger type, as mentioned in Section 3.1.

Symbolic Execution

At a high level, mixed concrete and symbolic execution can be viewed as achieving the same result as plain symbolic execution, but more efficiently. Thus, for ease of explanation, we explain in this section how we perform plain symbolic execution in our problem setting, and explain in Section 3.2 how we enhance the efficiency of plain symbolic execution using mixed concrete and symbolic execution.

Translating to an Intermediate Representation (IR). In order to perform sound symbolic execution, we must correctly interpret the semantics and effects of all assembly statements. The x86 instruction set is complex—many instructions have implicit side effects (e.g., `add` sets the `eflags` register on overflow), may have implicit operands (e.g., the memory segment selector), may behave differently for different operands (e.g., shifts by 0 do not set `eflags`), and there are even single instruction loops (e.g., `rep` instructions). Thus, to reduce the complexity of the symbolic execution logic, for each instruction that needs to be executed symbolically, we first translate it into a sequence of much simpler intermediate representation (IR) statements that we have designed. Our IR resembles a RISC-like assembly language, as shown in Table 1. The translation from an x86 instruction to our IR is designed to correctly model the semantics of the original x86 instruction, including making all the implicit side effects explicit (e.g., setting the `eflags` register). We then perform symbolic execution on the IR statements, instead of directly with the x86 instruction set.

$$Instructions\ i \quad ::= *(r_1) := r_2 | r_1 := *(r_2) | r := v | r := r_1 \square_b v$$
$$| r := \square_u v\ |\ \texttt{label}\ l_i\ |\ \texttt{jmp}\ \ell\ |\ \texttt{ijmp}\ r$$
$$|\ \texttt{if}\ r\ \texttt{jmp}\ \ell_1\ \texttt{else}\ \texttt{jmp}\ \ell_2$$
$$Operations\ \square_b ::= +, -, *, /, \ll, \gg, \&, |, \oplus, ==, != , <, \leq\ (\text{Binary operations})$$
$$\square_u ::= \neg, !\ (\text{unary operations})$$
$$Operands\ \ v \quad ::= n\ (\text{an integer literal})\ |\ r\ (\text{a register})\ |\ \ell\ (\text{a label})$$
$$Reg.\ Types\ \ \tau \quad ::= \text{reg64\_t}\ |\ \text{reg32\_t}\ |\ \text{reg16\_t}\ |\ \text{reg8\_t}\ |\ \text{reg1\_t}\ (\text{number of bits})$$

Table 1. Our RISC-like assembly IR. We convert all x86 assembly instructions into this IR.

Our IR has assignments ($r := v$), binary and unary operations ($r := r_1 \square_b v$ and $r := \square_u v$ where $\square_b$ and $\square_u$ are binary and unary operators), loading a value from memory into a register ($r_1 := *(r_2)$), storing a value ($*r_1 := r_2$), direct jumps (jmp ℓ) to a known target label (label ℓ_i), indirect jumps to a computed value stored in a register (ijmp r), and conditional jumps (if r then jmp ℓ_1 else jmp ℓ_2). Figure 3 shows a small portion of the x86 assembly for our running example translated into our IR.

```
// 4012b1: call  401810 <_GetLocalTime@4>
...
// 4012b9: cmpw $0x9,0xfffffffee(%ebp)
t0:=ebp+0xfffffffee;  t1:=*t0;  t2:=0x9 ≠ t1;
// 4012be: jne  40132d <_main+0xad>
if t2 ≠ 0 jmp 40132d else jmp 4012c0;
// 4012c0: cmpw $0xa,0xfffffff0(%ebp)
t3:=ebp+0xfffffff0;  t4:=*t3;  t5:=0xa ≠ t4;
// 4012c5: jne  40132d <_main+0xad>
if t5 ≠ 0 jmp 40132d else jmp 4012c7;
// 4012c7: cmpw $0xb,0xfffffffea(%ebp)
t6:=ebp+0xfffffffea;  t7:=*t6;  t8:=0xb ≠ t7;
// 4012cc: jne  40132d <_main+0xad>
if t8 ≠ 0 jmp 40132d else jmp 4012ce;
// 4012ce: cmpw $0x6,0xfffffff2(%ebp)
t9:=ebp+0xfffffff2;  t10:=*t9;  t11:=0x6 ≠ t10;
// 4012d3: jne  40132d <_main+0xad>
if t11 ≠ 0 jmp 40132d else jmp 4012d5;
// 4012d5: execute ddos code
// 40132d: do not execute ddos code
```

Fig. 3. The IR for the running example.

Symbolic Execution At a high level, symbolic execution builds up symbolic expressions for variables (such as registers and memory). In our setting, symbolic execution builds a path predicate for a chosen path, i.e., the formula that the trigger inputs need to satisfy in order for the code execution to go down that path. Intuitively, each conditional jump depending on trigger inputs along the chosen path places a constraint on the trigger inputs, since the different values of the trigger inputs will make the conditional jump go one way or the other. The path predicate is simply a conjunction of all these constraints.

We generate the symbolic formulas on-the-fly in a syntax-directed manner. Symbolic execution was first introduced by King [17]. Below we give a brief description of how we perform symbolic execution and compute the path predicate for the chosen path in our setting.

- For binary, unary, and assignment operations we generate a `let` expression. A `let` expression binds a unique variable name to the expression computed, e.g., in Figure 4 the name t_0 is bound to the expression "ebp + 0xfffffffee". Variable names are derived from the operand names, and renamed if necessary to be unique. For example, in Figure 4 we see that each incarnation of the virtual register t is uniquely named. Also note that each variable definition is properly scoped by the preceding statements.

```
let   Mᵢ = λ.x
 if x == (ebp+0xffffffee) then <wMonth>
 else if x ==  (ebp+0xfffffff0) then <wDay>
 else if ... else  Mᵢ₋₁ x
in
let t₀ = ebp + 0xffffffee in
let t₁ =  Mᵢ t₀ in
let t₂ = 0x9 ≠ t₁ in
let t₃ = ebp + 0xfffffff0 in
let t₄ =  Mᵢ t₃ in
let t₅ = 0xa ≠ t₄ in
let t₆ = ebp + 0xffffffea in
let t₇ =  Mᵢ t₀ in
let t₈ = 0xb ≠ t₇ in
let t₉ = ebp + 0xfffffff2 in
let t₁₀ =  Mᵢ t₉ in
let t₁₁ = 0x6 ≠ t₁₀ in
   (t₂ ==  0) // wDay is 9
   ∧ (t₅ ==  0) // and wHour is 10
   ∧ (t₈ ==  0) // and wMonth is 11
   ∧ (t₁₁ ==  0) // and wMinute is 6
```

Fig. 4. The path predicate generated.

- We symbolically execute loads and stores using λ-abstractions [21]. A store creates a new memory, which is a new λ abstraction. A load is modeled as a λ application to mimic reading from the current memory state. The λ-abstraction acts like an array: given an address, it returns the last value written to that address. Let $\mathcal{M}_0$ represent an initial memory state. Then a store $*a := v$ to memory address a with value v (in memory context $\mathcal{M}_0$) can be modeled as an if-then-else expression with argument x:

$$\mathcal{M}_1 \doteq \lambda x. \text{if } x == a \text{ then } v \text{ else } (\mathcal{M}_0 \; x)$$

This is a function which takes an argument — an address x — and returns the value associated with the address, e.g., v if $x == a$. A memory read of address a_r is performed by function application $(\mathcal{M}_i \; a_r) \doteq \text{if } a_r == a \text{ then } v \text{ else } (\mathcal{M}_{i-1} \; a_r)$. The application evaluates the if-then-else expression, returning the last-written value to the address a_r.

- When encountering a conditional jump, we generate two path predicates: one for the current path continuing with the true branch, and the other for the current path continuing with the false branch. For example, assuming the path predicate for the current path before the conditional jump is $\mathcal{F}$, for the conditional jump `if e then jmp L1 else jmp L2` we generate the path predicates $\mathcal{F} \wedge (e == 0)$ for the path continuing with the true branch, and $\mathcal{F} \wedge (e \neq 0)$ for the path continuing with the false branch. The generated path predicates will be then given to the Solver.

Figure 4 shows the path predicate generated for reaching the call to ddos (with $\mathcal{M}_i$ representing the state of memory after the call to GetLocalTime).

Mixed Concrete and Symbolic Execution

To enhance the efficiency of symbolic execution, we evaluate any instruction whose operands are not symbolic concretely on the real processor. For example, if $x = 5 + 6; x = x + x;$, there is no reason to build "let x = 5+6 in let $x_1 = x + x$" when we can evaluate it natively and generate $x = 22$. Also, for conditional jumps which do not depend on symbolic values, then we know the direction taken does not depend on the trigger, and thus we can just execute it concretely. Concrete execution reduces the size and complexity of the formula, but can *only* be performed if we know for certain that *all* operands are concrete. Conducting both concrete and symbolic execution is called mixed execution. In our setting, trigger inputs are represented as symbolic variables, and therefore any operand only has a symbolic value if it is derived from trigger inputs. Thus, the vast majority of instructions can potentially be evaluated concretely, offering significant performance improvements over plain symbolic execution.

To enable mixed execution, for each instruction issued, we first need to decide whether each operand is symbolic or not. For registers, we maintain a register status table which indicates whether a register holds a symbolic value, and if so, the corresponding symbolic variable. The register status table is updated during symbolic execution as writes to registers happen.

Memory operands are more complex, and it is important to distinguish between memory addresses and memory contents, each of which can be either symbolic or concrete. In the simplest case, all the memory reads and writes are to concrete memory addresses. In this case, we simply maintain a data structure which remembers which memory cells contain symbolic values and the corresponding symbolic values. A read of a memory cell of a concrete address whose content is symbolic loads the corresponding symbolic value. A write of a symbolic value to a concrete memory address similarly adds an association between the symbolic value and the concrete memory index into our data structure .

Reading or writing memory with symbolic addresses require more care because we do not know exactly what memory cells may be read or written. In these cases, since we cannot say definitively that all operands are concrete, we must perform the operation symbolically. In addition, after a write to a symbolic address, we must perform any subsequent instruction that may load a value from that cell symbolically (in the worse case, all subsequent instructions). Note that this way the correctness is guaranteed since the memory operations will be modeled as λ-abstraction as described in Section 3.2.

Thus, memory operations on symbolic addresses, especially stores to a symbolic address, pose a potential efficiency problem (though not a correctness problem). Since fewer instructions may be able to be executed concretely, this could increase the formula size, and potentially increase the difficulty for the Solver to solve for the formula. For example, in some cases, a read from a symbolic address may result in a case split when solving the formula: the Solver may need to create a separate formula to solve for each possible index read. Similarly, a write to a symbolic address will lead to a case split on subsequent reads since we need to consider the case where the index read coincides with the index written. We treat the Solver as a pluggable component, and can plug in the best solver capable of analyzing these situations.

However, in our tests, reads and writes with symbolic addresses happen rarely, thus the efficiency issue with memory operations on symbolic addresses currently does not prevent us from achieving results in practice from our experience. As future work, we do plan to build in the ability to reason about where the symbolic addresses might point to, i.e. alias analysis for binaries. Such reasoning is difficult since memory is treated as one contiguous array and we do not know where one object stops and another begins (unlike in source code). Although binary alias analysis is out of scope for this chapter, we have investigated how such alias analysis may be conducted [5]. We leave incorporating these ideas into our current infrastructure as future work.

3.3 The Solver

For each generated path predicate, the Solver checks whether it is *satisfiable*. One of three things can happen:

- The solver returns satisfiable, which means the path is feasible. In this case, the solver adds the feasible path to the set of paths to be further explored. In addition, the solver also generates an example set of input assignments, i.e., the trigger values, which will lead the program execution down the feasible path. The trigger values are then given to the Runner to concretely execute the program with the trigger values and observe the trigger-based behavior.
- The solver returns unsatisfiable. This means that the path is infeasible, i.e., no input will ever lead us down the exact specified path, and we mark the path as such.
- The solver takes too much time or memory. We do not consider this path further. Other choices are possible, e.g., increasing the time-out. One interesting possibility is to optimistically continue symbolically executing the path. If in subsequent execution we run into code that does not depend upon the trigger type, we can still concretely execute it. For example, in:

```
if(SHA1(x) == y)
    ddos()
```

we may not be able to solve for x for the comparison to be true, but we could still optimistically execute the ddos code. Technically we would not know whether the path is really feasible, thus do not know whether the malicious behavior will really be exhibited in this case. However, sometimes the information about the existence of such malicious behavior in a piece of malware may still offer value to the analyst.

Note that the practical power of our system would thus depend on the power of the solver. MineSweeper is extensible; we can plug in any Solver appropriate, and our system thus can automatically benefit from any new progress on decision procedures, etc. Currently in our implementation, we use STP as the Solver [6, 12].

3.4 The Path Selector

The Path Selector takes as input the set of currently discovered feasible paths to be explored, and outputs the next path selected to be explored. The Path Selector can use different heuristics to decide which path to pick from the set of feasible paths. For example, it can use breadth-first search, depth-first search, or other strategies. Ideally, we would like to have a strategy to help us uncover trigger-based behavior as early as possible.

In our approach, our strategy is to explore as many conditional jumps which depend upon trigger inputs as possible. Thus, we take a BFS-like approach where we will always try and explore a trigger-dependent branch that has never been seen before revisiting loop bodies.

When MineSweeper encounters a loop, it will initially try to explore both branches of the loop header (the loop header is the conditional jump which one branch executes the loop body, and the other branch leaves the loop). This mimics executing the loop once. Additional loop iterations will be added to the end of the path selection queue. We have found this strategy the most effective at quickly uncovering malicious behavior in our real world examples.

3.5 Runner

The runner takes as input the trigger values and executes the program with the trigger values in a controlled environment. In our design, the Runner intercepts any calls to the specified trigger types, and replaces the returned answer with the given trigger values. Note that since each trigger input has a fresh symbolic variable in the mixed execution, we will be able distinguish which trigger values to supply for which function returns. For example, the Solver may specify different assignment values for the first and second time a function call of a trigger type returns; in this case, the Runner will feed the different trigger values according to whether it is the first or second time the relevant function returned. In our running example, suppose the Solver output that the time should be 11/9 at 10:06 (in reality, the Solver would return an assignment of values to the trigger inputs, e.g., a value for byte 1-14 of the specified trigger type). The Runner would intercept the `GetLocalTime` call and replace the 14-bytes returned with the supplied time of 11/9 10:06.

4 Implementation and Evaluation

4.1 Implementation

We have implemented the above components in C/C++ and OCaml. We use QEMU [2], a whole system emulator, as the basis for dynamic binary instruction in the Mixed Execution Engine. Our implementation consists of about 41,000 lines of code.

Mixed Execution Engine Implementation. The translation from an x86 binary to our IR is about 20,000 lines of C/C++ code and 9000 lines of OCaml. Much of the complexity arises from the various flags and status registers different instructions may set and test. We have also developed an extensive testing infrastructure to verify the translation is correct: we can translate an x86 program into our IR, then back to x86, and have it run correctly.

The concrete and symbolic execution component is much smaller, compromising about 12000 lines of C/C++ code. In our implementation, we perform Mixed Execution Engine by a) translating the instruction into our IR, b) consulting our register and memory maps (as discussed in Section 3.2) to decide which operands are symbolic, and c) executing the instruction either symbolically or concretely. Also, as soon as we hit a symbolic memory address, we switch to the symbolic execution mode as described in Section 3.2. For efficiency, we process a block of instructions at a time. For us, a block consists of all sequential statements up to the next conditional jump. We load an instruction cache in the Mixed Execution Engine, then have it perform the above operations on a block at a time.

One potential issue is that we may encounter very long concrete runs after trigger-dependent branches. In our implementation, we use timeouts if there are other paths to explore so that we can move on and explore the new paths instead of continuing along very long runs that do not demonstrate any trigger-based behavior.

Solver Implementation. We use STP [6, 12], a decision procedure well suited for bit-vector operations commonly found in assembly, as our Solver. STP can reason about any formula over a finite domain. Since our paths are of finite length, and each variable can take on a finite value, STP could, in theory, answer any question we posed to it. However, in real life, STP may run out of memory, or take too long to return an answer. We found that formulas involving modulus or division operations can substantially increase the answer time. However, overall we have found STP effective in our experience.

Path Selector Implementation. Since trigger-based behavior is branch-based, our Path Selector follows a branch-based strategy. Conceptually, in our implementation, we would do this by forking the execution of our Mixed Execution Engine at every symbolic jump that we encounter. However, due to the size and complexity of saving, managing, and restoring all the state, we simulate this behavior by simply running the Mixed Execution Engine multiple times.

As part of our implementation, we also build a control flow like graph of conditional jumps which depend on the trigger inputs to provide visual feedback to the user. This graph provides visual feedback to the analyst as to the progress of MineSweeper. Vertices in the graph are conditional jumps which depend on the trigger inputs. The edges are the control flow relationship between such jumps. Figure 5 is an example of the graph generated for NetSky. By looking at the graph the analyst can get a good high level picture as to the progress of MineSweeper, the relationship among the path predicates for the trigger conditions, and the relationship among the possibly many trigger conditions themselves.

4.2 Evaluation

In order to test the effectiveness of our method, we have evaluated MineSweeper on real malware. Our real world examples include widely spread email worms (Net-Sky [16] and MyDoom [13]), DDoS tools (TFN [3]), and a keylogger (Perfect Keylogger [1]). All of our experiments were performed on a 2.8Ghz Pentium dual-core processor with 4GB of RAM. Our experiments demonstrate that our techniques are capable of automatically analyzing current real world malware examples. Our experiments also indicate that the total analysis time is quite small compared to an otherwise manual approach.

Program	Total Time	Total STP Time	Total Nodes	# Trigger Jumps	Percent Sym. Insn.
MyDoom	28 min	2.2 min	802042	11	0.00136%
NetSky	9 min	0.3 min	119097	6	0.00040%
Perfect Keylogger	2 min	<0.1min	4592	2	0.00508%
TFN	21 min	6.5 min	859759	14	0.00052%

Table 2. Our results on several real-world malware examples.

Results Summary. Table 2 shows the results of our experiments. In this table, the "Total Time" column is the total end-to-end experiment time for MineSweeper to analyze each malware, i.e., the time to explore all conditional branches which depend on the trigger inputs. Note that MineSweeper is an unoptimized prototype, and that subsequent optimizations will likely bring the total time down. We break out the total time spent in STP. In our experiments, we spent about 13% time on average solving the path predicates.

The "Total Nodes" column displays the number of STP nodes used in solving the formula. We use this as an indicator for the complexity of the formula that we generate.

The "# Trigger Jumps" column counts how many conditional jumps were based on trigger inputs. This number is important because it demonstrates that a relatively small number of branches need to be explored in order to uncover the trigger-based behavior in these experiments.

We also show the percent of symbolic vs. number of concrete (x86) instructions executed. These numbers indicate that mixed execution reduces the formula a significant amount. This demonstrates that mixed execution is a promising approach.

Below we discuss each experiment in more detail.

NetSky

Win32.NetSky is a Win32 worm that spreads via email. The NetSky worm was one of the most widely spread worms of 2004. NetSky is known to have time triggered functionality, however different variants trigger at different times. For example, the C variant is triggered on February 26, 2004 between 6am and 9am [9]. The D variant is triggered on March 2, 2004, when the hour is between 6am and 8am [16]. The NetSky binary we analyzed was packed to prevent static analysis.

In our analysis, MineSweeper output that the library call GetLocalTime is a potential trigger type. We specified GetLocalTime as the trigger type, which returns a data structure that contains fields for the current month, day, year, hour, and minute. MineSweeper then automatically explored NetSky and analyzed its trigger-based behavior. Figure 5 shows a graph of program paths which depend on the trigger. In this graph, node 1 represents the day comparison, node 2 the month, node 3 the year, and nodes 4 through 6 check the hour. As we can see, in order to generate an attack, the date must be February 26, 2004, between 6-9am. According to the Symantec advisory, this is when NetSky.C attacks [9]. We can also see that when the time doesn't match, Netsky will loop back to the beginning and check again.

Overall, MineSweeper was able to discover and uncover the trigger-based behavior in about 9 minutes. We verified that all known trigger-based behavior was discovered.

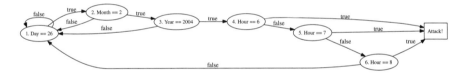

Fig. 5. MineSweeper generated graph showing NetSky's trigger-based behavior.

MyDoom

Win32.MyDoom [13] is another mass-mailing email worm with a built-in denial-of-service time-bomb. Different variants have different trigger dates. All variants launch DDoS attacks, most commonly against www.microsoft.com and www.sco.com. Additionally, most variants contain a termination date which causes them to stop propagating. The MyDoom binary we analyzed was packed. Overall, MineSweeper was able to discover and uncover the trigger-based behavior in MyDoom in about 28 minutes. We verified that all know trigger-based behavior was discovered.

MineSweeper output that the library call GetSystemTimeAsFiletime was a potential trigger type during its initial run. GetSystemTimeAsFiletime returns a structure which contains two 32 bit integers representing the current date and time. After adding this specification, MineSweeper discovered MyDoom's behavior depends upon 11 different comparisons with the current date. MineSweeper automatically generated the path predicates, which STP solved. After solving these values, we were able to discover the termination date (Feb 12, 2004) as well as two DDoS dates (Feb 1 and 3, 2004). Feeding these values into the MineSweeper confirmed the DDoS. In addition, these values are confirmed by Symantec as the DDoS dates for MyDoom [13].

Perfect Keylogger

Perfect Keylogger [1] is commercial software that has the ability to trigger itself based on window title (i.e. logging is activated and deactivated by the title of the window that is the target of the keystrokes).

MineSweeper identified `GetWindowTitle` as a possible trigger type. Once we added the trigger type specification, MineSweeper discovered that Perfect Keylogger checks if the current window name contains a pre-configured key string via the `strstr` library call. In our experiment, we found that MineSweeper branched heavily in the `strstr` call, e.g., checking if the first byte of the current window name was the same as the key's first byte, then checking if the second byte of the current window name was the same as the key's second byte, etc. In this scenario, MineSweeper continued to make progress, albeit very slowly.

However, since `strstr` is a standard library function, we can be more efficient by replacing `strstr` calls with calls to a *summary function*. The summary function concisely summarizes the effects of `strstr`. Note that summary functions need only be defined once, and can be reused when analyzing other examples, and that they are a widely adopted technique in programming language research [7,28]. Once we added this summary function, MineSweeper was able to quickly discover the trigger value in about 2 minutes. We verified that all know trigger-based behavior was discovered.

TFN: Tribe Flood Network

TFN [3] is a distributed denial-of-service attack zombie. Zombies are often found in the wild where the inner workings are unknown, e.g., the zombie may respond only to unusual messages. In the case of TFN, communication is carried out over ICMP. Different versions of TFN use different maps from command values to actions. Our goal in this experiment is to determine network inputs that would cause TFN to exhibit these different actions.

The original version of TFN that we located was Linux software. For our analysis, we have ported it to Windows since our current implementation is for Windows. Therefore, our version is not vanilla TFN, but it will still allow us to do the relevant analysis.

MineSweeper initially output that a raw ICMP network socket was the trigger type. After adding the appropriate specification, MineSweeper was able to identify and expand 14 conditional jumps that depend on network data. Using the solved formulas that we created, we were able to determine the various command values that this version of TFN would respond to. This complex data was easily generated in only 21 minutes using the MineSweeper system.

5 Discussion

In this chapter, we have shown that automatically analyzing trigger-based behavior in malware is possible and described our approach and system as a first step towards this goal. In this section, we discuss lessons we learned and limitations of the current MineSweeper system.

Evasion Attacks. Identifying trigger-based behaviors in malware is an extremely challenging task. Attackers are free to make code arbitrarily hard to analyze. This follows from the fact that, at a high level, deciding whether a piece of code contains trigger-based behavior is undecidable, e.g., the trigger condition could be anything that halts the program. Thus, a tool that uncovers all trigger-based behavior all the time reduces to the halting problem.

However, this theoretic result does not mean the task of providing automatic assistance to identifying trigger-based behavior is futile. First, as our experiment results demonstrate, our system is effective in identifying trigger-based behavior in malware in the real world. Secondly, even when the attacker tries to make the code difficult to analyze, e.g., to make the formula generated difficult for the Solver to solve, our system offers value over the hopeless alternative, manual analysis. When the formulas are difficult for a Solver to solve, it is most likely that it will be even more difficult for a human to think it through in his head. In addition, the formulas generated are valuable in themselves: they concisely summarize the conditions necessary for potential trigger-based behavior which can assist in further analysis.

One popular mechanism used to thwart analysis is static binary obfuscation or run-time packing. These techniques are designed to make static analysis difficult. Since MineSweeper analyzes malware as it runs, not statically, these evasion techniques do not pose a problem to our approach, as demonstrated by our experiments.

Limitations of Current Implementation and Future Work. The current implementation of MineSweeper has a few limitations. First, system calls with symbolic arguments are difficult, as they require either a) we build a symbolic formula over the relevant code executed by the kernel, or b) create function summaries. We choose to provide summary functions to keep the size of the generated formulas manageable, thus MineSweeper only supports system calls with symbolic arguments when we have defined the appropriate function summary. Summary functions need to be specified only once, and in general are useful and are widely adopted in research.

We iteratively explore paths of finite length, thus can iteratively reason about longer and longer inputs. Handling arbitrary length inputs is a difficult problem, and usually requires (in the worse case) manually supplying program invariants. Since we have found many triggers are small and can be handled via our iterative process, we leave adding support for invariants as future work.

Finally, we currently do not handle indirect jumps dependent upon trigger values, e.g., `t = GetLocalTime; jmp t->mDay;`. In order to handle such cases, we would need to reason about the possible values for the `mDay`. This is certainly possible: we use the Solver as an oracle to enumerate possibilities, and iteratively explore them. We leave incorporating this step as future work.

As mentioned in Section 3.2, our original support for memory reads and writes with symbolic indexes was handled inefficiently. However, we have recently improved our system to more efficiently handle these memory accesses. This technique is described in greater detail in a later work [4].

6 Related Work

Time-bomb analysis. Crandall *et al.* [8] recently proposed a virtual-machine-based analysis technique to analyze the timetable of malware. Their technique uses time perturbation to identify system timers in Windows. Their technique also uses limited symbolic execution and weakest precondition calculation to identify some time-related predicates. This is a good first step towards automatic analysis of time-bombs, however, compared to our holistic approach, their technique does not follow control flow, and can only perform limited symbolic execution, not a full system mixed concrete and symbolic execution. As a result, much of their analysis done in the chapter is manual, and their techniques miss several important time-related predicates. Additionally, while their technique is specialized for time-bombs, ours is designed to support more general trigger types.

Symbolic execution. Symbolic execution was first proposed by King [17]. Recently, symbolic execution has been used for automatic test case generation [14, 22, 29], sound replay of application dialog [20], vulnerability-based signature generation [14], and program verification, e.g., ESC/Java [10, 11].

Mixed Execution. DART and EXE have proposed mixed execution for finding bugs in software and have demonstrated that this approach is effective in increasing coverage for automatic testing [6, 14]. Their work is with source code: ours is with binaries. At a high level, the approaches for mixed execution on source code and binaries are similar in spirit. However, the techniques and engineering of a solution is considerably different. For example, as mentioned one big issue is to deal with the x86 instruction set. Though this may seem like a small side issue, in reality the engineering issues are quite immense. Another difference is source code mixed execution is usually performed by rewriting the source code so that appropriate constraints are generated as it executes. For us, we must perform the instrumentation on the fly.

Moser *et al.* [19] have independently and concurrently proposed a similar method of exploring multiple paths in a binary using symbolic execution. They have also demonstrated positive results using this approach. While our approach is similar, our system is capable of handling bit-level operations and more complicated, nonlinear formulas for symbolic variables within the system.

7 Conclusion

We have proposed that automatically analyzing trigger-based behavior in malware is possible, and designed and implemented a system using mixed execution as a first step towards this goal. Since often trigger-based analysis of malware is manual, any help provided by MineSweeper is of great use. In our experiments with real-world malware, we demonstrate MineSweeper is capable of a) detecting the existence of trigger-based behavior for specified trigger types, b) finding the trigger condition, c) Find input values that satisfy the trigger condition, when the trigger condition can be solved, and d) feeding the trigger values to the program, causing it to exhibit the trigger-based behavior, so that it may be analyzed in a controlled environment. Even when automatic analysis fails, MineSweeper can provide an analyst with valuable information about potential trigger-based behavior: information which previously would have to be manually obtained. Automatic trigger-based behavior detection is a challenging task, and we hope our work sheds new light and encourages further work in this area.

Furthermore, this approach is specifically relevant to analysis of botnets. As discussed, botnets are merely a specific example of the general class of malicious software containing hidden behaviors. We have further demonstrated this application in other work [4].

References

1. Blazingtools perfect keylogger. http://www.blazingtools.com/bpk.html.
2. QEMU. http://www.qemu.org.
3. Tribal flood network. http://www.cert.org/incident_notes/IN-99-07.html.
4. David Brumley, Cody Hartwig, Min Gyang Kang, Zhenkai Liang, James Newsome, Pongsin Poosankam, Dawn Song, and Heng Yin. Automatically dissecting malicious binaries. Technical Report CMU-CS-07-133, 2007.
5. David Brumley and James Newsome. Alias analysis for assembly. Technical Report CMU-CS-06-180, Carnegie Mellon University School of Computer Science, 2006.
6. Cristian Cadar, Vijay Ganesh, Peter Pawlowski, David Dill, and Dawson Engler. EXE: A system for automatically generating inputs of death using symbolic execution. In *Proceedings of the 13th ACM Conference on Computer and Communications Security (CCS)*, October 2006.
7. Edmund Clarke, Daniel Kroening, and Flavio Lerda. A tool for checking ANSI-C programs. In Kurt Jensen and Andreas Podelski, editors, *Tools and Algorithms for the Construction and Analysis of Systems (TACAS 2004)*, volume 2988 of *Lecture Notes in Computer Science*, pages 168–176. Springer, 2004.
8. Jedidiah R. Crandall, Gary Wassermann, Daniela A. S. de Oliveira, Zhendong Su, S. Felix Wu, and Frederic T. Chong. Temporal search: Detecting hidden malware timebombs with virtual machines. In *Proceedings of the Twelfth International Conference on Architectural Support for Programming Languages and Operating Systems (ASPLOS XII)*, October 2006.

9. Tony LeePeter Ferrie. Win32.Netsky.C. `http://www.symantec.com/security_response/writeup.jsp?docid=2004-022417%-4628-99`.
10. C. Flanagan and J.B. Saxe. Avoiding exponential explosion: Generating compact verification conditions. In *Proceedings of the 28th ACM Symposium on the Principles of Programming Languages (POPL)*, 2001.
11. Cormac Flanagan, K. Rustan M. Leino, Mark Lillibridge, Greg Nelson, James B. Saxe, and Raymie Stata. Estended static checking for java. In *ACM Conference on the Programming Language Design and Implementation (PLDI)*, 2002.
12. Vijay Ganesh and David Dill. STP: A decision procedure for bitvectors and arrays. `http://theory.stanford.edu/~vganesh/stp.html`.
13. Scott Gettis. W32.Mydoom.B@mm. `http://www.symantec.com/security_response/writeup.jsp?docid=2004-022011%-2447-99`.
14. Patrice Godefroid, Nils Klarlund, and Koushik Sen. DART: Directed automated random testing. In *Proc. of the 2005 Programming Language Design and Implementation Conference (PLDI)*, 2005.
15. Kevin Ha. Keylogger.Stawin. `http://www.symantec.com/security_response/writeup.jsp?docid=2004-012915%-2315-99`.
16. Neal Hindocha. Win32.Netsky.D. `http://www.symantec.com/security_response/writeup.jsp?docid=2004-030110%-0232-99`.
17. James King. Symbolic execution and program testing. *Communications of the ACM*, 19:386–394, 1976.
18. McAfee. W97M/Opey.C. `ttp://vil.nai.com/vil/content/v_10290.htm`.
19. Andreas Moser, Christopher Kruegel, and Engin Kirda. Exploring multiple execution paths for malware analysis. In *IEEE Symposium on Security and Privacy*. IEEE Press, 2007.
20. James Newsome, David Brumley, Jason Franklin, and Dawn Song. Replayer: Automatic protocol replay by binary analysis. In *Proceedings of the 13th ACM Conference on Computer and and Communications Security (CCS)*, October 2006.
21. Benjamin C Pierce. *Types and Programming Languages*. The MIT Press, 2002.
22. Koushik Sen, Darko Marinov, and Gul Agha. CUTE: A concolic unit testing engine for c. In *ACM SIGSOFT Sympsoium on the Foundations of Software Engineering*, 2005.
23. Symantec. Spyware.e2give. http://www.symantec.com/security_response/writeup.jsp?docid=2004-102614-1006-99.
24. Symantec. Xeram.1664. `http://www.symantec.com/security_response/writeup.jsp?docid=2000-121913-2839-99`.
25. United States Department of Justice Press Release. Former computer network administrator at new jersey high-tech firm sentenced to 41 months for unleashing $10 million computer "time bomb". `http://www.usdoj.gov/criminal/cybercrime/lloydSent.htm`.
26. United States Department of Justice Press Release. Former lance, inc. employee sentenced to 24 months and ordered to pay $194,609 restitution in computer fraud case. `http://www.usdoj.gov/criminal/cybercrime/SullivanSent.htm`.
27. United States Department of Justice Press Release. Former technology manager sentenced to a year in prison for computer hacking offense. `http://www.usdoj.gov/criminal/cybercrime/sheaSent.htm`.
28. Yichen Xie and Alex Aiken. Context- and path-sensitive memory leak detection. *ACM SIGSOFT Software Engineering Notes*, 30, 2005.
29. Junfeng Yang, Can Sar, Paul Twohey, Cristian Cadar, and Dawson Engler. Automatically generating malicious disks using symbolic execution. In *IEEE Symposium on Security and Privacy*, 2006.

Towards Sound Detection of Virtual Machines

Jason Franklin[1], Mark Luk[1], Jonathan M. McCune[1], Arvind Seshadri[1], Adrian Perrig[1], and Leendert van Doorn[2]

[1] Carnegie Mellon University, Pittsburgh, PA 15213
jfrankli@cs.cmu.edu, {mluk, jonmccune}@cmu.edu,
arvinds@cs.cmu.edu, perrig@cmu.edu
[2] Advanced Micro Devices, Austin, TX 78741
Leendert.vanDoorn@amd.com

Summary. We design, implement, and evaluate a practical timing-based approach to detect virtual machine monitors (VMMs) without relying on VMM implementation details. The algorithms developed in this paper are based on fundamental properties of virtual machine monitors rather than easily modified software artifacts. We evaluate our approach against two common VMM implementations on machines with and without hardware support for virtualization in a number of remote and local experiments. We successfully distinguish between virtual and real machines in all cases even with incomplete information regarding the VMM implementation and hardware configuration of the targeted machine.

1 Introduction

In their seminal work, Popek and Goldberg formally defined the essential properties that a program must satisfy to be termed a virtual machine monitor: efficiency, resource control, and equivalence [12]. In this article, we exploit the *timing dependency exception* to the equivalence property of a VMM to detect the presence of a virtual machine monitor (VMM) without relying on implementation details or software artifacts.

Virtual machine monitor detection has two direct implications for botnet remediation: first, it provides defenders with the ability to detect bots which utilize VMMs for improved stealth (e.g., VM-based rootkits [10, 18, 27]) and second, exploring VMM detection allows defenders to assess the extent to which intelligent bots can identify and potentially bias virtualized analysis environments such as high-interaction honeypots [9, 22, 26].

Due to the sophisticated nature of modern VMMs and significant variations between implementations, implementation-independent VMM detection is a difficult open problem. This difficulty is highlighted by the fact that most related work emphasizes implementation-dependent (software-artifact-based) techniques. These techniques have an inherent weakness: implementation-dependent detection techniques are easy to counter by modifying VMM implementations to mask or otherwise hide identifiable software artifacts.

In contrast to previous work, the detection algorithms developed in this paper are VMM implementation-independent and hardware-dependent. While the practicality of modifying VMM implementations to counter the multitude of current implementation-dependent detection techniques can be disputed, modifying the implementation of a VMM is inherently easier than modifying the underlying hardware, especially since in most cases the required software modifications are trivial. Our implementation-independent algorithms do not rely on software artifacts, making them difficult to counter without hardware modifications, a task which is difficult for organizations who rely on commodity hardware.

The main contribution of this article is the development of a class of implementation independent VMM detection algorithms whose execution is noticeably different when executed inside a virtual machine versus when executed directly on the underlying hardware. We describe the design and implementation of our algorithms, their success detecting a number of VMMs including VMware [23,25], the Xen VMM [2] on standard hardware, and the Xen VMM on a machine with hardware assistance for virtualization.

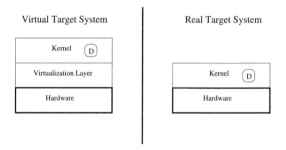

Fig. 1. VMM detection algorithm D on virtual and real target systems

We develop a class of VMM detectors that, when executing on a target system of unknown status (virtual or real) with access to a trusted external timer, can distinguish between a virtual and real target system (see Figure 1). Given the exact hardware specification and the specific VMM implementation that may be present, detection using timing is straightforward. However, given all known and possibly unknown VMM implementations, and all possible commodity hardware configurations, detecting the presence of a VMM on a platform with uncertain configuration is challenging. Hence, VMM detection spans a spectrum of scenarios, running from specific (easier to detect) to general (harder to detect) along two axes: VMM implementation ranging from known to unknown and hardware configuration ranging from known to unknown (see Figure 2). We explore this space of detection scenarios and address the challenges that lie within.

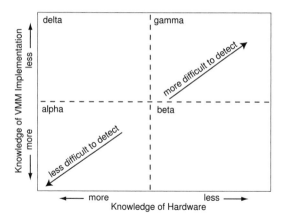

Fig. 2. Problem space

Complete knowledge of a system's hardware configuration is available in some scenarios, such as administratively controlled machines in corporations. As an example, consider the scenario where VM-based rootkits (VMBRs) become a significant threat in the wild. Anti-virus software makers, motivated to protect their users against such threats, could ask users to specify their hardware (e.g., Pentium 4 2.0 GHz) upon installation of a VMM detector such as the one developed in this paper. Servers run by the anti-virus company could then periodically challenge the users' systems to execute our hardware-specific VMM detector, designed to elicit a detectable performance degradation when running in a VMM. If performance is degraded sufficiently, the anti-virus software company could begin a recovery on the users' VM-based rootkit infected machines. A challenge in this naive model is that the information provided by the user about their system might be incorrect, incomplete, or unavailable.

The techniques described in this paper successfully detect the presence of a VMM on a target system even with uncertainty about the system's exact hardware configuration and specific VMM implementation. Our approach exploits VMM timing dependencies to elicit measurable VMM overhead, even in the face of limited hardware and software configuration information. Uncertainties with respect to hardware configuration include CPU microarchitecture, cache architecture, and clock speed. Uncertainties with respect to the VMM implementation include optimizations such as the use of binary rewriting or paravirtualization. Hardware support for virtualization, such as Intel's VT [8] or AMD's SVM [5] technologies, further complicate detection.

In our evaluation, we are able to identify sufficient hardware configuration information for target systems and to ultimately distinguish between virtual and real machines. Further, our approach continues to work against VMMs that utilize hardware support for virtualization. Our experiments demonstrate the viability of our approach over a range of uncertainty. As such, the algorithms developed in this paper represent a promising step towards general VMM detection techniques.

1.1 Context

The best way to understand VMM detection and to understand the relationship between this paper and past work is to describe the arms race which is VMM detection.
VMM detection is an arms race between detectors (which attempt to detect a VMM)
and VMMs (which attempt to evade detection). Below we describe the stages of the
arms race with each step labeled either current, emerging, or future to describe the
chronology of the race.

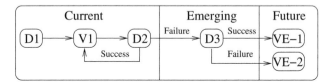

Fig. 3. VMM detection arms race

D1: Currently, detectors use software implementation-dependent artifacts such as
communication back doors, process names, and perturbed locations of system
components [19].

V1: VMMs evade detection by eliminating the specific artifacts used for detection.
For example, VMMs mask names and values (i.e., location of the IDT, special
processes, communication back doors etc...) or interpose on specific instructions
which are used in detection [10].

D2: Detectors search for previously unknown software artifacts. If found, return to
step V1 otherwise continue.

D3: In the absence of previously unknown software artifacts, detectors search for
implementation-independent perturbations such as timing (this article). If found,
continue, else jump to VE-2.

VE-1: Unable to evade implementation-independent detection, VMMs either remain
detectable or violate an assumption of the arms race. One possible violation
is that VMMs continue to operate on commodity hardware. It's possible that
hardware support for virtualization will eliminate VMM overhead. We suspect
this to be unlikely for multiple reasons: hardware-support is meant to fill holes
in current architecture's virtualization support and to ease the implementation of
VMMs, it is not designed to optimize or otherwise hide the presence of a VMM.
We evaluate the results of violating this assumption in Section 6.

VE-2: With both implementation-dependent and implementation-independent detectors eliminated, VMMs successfully evade detection.

Organization.   Section 2 discusses necessary background including the formal
properties of a VMM. Section 3 sketches a sound approach to VMM detection. Section 4 discusses the algorithm and protocol design for a class of VMM detection
algorithms. Section 5 describes the implementation of a detector. Section 6 presents

our experimental results. We present a security analysis in Section 7 and discuss limitations and possible extensions in Section 8. We cover related work in Section 9 and conclude in Section 10.

2 Background

We follow Popek and Goldberg in defining a virtual machine as an efficient, isolated duplicate of the underlying hardware [12]. This definition imposes the three properties that a control program must satisfy to be termed a virtual machine monitor: efficiency, resource control, and equivalence. To explain these three properties, we must first introduce some terminology.

2.1 Instruction Types

We classify the underlying instructions of a machine based on their behavior. An instruction is **privileged** if it can only be executed in the highest processor privilege level, and executing it at any other privilege level results in a trap to a higher privilege level. Privileged instructions are characteristics of the underlying hardware and are invariant over a particular instruction set architecture. An instruction is **sensitive** if it can interfere with the state of a memory-resident VMM. An instruction is innocuous if it is not sensitive.

2.2 Virtual Machine Properties

Informally, the **efficiency property** dictates that programs run in a virtualized environment show no more than minor decreases in speed. Since minor decrease in speed is difficult to quantify, a parallel requirement of the efficiency property is that a statistically dominant subset of the virtual processor's instructions be executed directly by the real processor.

The **resource control property** dictates that a VMM maintain complete control of system resources. This requires that it be impossible for an arbitrary program running in a VM on top of a VMM to affect system resources, e.g., memory and peripherals, allocated to a different VM or the VMM itself.

The **equivalence property** dictates that a VMM provide an environment for programs which is essentially identical to that of the original machine. Formally, any program P executing with a VMM resident in memory, with two possible exceptions, must perform in a manner *indistinguishable* from the case when the VMM did not exist and P had the freedom of access to privileged instructions that the programmer had intended. The two possible exceptions to the equivalence property result from resource availability and timing dependencies.

2.3 Exceptions

The **resource availability exception** states that a particular request for a resource may not always be satisfied. As a result, a program may be unable to function in the same manner as it would if the resource were made available. This exception exists because a VMM shares the underlying hardware and hence consumes resources.

The **timing dependency exception** states that certain instruction sequences in a program may take longer to execute. Hence, assumptions about the length of time required for the execution of an instruction might lead to incorrect results. This exception results from the possibility of a VMM occasionally intervening in certain instruction sequences.

These exceptions allow for the theoretical possibility of detecting a virtual machine monitor. If these exceptions did not exist, a VMM that perfectly satisfied the equivalence property would be impossible to detect. In this paper, we study how VMM detectors can be written which exploit these exceptions to unmask virtualized machines.

3 Approach

We sketch the design of a sound detection algorithm that exploits the timing dependency exception of a VM to distinguish between real and virtual machines.

3.1 Definitions

A *VMM detection algorithm* is a decision procedure which when given as input a target machine M outputs *accept* if M is a virtual machine and *reject* if M is a real machine. Let V be a virtual machine. A detection algorithm D is *sound* if and only if when $D(M)$ outputs *accept*, M is a virtual machine. A detection algorithm D is *complete* if and only if on input V, D halts and outputs *accept*. In order to eliminate any dependence on a particular VMM implementation, the approach described below is based on an idealization of a control program which satisfies the required properties of a VMM with the two previously mentioned exceptions. We term such a program an *idealized VMM*.

3.2 Intuition behind Detection Algorithms

Failure to control the execution of a sensitive instruction executed in a virtual machine (VM) can result in a loss of control over system resources. Since this is a violation of the resource control property, a VMM must strictly control the execution of sensitive instructions. The need to completely control system resources imposes stringent requirements on the execution of any instruction which has the potential to affect system resources.

Classes of instructions that can potentially affect system resources include sensitive-privileged instructions, sensitive-unprivileged instructions, and innocuous-privileged instructions. Innocuous-unprivileged instructions can be directly executed on the underlying hardware as they pose no risk of state corruption or control modification. It is the potentially control-modifying instructions that necessitate the existence of timing dependencies when a program executes in a VM.

When a VMM interposes on the execution of instructions that can affect system resources, VMM overhead is encountered. The VMM overhead of an instruction is the additional number of cycles required to execute the instruction in a VMM versus executing the instruction directly on real hardware. We exploit this overhead to distinguishing between real and virtual machines.

We give an intuition as to why positive VMM overhead is independent of VMM implementation. Assume positive VMM overhead does not exist. Then, either the VMM overhead is zero or it is negative. If the VMM overhead is negative, then the addition of a VMM actually increases the speed of the real machine, clearly a contradiction. If the VMM overhead is zero and instructions execute in a positive amount of time, then the VMM cannot interpose on instructions to maintain resource control. A program which does not maintain resource control is not a VMM, hence we arrive at a contradiction.

In our previous argument, we implicitly assumed that VMMs execute without hardware assistance for virtualization. The recent commoditization of hardware support for virtualization could reduce or in the extreme case eliminate VMM overhead. Previous work has show that even with current generation hardware support for virtualization, VMMs experience considerable performance overhead [1]. In addition, our experimental results confirm these observations. Since we cannot predict how future hardware might improve virtualization performance; the results of this paper only apply to current architectures.

3.3 VMM Detection Algorithm

We are interested in the class of detection algorithms that exploit the timing dependency exception to distinguish between real and virtual machines. We describe this class of algorithms as follows.

Let R_C be a real machine with configuration C and let M_C be a virtual or real machine with identical configuration C. Let Benchmark be a program with k control-modifying instructions each with VMM overhead o. Execute Benchmark on R. Store the time required for Benchmark to complete in $R_C(Benchmark)$. Execute Benchmark on M. Store the time required for Benchmark to complete in $M_C(Benchmark)$. Compare $M_C(Benchmark)$ and $R_C(Benchmark)$. If $M_C(Benchmark)$ is greater than $R_C(Benchmark)$ by at least $k * o$, output accept, else output reject.

4 Algorithm and Protocol Design

We present the design of our detection algorithm and protocol.

4.1 Algorithm Design

A number of complexities surface while implementing the detection algorithm developed in the previous section. First, a `Benchmark` with control modifying instructions must be constructed. Second, the execution time of a `Benchmark` on the real machine must be measured. Third, the execution time of a `Benchmark` on the target machine must be measured. Each of these entails additional complexities, explanations of which follow.

Designing for Overhead. As we previously argued, because of the inherent properties of a VMM, the VM should not be able to execute a program with control-modifying instructions as fast as the real machine. We design a `Benchmark` to include control modifying instructions empirically determined to have an overhead across implementations and validate our selection against a VMM of unknown implementation. We choose the particular control-modifying instructions and then tune their number such that the VMM overhead is remotely (e.g., across the Internet) noticeable.

Establishing Reference Times. The execution time of a `Benchmark` on R_C, denoted $Baseline(R_C)$ is our reference for distinguishing between virtual and real machines with hardware configuration C. The performance of our algorithm is directly related to the accuracy with which we can measure $Baseline(R_C)$. A central complexity in establishing an accurate reference time is how to establish this value for machines of unknown configuration.

Since the execution time of a `Benchmark` is dependent on the underlying hardware, clearly we require some knowledge of the hardware configuration to establish $Baseline(R_C)$. The greater the amount of information we have about the hardware configuration, the easier it is to distinguish between real and virtual machines, however, as we require more configuration information, the number of scenarios where our detector may work is reduced.

While our approach is independent of the mechanism used to determine the configuration of the machine in question, in order to develop an end-to-end VMM detection algorithm, we proceed as follows. To start, we assume we have no configuration information about the machine in question and that we cannot trust the machine's direct responses to configuration inquiries. Assuming we know the configuration of the machine in question greatly limits the scenarios in which our detection algorithm is applicable. Further, trusting a virtual machine's direct response to configuration questions can result in our acceptance of incorrect timing measurements.

We develop a heuristic approach to identify unknown hardware which works well in practice. Our heuristic, which we call hardware discovery, uses the existence of hardware artifacts that "shine through" a VMM. The hardware artifacts we discover are unique to a particular architecture and allow us to infer a portion of the configuration of the machine. This configuration information then allows for an estimation of $Baseline(R_C)$. We explain our techniques for hardware discovery and runtime estimation in the coming sections.

Measuring Execution Times in a VM. Timing the execution of a `Benchmark` on M necessitates the existence of a reliable timing source. If M is a virtual machine, the VMM may return timing measurements which do not accurately characterize the execution time [10]. To overcome this complexity, we allow the detector to contact an external timing source.

To remotely detect VMM overhead, we must develop a `Benchmark` with sufficient VMM overhead to overcome possible measurement noise. Potential sources of noise include variance in network latency, inaccuracies in timing, and variance in execution times resulting from caching. To overcome this noise, we develop techniques to configure the amount of VMM overhead to a nearly arbitrary extent.

4.2 `Benchmark` Design

Constructing a `Benchmark` requires that we determine which control-modifying instructions and the correct number of these instructions to execute. Below we discuss how a `Benchmark` can designed to have a variable amount of VMM overhead based on the specific instructions used and their number.

Selecting Instructions

To select the correct control-modifying instructions to induce VMM overhead, we measured the overhead of different sensitive-privileged instructions on several different VMMs. We use sensitive-privileged instructions, as opposed to sensitive-unprivileged instructions, because sensitive-unprivileged instructions violate the resource control property [14]. The results of these measurements are presented in Section 6.

Number of Instructions

After selecting particular instructions, we need to further tune the VMM overhead induced a `Benchmark` by selecting the number of instructions. There are two primary factors that affect the VMM overhead of a `Benchmark`. First, the processor configuration of a machine, for instance, Intel Pentium IV 2.0 GHz, has a direct effect on the execution time. Second, different VMM implementation techniques have different levels of overhead. The following analysis explains how we incorporate these two factors into our experiments in order to select the number of instructions in a `Benchmark`.

4.3 Measuring and Approximating Execution Times

First, we assume full knowledge of the configuration of the target machine. We then limit the amount of configuration information that is known and develop an approximation technique for estimating the runtime of a `Benchmark` over a class of machines.

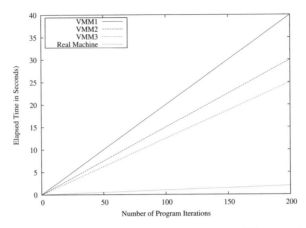

Fig. 4. Example VMM overhead of a `Benchmark`. Without a VMM executing, the instructions complete rapidly. With a VMM, there is noticeable overhead.

Timing With Complete Configuration Information

For purposes of demonstration, we imagine a scenario where we know the exact hardware configuration of the machine which we wish to distinguish as real or virtual, and we have access to a local machine of identical configuration. In this case, we can execute our detection code on the identically configured local machine and measure its execution time for use as a baseline for remote detection.

Given access to the local machine, we can determine the correct number of instructions to execute by estimating the noise in our experiments and running a number of experiments. We execute a `Benchmark` on the real hardware of the local machine and under different VMMs, while varying the number of instructions. The results look similar to Figure 4.

This graph is a hypothetical example based on our experimental results. The upper lines represent the runtimes of a `Benchmark` with a fixed set of control-modifying instructions under several different VMM implementations. The bottom line is the execution time on the real hardware. To determine the required number of instructions, we first fit equations to all the data points in the graph. We then use these equations to determine the minimum number of instructions required to overcome our noise estimate.

$$Let \quad Model(R_C) = \begin{cases} VMM_1(x) & = a_1 x \\ VMM_2(x) & = a_2 x \\ VMM_3(x) & = a_3 x \\ RealMachine(x) & = bx \end{cases}$$

with $a = min(a_1, a_2, a_3)$ and $FastestVMM(x) = ax$. Given a noise estimate of n, the minimum required number of iterations x such that $FastestVMM(x) - RealMachine(x) > n$ is $x > \frac{n}{a-b}$. Since n is small in practice and our VMM overhead is configurable to an almost arbitrary extent, selecting x based on local experiments presents few difficulties.

In the above example, which is based on our experimental results, we have $a = 0.125$ and $b = 0.01$. If we assume our experimental noise $n = 20ms$ (based on a network latency variation of 10 ms), a Benchmark must run at least 175 iterations.

Approximate Timing With Incomplete Configuration Information

We now examine the case where we have incomplete configuration information for the target machine. In this case, we determine the correct number of instructions to execute based on a number of estimates and experiments. We assume we have access to a machine with partial configuration information which matches that of the target machine.

As an example, imagine that the partial configuration information we have identifies just the processor type (e.g., Pentium IV). Since the remote machine we are attempting to distinguish as virtual or real may run at a different clock speed than the machine we are using for our experiments, we need to bound the runtime a Benchmark for different configurations and use these bounds for detection. In addition, since our baseline execution time will not be as accurate as in the full configuration information case, we must design the Benchmark such that its execution time is ordered as in Figure 5. Essentially, executing a Benchmark on the fastest VMM on the fastest real machine that matches the partial configuration information should take longer than executing the Benchmark directly on the slowest machine matching the partial configuration information.

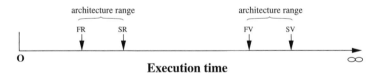

Fig. 5. The required order of execution times for a Benchmark for different configurations. Given some configuration information, FR is the fastest real machine, SR is the slowest real machine, FV is the fastest real machine running the fastest VMM, and SV is the slowest real machine running a VMM.

The approach we develop is to determine the range of processor speeds available given our partial configuration information and to use these values to approximate the execution time under different configurations. Since our detection code is CPU bound, it is possible to estimate the runtime of a Benchmark given only a few experiments on a single machine and a number of easily determined public values.

Given the partial configuration information we know, we determine the processor speed of the fastest machine available and denote this as F. While this value increases over time, the configurable nature of the overhead elicited by a Benchmark makes it possible to compensate for this increase. We denote the speed of the slowest machine satisfying our partial configuration information as S. The processor speed of the machine we are using for local experiments is denoted M. At the time of writing this paper, $F = 3.8GHZ$ and $S = 1.3GHZ$ for the Pentium IV[3].

As described above, we experimentally determine $FastestVMM(x) = ax$ and $RealMachine(x) = bx$ by running a small number of tests on the local machine M. We then use the ratio of the speed of the local machine to the speed of the slowest possible machine, $p = \frac{M}{S}$, to estimate the runtime a Benchmark on the real hardware of S. This gives us a runtime estimate on S of $SR = p*RealMachine(x)$. Similarly, we use the ratio of the speed of the local machine to the fastest machine, $u = \frac{M}{F}$, to estimate the runtime on the fastest virtual machine. This gives us $FV = d*FastestVMM(x)$. To determine the minimum number of instructions required to overcome our noise estimate, we require $FV > SR + n$ or equivalently, $x > \frac{n}{au-bp}$.

Returning to the above example and the Pentium IV, we have $a = 0.125$, $b = 0.01$, $M = 2.0$; GHz, $p = \frac{2.0}{1.3}$, and $u = \frac{2.0}{3.8}$. If we assume that our experimental noise $n = 20ms$ a Benchmark must run at least 471 iterations, more than twice as many as in the complete configuration information case.

4.4 Protocol Design

In our scheme, a trusted agent external to the target system denoted by V interacts with an instance of a detection algorithm D on a target machine M. V measures the start and end times of D by either invoking D remotely or receiving a communication immediately before D executes. After execution completes, D sends V a notification of completion.

D contains a specially crafted sequence of instructions called the Benchmark. The Benchmark is designed to elicit externally noticeable differences in execution time between virtualized and non-virtualized execution environments. D executes on the target host at the highest privilege level with interrupts turned off.

Upon receiving the notification of completion, V records the time elapsed since invocation of D. To determine if the detection algorithm D was executed in a VMM, V performs a lookup into a precomputed table of baseline execution times for the target host's hardware platform. If the execution time exceeds the threshold set for the slowest real machine of the specified configuration, the target machine M is considered to be a virtual machine.

5 Implementation

We detect the presence of a VMM based on performance measurements of instruction sequences, which we execute in a loop called the benchmarking loop. We use a sequence of instructions inside of a loop rather than as a straight line program to ease experimentation. We iterate the loop containing control-modifying instructions

---

[3] http://www.intel.com/products/processor/pentium4

until we generate enough overhead for detection. Unless stated otherwise, our loop iterates 2^{17} times. We experimentally selected this value.

We implemented our `Benchmarks` as Linux kernel modules. Their instructions always execute at the same privilege level as the kernel itself, which depends on the hardware architecture and the presence or lack of a VMM. To measure execution time locally, we use the `rdtsc` (read time-stamp counter) instruction before and after the benchmarking loop. To obtain measurements using an external or remote verifier, a user-level program `measured` runs on the target system and listens for a TCP connection from the verifier. When a connection is established, `measured` immediately tries to open a file that our kernel module adds to the `/proc` filesystem. This results in a call to a function in our module, which immediately suspends the calling process, disables interrupts, and begins execution of the benchmarking loop. When the benchmarking loop finishes, interrupts are re-enabled, the calling process gets woken up, and its file-open succeeds. Without even reading any data from the file, `measured` sends a packet back across its TCP connection, indicating to the verifier that execution of the benchmarking loop is complete.

6 Evaluation

We first describe the VMMs evaluated in our experiments and our experimental setup, then the actions necessary to ensure timing integrity for our experiments. Mechanisms that can detect the hardware architecture of an unknown remote system are presented next. Finally, we provide the results of both local and remote experiments, culminating in successful detection.

6.1 VMM Implementations

We evaluate our approach against two common virtual machine monitor implementation techniques [15]: full virtualization and paravirtualization. Both of these techniques are used to virtualize operating system instances rather than processes on one operating system; however, they differ in their approach to achieving this goal.

In full virtualization, the virtual replica of the underlying hardware exposed is functionally identical to the underlying machine. This allows operating systems and applications to run unmodified. Full virtualization is typically implemented in one of two ways: (1) with full support from the underlying hardware, affording maximum efficiency; and (2) without full support from the underlying hardware, requiring sensitive instructions to be emulated in software.

A popular full system virtualization VMM is VMware Workstation [23,25], hereafter referred to as simply VMware. VMware runs inside of a host operating system – as opposed to running on the raw hardware – and exposes an accurate representation of the x86 architecture to guest operating systems. This causes VMware to suffer a performance overhead during the execution of certain privileged instructions, since they must be emulated in software.

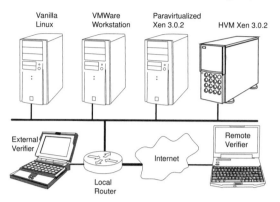

Fig. 6. Experimental machine and network setup

In paravirtualization, the virtual replica of the underlying hardware exposed is similar to the underlying machine, but it is not identical. This is done when the underlying machine architecture consists of sensitive instructions which are not privileged. Paravirtualized VMMs have the drawback that operating systems must be modified to run on them; however, they enable efficient virtualization to be performed even when hardware support for full virtualization is unavailable.

Xen is an open-source x86 virtual machine monitor that uses paravirtualization to achieve high performance [2]. Xen presents a software interface to the guest OS that is not identical to the actual hardware. Therefore, the guest operating system needs to be modified before it can run on Xen. Paravirtualization is trivially detectable from within a guest OS, as certain features of the underlying hardware will be broken or missing. Full virtualization on Xen can be accomplished with hardware support, e.g., Intel Vanderpool Technology (VT) [8] or AMD SVM [5].

6.2 Experimental Setup

We use six machines in our VMM detection experiments. Figure 6 shows these machines and their network connectivity. Three of the machines are identical 2.0 GHz Intel Pentium IV systems. These systems run vanilla Linux, VMware Workstation, and paravirtualized Xen 3.0.2, respectively. The fourth machine has hardware extensions to support virtualization (e.g., Intel VT [8] or AMD SVM [5]) and runs Xen 3.0.2. The last two machines are used as verifiers in experiments where timing measurements are made remotely. One of these is on a separate subnet from our machines running VMMs, separated by one hop through a router, which we call the *external* verifier. The other is located remotely at another university, which we call the *remote* verifier. Average ping times to the external and remote verifiers are 0.4 ms and 16 ms, respectively. All CPU-scaling and power-saving features are disabled on the external and remote verifiers during experiments to prevent the clock frequency of the CPU in the verifier from changing.

In the remainder of the paper, we sometimes refer to a target host as "VMware" or "Xen", when in fact we mean the guest OS running on VMware or Xen. All experiments run against Xen, with or without HVM support, are run against an unprivileged user domain which is the only other domain running besides the privileged domain 0.

In our experiments, we execute the benchmarking loop in the same privilege level as the OS kernel. Once the benchmarking loop executes on the target host, it turns off interrupts and executes a sequence of instructions that will experience detectable performance differences depending on the presence or absence of a VMM. Interrupts were disabled to improve the accuracy of timing measurements. Once the sequence of instructions executes, the VMM detection code re-enables interrupts and sends a notice of completion to the verifier.

We must address one more issue before delving into our benchmarking loops: the issue of a heavily loaded target host. We compare the case where the target host is not running a VMM with the case where it is. If there is no VMM, then disabling interrupts in the benchmarking loop truly disables them. The benchmarking loop executes to completion without interruption, rendering the load on the target host irrelevant. If the target system is a guest running on a VMM, interrupts are *at least* disabled in that guest VM. Thus, only code executing in other guest VMs on the same VMM can affect performance. If another heavily loaded guest exists alongside the target guest, the performance of the target guest may be degraded. This performance degradation only applies on systems running VMMs, and will thus *improve* our chances of successfully detecting the VMM. All of our experiments are run without any extra load on the VMMs, hence we evaluate our VMM detection approach in the worst-case of an unloaded system.

6.3 Timing Integrity

A VMM has total control over instructions executed by the guest OSes. Thus, we cannot trust a VMM to return valid answers to `rdtsc` "in the wild" [10]. Figure 7 compares internal (local) versus external timing measurements for the exact same experiment run on two variants of HVM Xen. One variant is the standard 3.0.2 release. The variant labeled as "Low-Integrity" in the figure is actually an unstable development release of Xen with a bug in the code which handles `rdtsc`. It is illustrative here because a party who wishes to thwart local VMM detection may intentionally modify their VMM to return such invalid timing measurements.

Figure 7(a) shows the internal timing measurements for a loop of a sequence of arithmetic instructions which clears interrupts at the beginning of each loop iteration. Xen 3.0.2 behaves as expected, with longer instruction sequences requiring longer to execute. In contrast, "Low-Integrity" Xen does not show any overhead whatsoever. In fact, some of the elapsed times are negative. Figure 7(b) shows a rerun of the same experiment, except that timing is performed by an external verifier. Local `rdtsc` calls are now unnecessary, and the runtime of the two experiments is nearly identical.

VMware Workstation can be made to demonstrate similar behavior. In fact, VMware provides a configuration option for VMs called

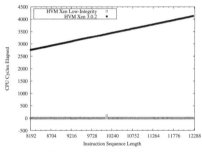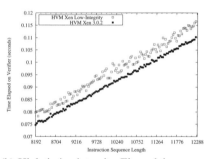

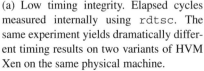

(a) Low timing integrity. Elapsed cycles measured internally using `rdtsc`. The same experiment yields dramatically different timing results on two variants of HVM Xen on the same physical machine.

(b) High timing integrity. Elapsed time measured via an external verifier. The same experiment yields similar results, even though one VMM was returning incorrect responses to `rdtsc` instructions.

Fig. 7. Timing integrity using internal versus external verifiers

`monitor_control.virtual_rdtsc` [24]. When set to `true`, a virtual counter in the VMM is used to provide values for guest OS calls to `rdtsc`. When set to `false`, VMware allows guest OS calls to `rdtsc` to access the CPU's true timestamp counter.

6.4 Identifying Remote Architectures

Inducing significant overhead in a VMM can result in long runtimes, which we detect by measuring runtime from a separate system. However, without some idea of the hardware architecture of the remote system in question, it is difficult to interpret timing results correctly. In this section, we describe a technique which is useful for identifying an unknown remote system as having an Intel Pentium IV CPU. If a system is known to be equipped with a Pentium IV, we can bound its expected performance (as demonstrated in Section 4). This bound is what allows for the establishment of a runtime threshold, above which it is likely that the target system is running a VMM. The Netburst Microarchitecture of the Intel Pentium IV family includes a trace cache with consistent specifications across all currently-produced Pentium IV CPUs [3]; our hardware discovery heuristics detect the presence of the trace cache. Other relevant characteristics of the Pentium IV microarchitecture include an out-of-order core and a rapid execution engine.

The trace cache stores instructions in the form of decoded μops rather than in the form of raw bytes which are stored in more conventional instruction caches [17]. These *traces* of the dynamic instruction stream permit instructions that are noncontiguous in a traditional cache to appear contiguous. A trace is a sequence of at most n instructions and at most m basic blocks (a sequence of instructions without any jumps) starting at any point in the dynamic instruction stream. An entry in the trace cache is specified by a starting address and a sequence of up to $m - 1$ branch outcomes, which describe the path followed. This facilitates removal of the instruction

```
rdtsc                         ;; get start time

mov $131072, %edi ;; n = 131072

loop:

xorl %eax, %eax     ;; begin special

addl %ebx, %ebx     ;; instr. seq.

movl %ecx, %ecx

orl %edx, %edx

...                           ;; 1K – 16K instr.

sub $1, %edi          ;; n = n − 1

jnz loop                 ;; until n = 0

rdtsc                        ;; get end time
```

Fig. 8. Example assembly code used to fill trace cache with register-to-register arithmetic instruction sequences without data hazards. These arithmetic instructions each decode to a single μop on Intel Pentium IV CPUs.

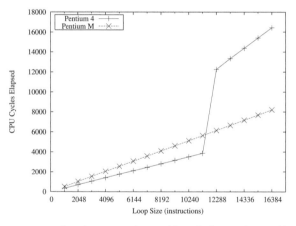

Fig. 9. When sequences of register-to-register arithmetic instructions without data hazards populate the trace cache of an Intel Pentium IV, a CPI of $\frac{1}{3}$ is attainable. Once an instruction sequence exceeds the trace cache's maximum size of 12KB, the CPI becomes 1. No such effect is visible on a Pentium M (an architecture without a trace cache). Cycles measured locally with rdtsc.

decode logic from the main execution loop, enabling the out-of-order core to schedule multiple μops to the rapid execution engine in a single clock cycle. In the case of register-to-register arithmetic instructions without data hazards, it is possible to retire three μops every clock cycle. Register-to-register x86 arithmetic instructions (e.g., add, sub, and, or, xor, mov) decode into a single μop. Thus, it is possible to attain a Cycles-Per-Instruction (CPI) rate of $\frac{1}{3}$ for certain sequences of instructions.

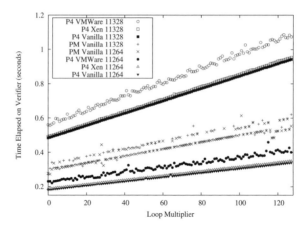

Fig. 10. Trace cache overhead timed remotely from another university. Sequences of either 11264 or 11328 arithmetic instructions with no data hazards are executed in a loop. The number of loop iterations is defined by $2^{17} + 2^{10}k$, where k is the Loop Multiplier on the X-axis. With and without a VMM, the Pentium IV architecture shows a considerable jump in overhead for a small number of additional instructions. In contrast, the Intel Pentium M (legend: PM) shows no such jump.

Intel has published the size of the trace cache in the Pentium IV CPU family – 12K μops. However, the parameters m and n, as well as the number of μops into which x86 instructions decode, have not been published. We performed an experiment where we executed loops of 1024 to 16384 arithmetic instructions devoid of data hazards on Pentium IV systems running vanilla Linux 2.6.16. Figure 8 shows the structure of our benchmarking loop. Figure 9 shows the results of this experiment when run using the `rdtsc` – read time-stamp counter – instruction to measure the elapsed CPU cycles locally. On the Pentium IV, the CPI is $\frac{1}{3}$ until the number of instructions reaches Intel's published trace cache capacity of 12K μops. We also ran this experiment locally on a laptop equipped with a Pentium M CPU; no unusual caching effects are observed (note that a CPI of less than 1 is obtained for the entire loop).

At this point we know enough about the trace cache in Pentium IV CPUs to construct a loop that has sufficient trace cache overhead to be detectable over the Internet. As described above, the exact details of how the trace cache generates its traces are not published. We performed additional experiments like those of Figure 9 locally and determined that a benchmarking loop composed of a sequence of 11264 arithmetic register-to-register instructions fits inside the trace cache, but that a sequence of 11328 instructions does not fit. That these figures are less than 12K is expected, as there are additional instructions executed to maintain loop counters and jump back to the beginning of the loop. Thus, executing these sequences multiple times should cause the performance of the larger loop to suffer disproportionately with respect to its added length.

Since the benchmarking loops contain only innocuous instructions, VMMs allow them to execute directly. The exaggerated performance difference between the two loops is largely unaffected by the presence of a VMM. Figure 10 shows the results of an experiment designed to demonstrate this effect. The top three lines are the execution time for the smaller sequence (11264 instructions per loop iteration) on vanilla Linux, paravirtualized Xen, and VMware Workstation. The bottom three lines show the same with the larger sequence (11328 instructions per loop iteration). The middle two lines show the two sequences executed on a Pentium M running vanilla Linux; this serves to illustrate how minimal the runtime difference between the loops is when there is no trace cache involved. The gap between the execution time of loops of the smaller sequence and loops of the larger sequence is considerable making this overhead identifiable across the Internet.

6.5 Inducing Detectable VMM Overhead

Given the results of the previous section, we have partial configuration information about the remote architecture of the target host. For example, we know the CPU is a member of the Pentium IV family. As described in Section 4.3, we need sufficient overhead to distinguish between the slowest member of the CPU family running a native OS and the fastest member of the CPU family running a guest OS on a VMM.

Recall that to detect a VMM, we must induce significant performance overhead. As described in Section 4, we use sensitive-privileged instructions which result in the execution of additional code inside the VMM. While we do not have space to exhaustively treat all sensitive instructions, we select a few and analyze their overhead on Xen 3.0.2 and VMware Workstation on an Intel Pentium IV. The instructions we consider are `cli` (clear interrupts), `mov %cr0, %eax` (read processor control register 0), `mov %cr2, %eax` (read processor control register 2), and `mov %cr3, %eax; mov %eax, %cr3` (read and write processor control register 3, which contains the physical address of the base of the page directory).

We next analyze these selected instructions locally on Xen 3.0.2, VMware Workstation, and vanilla Linux to understand their behavior (Section 6.5). Armed with this knowledge, we construct a remote attack that successfully detects the presence of a VMM across the Internet (Section 6.6).

Per-Instruction Overhead

We configured VMware with the configuration setting `monitor_control.virtual_rdtsc = false` to provide guest OSes with direct access to the CPU's timestamp counter. Paravirtualized Xen 3.0.2 allows its guests to access the time stamp counter by default. Thus, we can run local experiments to analyze per-instruction overhead. Our analysis is based on experiments where a small number of one of the sensitive instructions in question are inserted in between sequences of register-to-register arithmetic instructions. For each sensitive instruction, we evenly space 1, 2, 4, 8, or 16 instances of that instruction among 12,256 arithmetic instructions. We selected 12,256 to ensure that trace cache effects

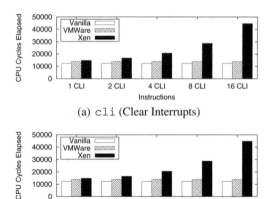

(a) `cli` (Clear Interrupts)

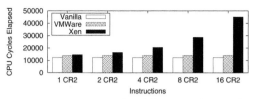

(b) `mov cr0, %eax` (Read Processor Control Register 0)

(c) `mov %cr2, %eax` (Read Processor Control Register 2)

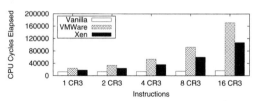

(d) `mov %cr3, %eax; mov %eax, %cr3` (Read and then write Processor Control Register 3)

Fig. 11. Local execution times for selected sensitive instructions

would not add noise to our results. We cannot be sure how the trace cache would impact a smaller sequence of instructions because the exact μop structure of these sensitive instructions is not published.

Figure 11 shows the results of local performance measurements. Figures 11(a), 11(b), and 11(c) yield very similar results. VMware Workstation shows a consistent minor overhead above vanilla Linux. In contrast, Xen's performance degrades significantly with each additional sensitive instruction. However, for CR3, we read its current value and then rewrite that value. CR3 contains the physical address of the base of the page directory, thus the VMM must interpose on access to CR3 to uphold

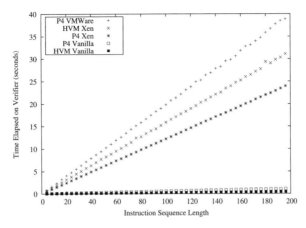

Fig. 12. Overhead resulting from reading and writing x86 Control Register 3 multiple times consecutively. Without a VMM executing, these instructions complete rapidly. With a VMM, there is sufficient overhead for remote detection via thresholding. Timed remotely from another university.

the resource control property. As Figure 11(d) shows, VMware Workstation incurs considerable overhead when it handles a write to CR3.

While reading and writing CR3 does not induce the worst overhead on Xen, the overhead is still significant. In the next section, we show how we use reads and writes to CR3 to detect a VMM across the Internet.

6.6 Successful Detection

We have established that an instruction sequence of reads and writes to CR3 results in VMM overhead when the target system is running either VMware or Xen. We used a loop containing a sequence of such instructions in our remote detection experiment. Although we did not include HVM Xen in our analysis of per-instruction overheads in the previous section, we include it in this experiment to validate our approach.

Figure 12 shows the results of our experiment, where the remote verifier is located at another university. We are able to induce extremely high overhead; code which executes in under 2 seconds on a native system takes more than 20 seconds to execute when running on either paravirtualized Xen, HVM Xen, or VMware Workstation. This is far above the amount of overhead necessary to overcome network latencies, allowing us to conclude that our approach to VMM detection is feasible.

7 Security Analysis

We have shown in the previous sections that it is possible to craft code which has pathological performance on a VMM, while still executing efficiently on bare hardware. This discrepancy provides an avenue through which motivated parties can detect VMMs. Recall that the execution of a detection algorithm has three logical stages:

Stage 1. For a target machine R_C, locate a hardware artifact to establish the configuration C of the machine.

Stage 2. Establish a reference time, $Baseline(R_C)$, for distinguishing between virtual and real machines with hardware configuration C.

Stage 3. Develop and execute a `Benchmark` which when running on top of a VMM on the fastest available machine for the architecture in question executes sufficiently slower than the `Benchmark` running in a native OS on the slowest available machine for the architecture in question.

We analyze the security of each stage individually, describing techniques which a VMM might deploy to evade or resist detection.

7.1 Stage 1 and 2 Evasion

A VMM can corrupt the results of stages 1 and 2 by masking all possible hardware artifacts that are observable through the VMM and simulating alternative artifacts from a slower machine. If a VMM were able to successfully simulate a slower machine, the baseline value established in stage 2 would be larger than necessary. This larger value might allow a VMM to execute a `Benchmark` without sufficient overhead to identify its presence.

Consider the case of a VMM running on an Intel Pentium IV. If this VMM is able to hide the existence of the trace cache, perhaps by masquerading as an Intel Pentium 3, then as a result of the speed difference between the Pentium IV and the Pentium 3, a detection attack may complete before the detection threshold for the Pentium 3, even with the overhead of the VMM.

For a VMM to successfully masquerade as a different architecture requires the following to be true: the configuration of the target machine is not known a priori and the VMM is able to simulate a slower device during stage 1 while still running at normal speed during stage 3. To successfully hide all hardware artifacts, the VMM would need to be a full system simulator. To execute at normal speed during stage 3, the VMM would have to be able to identify when the detection code is running since running a cycle-accurate simulator on its own incurs delays that are orders of magnitude larger than the overhead of any modern VMMs, making the simulator timings off the charts [16].

7.2 Stage 3 Evasion

To describe our assumptions with respect to a VMM's ability to evade detection, we specify two models of VMM behavior: experiential VMMs and propositional VMMs. Our models follow from partitioning the arms race of Section 1.1 based on a VMM's level of omniscience.

Experiential VMM. An experiential VMM has posteriori knowledge of experientially observed detectors but lacks identifiable information (i.e. process name, code signatures, etc.) for all detectors. It may deploy general countermeasures to evade detection such as virtualizing local timing sources (i.e., rdtsc, performance counters, etc.), but isn't able to analyze programs to infer their intent. Experiential VMMs may have a finite list of signatures to identify detectors, but are unable to prevent all detection attempts.

Propositional VMM.   A propositional VMM has a priori knowledge of detectors and evades detection by disabling or tampering with detection attempts either before or during its execution.

A propositional VMMs is the case where the VMM can identify all detection algorithms and trivially thwart detection. Recent work on verifiable code execution on untrusted devices assumes a similar model of adversarial omniscience, however is not useful for VMM detection because it does not work across an uncontrolled network, such as the Internet [21].

Correctly identifying a detection attack makes it possible for the VMM to interpose and tamper with the execution of the attack. If the VMM realizes it is under a detection attack prior to the execution of the benchmarking loop, it may be able to prevent the detection attack from executing correctly, perhaps returning a valid response in the correct amount of time for a non-virtualized host.

Identifying that a particular code segment is a detection algorithm may be difficult. One potential approach is to rely on the unique structure of our detectors, for example, long sequences of the same operations, few or no I/O operations, and control-flow graphs with limited branching. These properties might provide sufficient invariants to generate signatures that match detection algorithms.

Even with the unique properties of our benchmarking loop, there are a number of difficulties inherent in evading detection. First, identification techniques could introduce false positives which would affect benign applications, secondly, a single false negative allows for the detection of the VM.

8 Discussion

We discuss limitations and potential extensions of our approach.

8.1 VMM Implementation Independence

While commodity VMMs aren't VMBRs specifically designed to thwart detection, they are implemented using the same techniques. As discussed in Section 3, these techniques necessitate the existence of VMM overhead. If hardware assisted VMMs become more common, then this overhead may be reduced, however our results show that current generation systems provide sufficient overhead for detection.

8.2 User-Level Detection

The detectors developed in this paper run at kernel-level rather than at user-level. In most scenarios, running a kernel-level detector is a reasonable assumption since the system's administrator is interested in detecting VMBRs. Administrators and users regularly run kernel-level integrity checkers and attackers continue to perform remote root exploits to gain administrator status. Statistical techniques may be necessary to overcome the resulting noise that user-level detection would incur.

8.3 Local VMM Detection

Rather than identify a target host as virtual or real by using an external source of time, local VMM detection aims to demonstrate to a user if their platform is virtual or real without a trusted time source. One potential approach is for a detector to observe the relative inter-leavings of short code sequences which are executed concurrently as a relative timing attack. If code sequences can be developed whose inter-leavings are virtualization sensitive, such an approach may be able to eliminate the requirement of a trusted time source.

8.4 Widespread Virtualization

As more and more machines run VMMs, the existence of a VMM becomes less of an anomaly. However, to dismiss VMM detection as useless in the face of widespread virtualization is too harsh. Legacy machines without VMMs will likely persist for many years to come. VMM detection algorithms like the ones developed in this paper can help protect these machines against VMBRs when upgrading is not an option. We believe that VMM detection will remain useful as long as non-virtualized platforms exist.

9 Related Work

Most related work either detects VMMs based on implementation details, use techniques which make assumptions that limit their applicability, or relies on the integrity of values returned from the VMM. In contrast, our detection algorithm has a higher degree of independence with respect to the implementation of the VMM on the target host, uses a hardware discovery heuristic to identify the configuration of remote devices, and incorporates a remote timing and decision maker to eliminate the need to trust the VMM.

Delalleau proposed a scheme to detect the existence of a VMM by using timing analysis [4]. The proposed scheme requires a program to first time its own execution on a VMM-free machine in a learning phase. Then, when the program infects a suspect host of known configuration, its execution time is compared against the results from the learning phase. Because the result of the learning phase is dependent on the exact machine configuration and the scheme is not designed to produce a configurable overhead, it is unclear how practical it is to deploy such a detection algorithm in practice.

Execution path analysis (EPA) [20] was first proposed in Phrack 59 by Jan Rutkowski as an attempt to determine the presence of kernel rootkits by analyzing the number of certain system calls. Although the main idea can also apply to detect VMMs, EPA has several severe drawbacks. The main drawback is that it requires significant modification to the system (debug registers, debug exception handler) that could be easily detected and consequently forged by the underlying VMM.

Pioneer [21] is a primitive which enables verifiable code execution on remote machines. As part of the inherent challenge of verifiable code execution, Pioneer needs to determine whether or not it is running inside a VMM. The solution in Pioneer is to time the runtime of a certain function that also reads in the interrupt enable bit in the EFLAGS register. This function is pushed into the kernel and is expected to run with interrupts turned off. However, if it was running inside a VMM, the output of the EFLAGS register would be different than expected. Although promising, Pioneer assumes that the external verifier knows the exact hardware configuration of the target host. We eliminate this assumption and rely on hardware artifacts to discover the target host's hardware configuration. In addition, the minimal timing overhead of the Pioneer checksum function makes remote usage of Pioneer difficult.

There are a number of previously developed techniques from the blackhat community. Redpill[4] is an example detection algorithm used to detect the VMware virtual machine monitor. Redpill operates by reading the address of the Interrupt Descriptor Table (IDT) with the SIDT instruction and checking if it has been moved to certain locations known to be used by VMware. This algorithm can be easily fooled since it relies on the VMM to return the correct address of the IDT [10]. Similar to Redpill, VMware's Back[5] is a software-dependent detection attack which uses the existence of a special I/O port, called the VMware backdoor. This I/O port is specific to the VMware virtual machine and hence can be used to detect VMware.

Holz and Raynal describe some heuristics for detecting honeypots and other suspicious environments from within code executing in said environment [7]. Dornseif et al. study mechanisms designed specifically to detect the Sebek high-interaction honeypot [6]. Unlike these approaches, the detection algorithm we have constructed are not based upon specific software artifacts.

Vrable et al. touch briefly on non-trivial mechanisms for detecting execution within a VMM [26]. They allude to the fact that although a honeynet may be able to perfectly virtualize all hardware, an attacker may be able to infer that it is executing inside a VMM through side channel measurements.

Robin and Irvine analyzed the Intel Pentium's architecture and ISA [14] and pointed out problems in implementing a secure VMM on the Intel Pentium architecture. For instance, certain instructions break hardware virtualization requirements because they read sensitive registers and/or memory locations (e.g., the clock register and interrupt registers), but are not privileged instructions. Execution of such instructions does not raise an exception, and thus allows the attacker to read sensitive system data. However, the VMM can perform binary translation when it loads the process into memory, and change all such instructions into system calls. Alter-

---

[4] http://invisiblethings.org/redpill.html
[5] http://chitchat.at.infoseek.co.jp/vmware/

natively, the VMM can expose a paravirtualized version of the underlying hardware, which Xen does on the Intel x86 architecture [2].

Remote physical device fingerprinting can be used to detect VMMs if the external verifier can directly interact with two different virtual machines running on the same host [11]. Our approach only requires the existence of a single VM and hence is useful in the case of virtual machine based rootkits [10]. Also, defending against remote physical device fingerprinting is as simple as disabling or masking the TCP option timestamps. HoneyD is an example virtual honeypot which defends against remote physical device fingerprinting [13].

10 Conclusions

The main contribution of this article is the development of a detection algorithm whose execution differs from the perspective of an external verifier when a target host is virtual (versus when it is executed directly on the underlying hardware). Our detection algorithm is based on the timing dependency exception property of a virtual machine monitor. We presented results where a single benchmarking program generates sufficient overhead on several different virtual machine monitors to be remotely detectable across the Internet. Included in our analysis is a machine with hardware virtualization support. The success of our detection algorithm against this platform demonstrates that hardware support for virtualization is not sufficient to prevent VMM detection.

11 Acknowledgments

We thank Garth Gibson and Adam Pennington for their instruction and guidance in the early stages of this project. We thank Michael Kozuch for his insightful comments and useful discussions. Finally, we thank Ahren Studer for his assistance preparing a preliminary version of this paper.

References

1. K. Adams and O. Agesen. A comparison of software and hardware techniques for x86 virtualization. In *Proceedings of the ACM Conference on Architectural Support for Programming Languages and Operating Systems*, October 2006.
2. P. Barham, B. Dragovic, K. Fraser, S. Hand, T. Harris, A. Ho, R. Neugebauer, I. Pratt, and A. Warfield. Xen and the art of virtualization. In *Proceedings of the Symposium on Operating Systems Principles (SOSP)*, 2003.
3. D. Boggs, A. Baktha, J. Hawkins, D. T. Marr, J. A. Miller, P. Roussel, Singhal R, B. Toll, and K. S. Venkatraman. The microarchitecture of the Intel Pentium 4 processor on 90nm technology. *Intel Technology Journal*, 8(1), February 2004.
4. G. Delalleau. Mesure locale des temps d'execution: application au controle d'integrite et au fingerprinting. In *Proceedings of SSTIC*, 2004.

5. Advanced Micro Devices. AMD64 virtualization: Secure virtual machine architecture reference manual. AMD Publication no. 33047 rev. 3.01, May 2005.

6. M. Dornseif, T. Holz, and C. Klein. Nosebreak - attacking honeynets. In *Proceedings of the 2004 IEEE Information Assurance Workshop*, June 2004.

7. T. Holz and F. Raynal. Detecting honeypots and other suspicious environments. In *Proceedings of the IEEE Workshop on Information Assurance and Security*, June 2005.

8. Intel Corporation. Intel virtualization technology. Available at: http://www.intel.com/technology/computing/vptech/, October 2005.

9. X. Jiang, D. Xu, H. J. Wang, and E. H. Spafford. Virtual playgrounds for worm behavior investigation. In *8th International Symposium on Recent Advances in Intrusion Detection (RAID '05)*, 2005.

10. S. T. King, P. M. Chen, Y.-M. Wang, C. Verbowski, H. J. Wang, and J. R. Lorch. SubVirt: Implementing malware with virtual machines. In *Proceedings of the IEEE Symposium on Security and Privacy*, May 2006.

11. T. Kohno, A. Broido, and K. Claffy. Remote physical device fingerprinting. In *IEEE Symposium on Security and Privacy*, May 2005.

12. G. J. Popek and R. P. Goldberg. Formal requirements for virtualizable third generation architectures. *Communications of the ACM*, 17, July 1974.

13. N. Provos. Honeyd: A virtual honeypot daemon. In *Proceedings of the 10th DFN-CERT Workshop*, 2003.

14. J. S. Robin and C. E. Irvine. Analysis of the intel pentium's ability to support a secure virtual machine monitor. In *Proceedings of the USENIX Security Symposium*, 2000.

15. R. Rose. Survey of system virtualization techniques. Available at: http://www.robertwrose.com/vita/rose-virtualization.pdf, March 2004.

16. M. Rosenblum, S. A. Herrod, E. Witchel, and A. Gupta. Complete computer system simulation: The SimOS approach. *IEEE Parallel and Distributed Technology: Systems and Applications*, 3(4):34–43, Winter 1995.

17. E. Rotenberg, S. Bennett, and J. E. Smith. Trace cache: A low latency approach to high bandwidth instruction fetching. In *Proceedings of the 29th Annual International Symposium on Microarchitecture*, November 1996.

18. J. Rutkowska. Subverting Vista kernel for fun and profit. Presented at Black Hat USA, 2006.

19. J. Rutkowska. Red Pill... or how to detect VMM using (almost) one CPU instruction. http://invisiblethings.org/papers/redpill.html, 2004.

20. J. Rutkowski. Execution path analysis: finding kernel rootkits. *Phrack*, 11(59), July 2002.

21. A. Seshadri, M. Luk, E. Shi, A. Perrig, L. VanDoorn, and P. Khosla. Pioneer: Verifying integrity and guaranteeing execution of code on legacy platforms. In *Proceedings of the Symposium on Operating Systems Principals (SOSP)*, 2005.

22. S. Staniford, V. Paxson, and N. Weaver. How to 0wn the internet in your spare time. In *Proceedings of the 11th USENIX Security Symposium (Security '02)*, 2002.

23. G. Venkitachalam and B. Lim. Virtualizing I/O devices on VMware workstation's hosted virtual machine monitor. In *USENIX Technical Conference*, 2001.

24. VMWare. Timekeeping in VMWare virtual machines. Technical Report NP-ENG-Q305-127, VMWare, Inc., July 2005.

25. VMWare. VMWare Workstation. Available at: http://www.vmware.com/, October 2005.

26. M. Vrable, J. Ma, J. Chen, D. Moore, E. Vandekieft, A. C. Snoeren, G. M. Voelker, and S. Savage. Scalability, fidelity and containment in the potemkin virtual honeyfarm. In *Proceedings of the Symposium on Operating Systems Principals (SOSP)*, 2005.

27. D. D. Zovi. Hardware virtualization-based rootkits. Presented at Black Hat USA, August 2006.

Botnets and Proactive System Defense

John Bambenek and Agnes Klus

Coordinated Science Laboratory, University of Illinois at Urbana-Champaign, Urbana, IL 61801
{bambenek,aklus}@uiuc.edu

1 Introduction

In the early days of the Internet, the core application was the exchange of information. Sendmail, gopher and other tools were designed so that researchers and other academics could exchange information. Even after the advent of the webserver and web browser in 1993 with NCSA Mosaic, the core activity remained the exchange of information. It should come as no surprise that malicious individuals on the Internet at that time were primarily concerned with gaining that information illicitly. Starting around 1995, more sites came online that dealt more with commerce. Companies such as eBay and Amazon.com used the web to do business anywhere in the world 24 hours a day. To make this happen, they adapted the current credit card system for online use.

As the "dot-com" era began, more and more new companies cropped up and more and more old companies adapted their business to take place online. Soon online bill payment, online banking and online investment services became the norm. According to a study by Pew Internet, approximately 43% of all Americans were banking online in 2005 [1]. The primary purpose of the Internet became less about the exchange of information, though it still plays a key role, and more about economic transactions online. Even the exchange of information was leveraged by companies for advertising purposes. For example, Google makes most of its revenue by providing its information with context appropriate advertising. This change in purpose for the Internet also led to a change in the primary reason malicious users engaged in hacking activities online as well.

2 Paradigm Shifts in Commerce

Originally, credit card transactions were performed manually by a consumer handing the card to a merchant, the merchant making an imprint of the card and the calling in authorization for that credit card to be used. Fraud still happened, sure, but it was difficult to do on a large scale because it required not only a physical credit card but to be physically present for each purchase where a merchant would be likely to catch on to odd transactions. Merchants could steal credit card information and manually process fake transactions but even they would be physically tied to a location which could be very easily tracked. Authentication for financial transactions was basically two-factor, you *have* to have your credit card and you have to be able to *know* how to replicate the signature. While phone orders were made without the physical presence of the consumer, using fraudulent financial information was still time consuming to repeat.

With the transition to an online economy, having a physically present consumer was no longer practical. Further, it was not practical to give ever consumer a credit card processing terminal to attach to the computer to process transactions. Consumers would simply enter in their credit card information and perhaps some other personal information and a transaction would be approved. With the transition between in-person transactions and online transactions, authentication went from two-factor to single-factor. Online transactions only require you to *know* enough information.

With financial transactions being placed over computer systems, the possibility of massive fraud become plausible. Replicating thousands of credit cards and then running around town to buy things fraudulently took a great deal of time. However, using computers you can steal thousands of credits cards simply by sending out the right malware and repeating mundane tasks in quick succession over a short period of time is something computers are good for.

3 Fundamental Flaws in Current System

There are four main flaws in the current system on online financial transactions that lead to the possibility of mass exploitation. First, the authentication for most financial transactions (specifically credit card transactions) is based solely on knowing the right information. Second, transactions take place using consumer personal computers which cannot be secure and are not trustworthy. Third, the basis of identity in the United States is a unique 9-digit number called a Social Security Number which is inherently insecure and easy to steal. Fourth, information security, particularly patching vulnerabilities and creating anti-virus/anti-spyware signatures is a reactive process.

The current system on online financial transactions is bases authentication solely on knowing enough information. If a person knows the correct 16-digit credit card number with CVV2 number, the correct login and password, and the address of the victim, an attacker can make transactions in the name of the victim. While banks are moving to two-factor authentication to perform transactions, the transition is slow and voluntary. Many banks simply require a username and password and balance transfers or online bill payment services can be accessed. There is no clear attempt to move to two-factor authentication for commerce online. The leaves a system where fraudulent financial transactions can be made by an attacker who happens to get enough information, some of it public domain. Further, there are no small amount of online locations that store credit card information (Google "5424 cvv2") where a lazy attacker could just poach another attacker's work.

To make matters easier for an attacker, most people who engage in electronic commerce do so from their home personal computers. Few people in the information technology industry are fully qualified to harden a machine against attacks on the Internet and those are computer experts. Most consumers are not fully versed in the full functionality of the computers, much less how to secure them. Nor should they be experts in information security. However, our current system assumes that the consumer's PC is secure. A keylogger on a consumer PC makes it trivial to steal financial information. Even encrypted traffic can be stolen relatively easily when one of the end-points (i.e. the consumer PC) has been compromised [2].

This problem of insecure personal computers is only enhanced by consumers who aren't aware, much less, practice safe online browsing and e-mail practices [3]. According to the Bentley survey conducted in 2004, only 46% always update their anti-virus software. Between 30% and 60% of people simply had little to no knowledge about basic computer security issues such as viruses, spyware and safe web browsing. Most computers ship with trial anti-virus software which surely helps but these numbers indicate that most home users simply do not pay for updates after the trial period ends. Only recently have Microsoft and anti-virus vendors integrated an anti-spyware strategy into their products. Likely many more users have not installed anti-spyware software even though many programs are free to download.

What this creates is a ripe environment for attackers to operate. There are computers out there with financial data that do not have adequate protection, are operated by unsophisticated users, and likely aren't patched as frequently as those in a corporate environment. Even corporate environments have a hard time keeping up with their protection, it simply isn't a feasible strategy to assume consumers, with less resources than large companies, can keep pace with a constantly changing information security landscape.

The entire identity regime in the United States is based on a unique 9-digit number called a Social Security number. This number is required to open bank accounts, it is used for identifying credit files, it is often used to identify medical records, it is required by educational institutions, in short this number is used as a unique identifier which is the basis of all other identifying documents. The problem is that this identifier is used so ubiquitously that it becomes easy to steal. Several sites even use Social Security Numbers as logins (most infamously, student loan agencies)!

Every month it seems there is another story in the press about a laptop getting stolen or backup tapes getting lost that include Social Security Numbers or other financial information. Some of these instances, such as the Department of Veteran's Affairs, impacted tens of millions of Americans. With the amount of instances of theft and compromise of Social Security Numbers we are approaching a situation of complete compromise of the entire balance of Social Security Numbers.

The theft of a Social Security Number would not be such a big deal if it were not for the fact that knowledge of that number allowed malicious individuals to access credit records, open financial accounts or even steal the identity of the victim. Though identity theft can take place, and mostly does take place, using offline methods, the ability of massive compromise of a large number of victims in a short time via the internet cannot be ignored. In 2002, one estimate places identity theft loses at $24 billion. In 2003, that estimate is $73 billion [4] from both online and offline attacks.

Lastly, information security tends to be practiced in a reactive manner. A new virus is released and caught by an anti-virus company who begins to work on a signature. Usually with 24 hours they have a signature out with most anti-virus software updating their signatures daily. This gives a maximum of 47 hours where a virus is *known* and operating in the wild successfully compromising machines that are protected. Even before detection, exploitation is occurring. This means machines are being compromised and information stolen hours if not days before protection is available.

In addition, personal computers in general will trust all software unless it is specifically rejected by the anti-virus or anti-spyware systems. Instead of a regime of least privilege, where only trusted software can run, these computers run under a regime of most privilege where anything, including unknown but malicious code, can run without obstruction.

That patch cycle also creates problems. If the vulnerability stays secret before the patch is released there is about four days, at best, between the patch being released and the exploits being seen in the wild. If the vulnerability gets out before a patch is released it could be some time where the exploit has free reign to attack machines. The worst recent example of this window of vulnerability was with the WMF exploit [5]. There was over two weeks between the discovery of the WMF exploit and the out-of-cycle patch being issued by Microsoft. In the meantime, over 200 different attacks were used in the wild to exploit this vulnerability, some of which created botnets. While there is about 4-6 days between an exploit being released after a vulnerability is known, the time to develop a patch is about 40-60 days [7].

The reactive nature of signature-writing and patching means that attackers will be successful for some variable span of time in exploiting and taking over machines. While research continues to make that span of time shorter, the window of vulnerability still exists. There are also new techniques emerging that avoid detection of an exploit by anti-virus/anti-spyware vendors which would increase the window. Sun Tzu in The Art of War says that victory in war is impossible once the initiative has been surrendered. For the most part, the initiative has been handed over to the attackers which is why they keep winning.

4 Growth and Changes in Malware

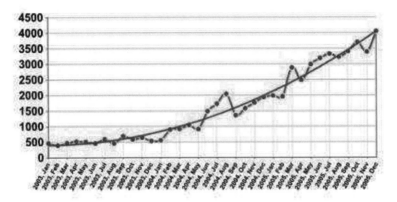

Fig. 1. Number of trojans intercepted by Kaspersky Labs (retrieved May 20, 2007) [11].

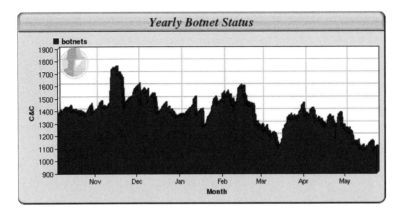

Fig. 2. Number of botnets detected by Shadowserver foundation (retrieved May 20, 2007) [9].

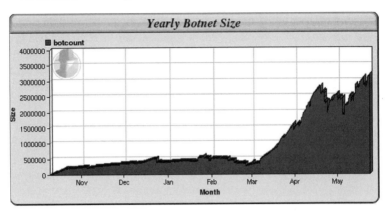

Fig. 3. Number of bot clients detected by Shadowserver foundation (retrieved May 20, 2007) [10].

As long as there has been commerce on the Internet there has been spam. Around 2003, those spammers branched out their operations to include spyware, phishing and botnets to further their money-making activities online. Despite spam being a decade old problem, spam has grown and flourished despite the enormous amount of money being spent trying to keep it under control. Despite the effort, spam continues unabated because it keeps working; people are making money with it. Now they've parlayed their efforts into general malware and phishing to keep the money flowing in.

Phishing, as a form of social engineering, is a logical outgrowth of spamming. More precisely it is a specific use of spam to trick a victim into doing something, whether it be give up their personal or financial information, install software, or run an exploit. Phishing need not be solely an e-mail operation, there have been plenty of phishing attempts using instant messaging and with the growth of social networking, that will likely be a vector that will be exploited.

The important feature of the growth of this form of Internet attacks is that it comes from those with a financial incentive. For instance, "Spamford Wallace", a well-known spammer, was fined for massive spyware operations to the tune of $4 million [6]. Malware developers are motivated by the ability to make money, whether it be through Denial of Service extortion, click fraud, spam or stealing financial information.

Like spam, botnets and phishing are still growing despite the massive amount of time and money being spend on the problem. In the 1990s, there were a handful of rootkits available so attackers could maintain control of a machine. However, control was a one-to-one operation, specifically, an attacker could only manage one node at a time. The evolution of botnets allowed an attacker to not only exploit many machines simultaneously but to maintain control of those machines once they have been exploited. While there has been some experimentation of protocols to maintain control of those machines (for instance, older distributed denial of service tools used a client-server model), IRC seems to be the de facto norm.

The reason for using IRC as the botnet controlling protocol is based on several factors. First, it is a known and otherwise "normal" protocol. People still use IRC for chatting to this day, though its popularity has waned with instant messaging and on-line forums. Second, there already existed IRC bots that were in use, most commonly to keep control of an IRC chatroom. Third, IRC has the ability of having many people in a chatroom at the same time with low bandwidth utilization. Lastly, it provided an attacker with the ability to have real-time information flow with all of his client machines whether they number in the thousands, tens of thousands, or in one case, 1.5 million [8].

The growth of trojan software and botnet clients has been been very steep. In January 2003, Kaspersky Labs detected approximately 500 trojans. By the end of December 2005 that number had grown to over 4000 (see Fig. 1). In 2006-2007, despite the number of botnets being relatively stable between 1100-1400 (see fig. 2) but the number of bot clients 500,000 to 3 million (see fig. 3) according to the Shadowserver Foundation. This seems to indicate that the size of botnets is growing. Growth has taken place despite the advances in Windows XP Service Pack 2 and Windows Vista though those developments did slow growth down for a time.

Another important fact is that even for known malware, not all of it is detected. Some vendors are better than others, but at any given time about 20% of malware is not detected [12]. This 80% detection is only relevant for environments that have full anti-virus/anti-spyware protection and update their signatures on a relatively frequent basis. The best case is that 20% of all malware will still manage to get through even with "perfect" users and a "perfect" configuration.

Most of the botnet software comes with keyloggers built-in so attackers can steal credit card information, usernames and passwords or potentially any other information they want. The botnet controller has the ability to issue instructions to the clients that can change their configurations at any time as to what they are looking for or where they send their data to. Many bot clients can also act as e-mail relays for spammers with the added advantage of not compromising their home IP space.

5 Future Trends of Botnets

There are six characteristics that can be identified as desirable for botnets. These criteria are based on the assumption that an attacker wants to achieve maximum financial gain or have maximum adverse impact to a target. They are: high capacity, low overhead, fast responding, flexible, anonymifying and quiet.

A botnet should have the capacity to hold as many hosts as it possible can. The more hosts that are controlled the more financial information can be stolen, the more machines can be leveraged in a distributed denial of service and so on. An attacker must have some means of controlling all these machines in a relatively easy and "low maintenance" way. IRC was a good protocol for that up to this point because many thousands of machines could join the same channel and simple commands could be issued to them all simultaneously.

Going along with high capacity, a botnet needs to have low overhead. The controlling protocol needs to use as little bandwidth as possible and send out as little as possible. Part of this is to maximize capacity, part is to prevent detection, and part is to maintain usefulness. A botnet isn't useful to an attacker if they get DoS'd off the network every time they try to get information from their clients.

Botnets also need to be fast responding so that an attacker is able to get the bot clients to act in unison in a somewhat coordinated manner. Once a botnet is discovered, a botnet operator has only a brief period of time to get the word out to his clients to move to another network before he gets shut down. Or, as another example, if an attacker wants to launch a distributed denial of service attack, it would not be as effective if all the clients started flooding a victim starting at random points over an hour. A distributed denial of service attack only works when the machines are more or less acting in unison.

An attacker would want his botnet to be flexible, namely, he should be able to deploy and redeploy his botnet in a variety of tasks with relative ease. An attacker may want to have his bot clients keylog credit card information one day, and when he has too much credit card information to sell off, he may wish to switch to stealing bank account login information. He may wish to install additional software on the clients, perhaps a browser helper object to steal SSL-encrypted information in web browsing sessions, and so on.

One of the most important features of a botnet is that it must be controllable in such a way as to hide the identity of the attacker. A botnet is little user to an attacker if his "real life" identity is broadcast to the world making it easy for the FBI to pay him a visit. The less traceable a botnet is to its owner, the better.

Lastly, a botnet must be quiet on the network. That is to say that it should be as undetectable as possible to intrusion detection mechanisms. Once a bot client is discovered, the process of reverse engineering the malware begins which ultimately point to where the botnet is controlled and that endangers the viability of the botnet as a whole. A good botnet will be able to operate for long periods of time "in plain site" without being noticed by network monitoring software, and ideally, from host monitoring software.

IRC was a natural choice to begin with for botnets. It is text-based so it is both high-capacity and low-overhead. Machines are connected in real-time to the chatroom so the clients are fast responding. Many of the botnet features already existed in IRC bots, attackers simply retasked the same software, made some modifications and rolled it out to victims. Because of the number of machines that connect to a botnet, assuming it is one of the already existing IRC networks, tracking a connection is difficult (but not impossible). Lastly, since IRC is a "normal" protocol it wouldn't arouse suspicion.

However, now that everyone knows botnets typically use IRC, administrators and ISPs are on the lookout. Further, IRC is generally unencrypted and text-based which makes it visible to network inspection now that administrators know what to look for. The long-term viability of IRC as a botnet protocol is not high. There have been some attempts at finding alternatives such as with peer-to-peer applications, however, peer-to-peer is already suspect traffic even before botnets are a consideration.

The above considerations point towards the use of XML and RSS as future directions of controlling botnets. The ubiquity of RSS feeds has far eclipsed the use of IRC as a protocol (though the purposes differ between them). RSS feeds are text-based, have low overhead, and have the potential of reaching many clients quickly. The communication would be asynchronous, namely, that the clients would have to respond through some other mechanism if appropriate. As an example, many popular blogs have RSS feeds that are public that no one would suspect would contain malicious traffic. Some of those sites include comments in their RSS feeds. An attack could place a comment on the blog that would appear normal but would contain commands for the bot clients. Those bot clients would check the RSS feed are set intervals and would pick up those commands. There would be a delay and once the commands were figured out the game would be over, but it would present a difficult problem to detect the first time. Once detection took place, the command syntax could be changed in future botnets so that newer botnets would still go undetected.

Another direction attackers could take is leveraging the XML features of Google's Mail service (Gmail). Google mail accounts are free and no network detection (except in very specific environments where free e-mail services are already banned by police) would pick up on it. An interesting but unpublished feature of Gmail is that it can be accessed over an SSL connection instead of the standard HTTP which would make it even harder to detect malicious traffic. This would present bidirectional communication between client and master.

The more normal the traffic appears and the lighter-weight the protocol is, the more likely it will be used by botnet operators. There are a variety of different possibilities but the direction is unmistakably going to be towards more "modern" protocols that will do an even better job at evading intrusion detection systems or other network monitoring.

Botnets will likely also branch out in the kinds of activities they are used in. Having control of hundreds of thousands of machines could make a serious economic warfare attack plausible. For instance, bot clients entering in fake transactions in the name of the victim across 100,000 unique victims could seriously undermine the confidence in electronic commerce forcing a rollback of those economic developments.

Another potential and under-used attack would be the development of botnets for corporate espionage. Namely, malware would be developed explicitly only to work within one organization or self-destruct. That malware then could be used to steal internal passwords, steal confidential intellectual property or for general eavesdropping.

6 Remediation of Core Vulnerabilities

Consumers are a key component of remediating these problems with online commerce. Not only is it their computers but without their buy-in, few options remain on the table. They are also generally unsophisticated when it comes to their computers so solutions must be simple and require as little effort on the part of the consumer as possible. In short, any solution must be convenient and "free". Banks and financial institutions bear the cost of protecting against financial fraud (which they pass down to the consumer in increased fees) and in some cases the costs are borne by merchants who are also victims of fraud. They also have a vested interested in preventing fraud.

Consumer personal computers must be treated as untrustworthy for the purposes of electronic commerce. There are far too many ways to compromise them and far to many uncontrolled variables to view it any differently. By way of analogy, sniffing network traffic is a pretty easy task. As a result, SSL encryption is required for all sensitive transactions so they cannot be intercepted. Data traveling through the Internet is not viewed as taking a safe path. Likewise, data going through a consumer PC cannot be viewed as traveling on a safe path.

Sensitive financial and personal information should be encrypted before it touches a potentially unsafe computer. Further, limiting the amount information on the computer or that needs to be entered into the computer would provide an extra layer of security. Banks already are starting this to some degree requiring one-time passwords with keyring tokens or other devices so that even if an attacker gets the one-time password, they cannot compromise the account.

The fact that anti-virus and anti-spyware operate on a most privilege dynamic ("allow all") means that any malware developed will run on a machine until a signature is developed to stop it. Operating systems likewise trust all software installed by any user with sufficient permissions to do so. The problem is that about 10% of all people on the Internet will at one time or another click or otherwise install malware unknowingly from generally phishing attacks. When social networks are used for phishing, that number rises to over 70% [13].

Anti-virus and anti-spyware applications should move towards a least privilege or "deny all" dynamic or at least a "deny most". There are a finite number of reputable software vendors and applications out there and far more disreputable software vendors and applications. Managing a system where software has to be "trusted" before it can be run makes the attackers job more difficult. Additionally, there is less of a time-crunch involved when someone wants to deploy new software compared to when malware is already in the wild and needs to be stopped yesterday. Signed software provides a general mechanism by which to accomplish this.

As an additional step, free and consensus-based hardening scripts should be developed for the consumer and unprotected computer space. Once developed, these scripts could be sent out on CDs by banks, credit card companies and ISPs to their customers. Consumers will run free software if they think it will protect them and if all they have to do to install it is click "Next" a handful of times.

The last mechanism of protection of computers should be remote validation of the system for its relative safety for financial transactions. Many VPN applications will determine if a machine is patched, running anti-virus and has appropriate security settings before letting it remotely connect to an office. This model could be adapted such that a computer is checked for basic security before a website allows the consumer to place a transaction.

These steps should not exclude other network-based or host-based detection and prevention technologies but should supplement them. Defense-in-depth allows for a more secure environment by relying on multiple layers of security technologies to protect information. The current situation is that consumer computers are "protected" by the hope that a consumer will take the time to do so. All an attacker has to do is undermine one layer of ineffective security. A defense-in-depth will make it more difficult for attackers to break-in. The more effort they have to take, the less money they can make and the more they'll get out of the business.

As a non-technical step, the national identification system in the United States needs to be reexamined. While the current debate is on the concept of whether or not a national ID is appropriate or desirable, the point is missed that there is already a national ID. The Social Security Number as an identifier has fared extremely poor against the development of identity fraud. Either other forms not involving a national ID need to be developed that don't include such a simple number or an actual national ID that can be used effectively as an identifier needs to be created.

7 Risks to the System without Change

All of the above changes comes with significant costs to banks, financial institutions, software developers, merchants and the government. To help justify those costs an examination must be made as to what is really at risk.

According to the Consumer Internet Barometer [14] 67.5% of American households are shopping online yet only 25.6% of them have trust in the system. With over 111 million households in America that makes about 75 million who shop online. Assuming that only 10% of those consumers have malware on them that steal financial and identity information, that would make 7.5 million households that have had their identities compromised. According to a Federal Trade Commission report [15], an average loss with identity theft is $10,200 per victim. Using the numbers above, over $75 billion could be stolen. Without action, these numbers will only continue to rise.

The mitigating factor preventing identity thieves from stealing that much money is that it would be immediately noticed and shut down by financial institutions using their fraud models. The straw is only so big. However, if the motive isn't to make money but to disrupt an economy, a lot of damage could be done playing with that amount of consumer's money. If botnets were used simply to place lots of small but fraudulent transactions to reputable vendors without an attempt to get the money, it could reduce the confidence in online commerce to catastrophic levels where consumers simply decline to shop or otherwise transact business online. That would be a dramatic economic effect in both lost time and lost efficiency and would have wide economic repercussions.

8 Conclusions

The core vulnerabilities with economic commerce have yet been adequately addressed. Those vulnerabilities stem from apply an older economic model of in-person transactions to an online setting without thinking through the security implications. Authentication for basic financial transactions still relies on one-factor authentications, simply knowing enough information is all that it takes to authorize a transaction.

Fraud and identity theft will continue to be the primary drivers of botnet growth and development. They key to reducing those threats is to take the financial motivation out of compromising consumer computers. If the data that can be stolen from a computer system is not enough to place a transaction, would be attackers would be forced to use other tactics. The financial incentive allows for not only attackers to make money, but for entrepreneurial software rights with flexible morality to make money be enabling these attackers with new software. If no money or little money can be made, less people will be interested in botnets.

Botnets will continue to develop and grow. The botnets will generally have more clients per net as attackers grow the size of their botnets. It takes some level of sophistication to move money and not be caught so bot clients will be passed on to someone able to truly leverage them. Eventually botnets will become harder to near-impossible to detect on the network as the money allows for software writers to earn a living while refining their craft. Eventually IRC will outlive its usefulness as a botnet protocol and a shift will be made to other modern protocols.

Proactive steps that change the dynamics of financial fraud and identity theft will force the attackers to rethink their strategy and attempt to develop entirely new methods of attack. There are no methods to permanently stop hacking but there are ways to change the rules of the game that force the attackers to come up with something new. This will help move information security professionals out of the patch-cycle and signature-development cycle that always keeps information security days behind attackers.

Without an ability to make serious money with botnets and similar technology, organized crime and other institutional players with the resources to really develop these attacks will not be interested in participating because they won't have a good return on their time. The less sophisticated the adversary in the botnet game will make it easier for security professionals to stay ahead.

Lastly, a defense-in-depth dynamic will need to be established for the unprotected wild of consumer PCs. Those machines remain easy to exploit and are a counter-incentive to full participation in the online economy by those consumers. The more usable their machines are, the more they'll be willing to buy, sell and trade online. Those machines will be less available for not only fraud and identity theft, but for use as distributed denial of service drones, spamming machines or other hostile activities. This will help secure the weakest link in the cyber security puzzle.

References

1. Susannah Fox and Jean Beier, " Online Banking 2006: Surfing to the Bank," *Pew Internet and American Life Project*, June 14, 2006. http://www.pewinternet.org/pdfs/PIP_Online_Banking_2006.pdf.
2. John Bambenek, "Defeating Encryption," *Infosec Writers*, November 11, 2004. http://www.infosecwriters.com/text_resources/pdf/Defeating_Encryption.pdf.
3. Mary Culnan, "Bentley Survey on Consumers and Internet Security," *Securing the Weak Link in Cyberspace*, November 17, 2004. http://www.bentley.edu/events/iscw2004/survey_findings.pdf.
4. Roger Thompson, "Cybersecurity & Consumer Data: What's at Risk for the Consumer?," Prepared Witness Testimony, House Committee on Energy and Commerce. November 19, 2003. http://energycommerce.house.gov/reparchives/108/Hearings/11192003hearing1133/Thompson1799.htm.

5. Sophos Labs,"Microsoft WMF vulnerability exploited in over 200 different attacks." Janurary 4, 2006. `http://www.sophos.com/pressoffice/news/articles/2006/01/wmfexploit.html`.
6. John Leyden,"'Spamford' Wallace fined \$4m over spyware biz," *The Register*, May 5, 2006.
7. Johannes Ullrich,"The Disappearing Patch Window," `http://isc.sans.org/presentations/MITSecCampISCPresentation.pdf`.
8. Internet Storm Center,"Handler's Diary," October 20, 2005, `http://isc.sans.org/diary.html?storyid=778`.
9. Shadowserver Foundation,"Botnet Charts,", May 20, 2007, `http://www.shadowserver.org/wiki/pmwiki.php?n=Stats.BotnetCharts`.
10. Shadowserver Foundation,"Bot Counts,", May 20, 2007, `http://www.shadowserver.org/wiki/pmwiki.php?n=Stats.BotCounts`.
11. Viruslist.com,"Malware Evolution: 2005," `http://www.viruslist.com/en/analysis?pubid=178949694`.
12. Andy Patrizio, "New Means to Root Out Malware,", *Internet News*, June 13, 2006, `http://www.internetnews.com/security/article.php/3613236`.
13. Tom Jagatic, Nathaniel Johnson, Markus Jakobsson and Filippo Menczer, "Social Phishing," *Communications of the ACM*, pre-print, `http://www.indiana.edu/~phishing/social-network-experiment/phishing-preprint.pdf`.
14. Consumer Internet Barometer, May 20, 2007, `http://www.consumerinternetbarometer.us/`.
15. Federal Trade Commission, "Identity Theft Survey Report," September, 2003, `http://www.ftc.gov/os/2003/09/synovatereport.pdf`.

Detecting Botnet Membership with DNSBL Counterintelligence

Anirudh Ramachandran, Nick Feamster, and David Dagon

School of Computer Science, Georgia Institute of Technology, Atlanta, GA 30332
{avr,feamster,dagon}@cc.gatech.edu

1 Introduction

Internet malice has evolved from pranks conceived and executed by amateur hackers to a global business involving significant monetary gains for the perpetrators [20]. Examples include: (1) unsolicited commercial email ("spam"), which threatens to render email useless by immensely decreasing the signal-to-noise ratio of traffic [18]; (2) denial of service attacks, which have become common [13], and (3) click fraud, whereby a group of attackers send bogus "clicks" for online advertisements that mimic legitimate request patterns, swindling advertisers out of large sums of money [5].

Botnets are a root cause of these problems [9], since they allow attackers to distribute tasks over thousands of hosts distributed across the Internet. A botnet is network of compromised hosts ("bots") connected to the Internet under the control of a single entity ("botmaster", "controller", or *command and control*) [6]. The large cumulative bandwidth and relatively untraceable nature of spam from bots makes botnets an attractive choice for large-scale spamming. Previous work provides further background on botnets [6, 7].

If network operators and system administrators could reliably determine whether a host is a member of a botnet, they could take appropriate steps towards mitigating the attacks they perpetrate. Although previous work has described an *active* detection technique using DNS hijacking technique and social engineering [7], there are few efficient methods to *passively* detect and identify bots (*i.e.*, without disrupting the operation of the botnet). Indeed, detecting botnets proves to be very challenging: a victim of a botnet attack can typically only observe the attack from a single network, from which point the attack traffic may closely resemble the traffic of legitimate users. Regrettably, the state-of-the-art in botnet identification is based on user complaints, localized honeypots and intrusion detection systems, or through the complex correlation of data collected through darknets [14].

We propose a set of techniques to identify botnets using *passive* analysis of DNS-based blackhole list (DNSBL) lookup traffic. Many Internet Service Providers (ISPs) and enterprise networks use DNSBLs to track IP addresses that originate spam, so that future emails sent from these IP addresses can be rejected. For the same reason, botmasters are known to sell "clean" bots (*i.e.*, not listed in any DNSBL) at a premium. This paper addresses the possibility of performing *counter-intelligence* to help us discover identities of bots, based on the insight that *botmasters themselves must perform "reconnaissance" lookups to determine their bots' blacklist status*. The contributions of this paper include:

1. Passive heuristics for counter-intelligence. We develop heuristics to distinguish DNSBL reconnaissance queries for a botnet from legitimate DNSBL traffic (either offline or in real-time), to identify likely bots. These heuristics are based on an enumeration of possible lookup techniques that botmasters are likely to use to perform reconnaissance, which we detail in Section 2. Unlike previous detection schemes, our techniques are *covert* and do not disrupt the botnet's activity.

2. Study of DNSBL reconnaissance techniques. We study the prevalence of DNSBL reconnaissance by analyzing logs from a mirror of a well-known blackhole list for a 45-day period from November 17, 2005 to December 31, 2005. Section 4 discusses the prevalence of the different types of reconnaissance techniques that we observed. Much to our surprise, we find that bots are performing reconnaissance on behalf of other (possibly newly infected) bots. Although some bots perform a large number of reconnaissance queries, it appears that much of the reconnaissance activity is spread across many bots each of which issue few queries, thus making detection more difficult.

3. Identification of new bots. We analyze DNSBL queries that are likely being performed by botmasters to identify "clean" bots. Such reconnaissance usually precedes the use of bots in an attack, suggesting the possibility that this DNSBL counter-intelligence can be used to bolster responses. Section 3 demonstrates the possibility of such early warning. To validate our detection scheme, we correlate the IP addresses of these likely bots with data collected at a botnet sinkhole (sinkholing technique explained in previous work [7]) over the same time period (this dataset has been used as "ground truth" for botnet membership in previous studies [7, 18]).

4. DNSBL-based countermeasures. Our heuristics could be used to detect reconnaissance in real-time. This ability potentially allows for active countermeasures, such as returning misleading responses to reconnaissance lookups, as shown in Figure 1. We revisit this topic in Section 5.

2 Model of Reconnaissance Techniques

This section describes our model for DNSBL reconnaissance techniques (*i.e.*, the techniques that botmasters may be using to determine whether bots have been blacklisted). Our goal in developing these models and heuristics is to distinguish DNSBL queries issued by botmasters from those performed by legitimate mail servers.

DNSBL queries issued by mail servers are often performed by directly querying the DNSBL, rather than relying on a local resolver. For example, SpamAssassin [21] implements its own recursive DNS resolver. Hosts performing reconnaissance are

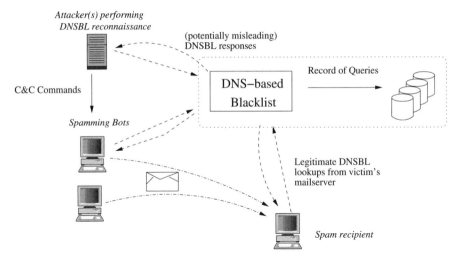

Fig. 1. DNSBL-based Spam Mitigation Architecture.

also unlikely to query DNSBLs using local resolvers. Thus, in both cases, the querying IP address observed at the DNSBL correctly reflects the end-host performing the query.

2.1 Properties of Reconnaissance Queries

Our detection heuristics are based on the construction of a *DNSBL query graph*, where an edge in the graph from node A to node B indicates that node A has issued a query to a DNSBL to determine whether node B is listed. After constructing this graph, we develop detection heuristics based on the expected *spatial* and *temporal* characteristics of legitimate lookups versus reconnaissance-based lookups. These characteristics hold primarily in cases when members of the botnet are not performing queries on behalf of each other, a case that makes detecting reconnaissance more difficult, as we explain in Section 2.2. As we describe below, our detection heuristics exploit both spatial and temporal properties of the DNSBL query graph.

Property 1 (Spatial relationships). A legitimate mail server will perform queries *and* be the object of queries. In contrast, hosts performing reconnaissance-based lookups will only perform queries; they will *not* be queried by other hosts.

This heuristic assumes that networks generally use the same host for both inbound and outbound mail servers. Although this configuration is common, some large networks separate the hosts responsible for inbound and outbound mail servers. In this case, queries from the inbound mail server might be misinterpreted as a reconnaissance attempt.

In other words, legitimate mail servers are likely to be queried by other mail servers that are receiving mail from that server. On the other hand, a host that is not itself being looked up by any other mail servers is, in all likelihood, not a mail server. We can use this observation to identify hosts that are likely performing reconnaissance: lookups from hosts that have a high *out-degree* in the DNSBL query graph (*i.e.*, hosts that are performing many lookups) but have a low *in-degree* are likely unrelated to the delivery of legitimate mail. To quantify this effect, we define the *lookup ratio*, λ, of some node n as follows:

$$\lambda_n = \frac{d_{n,out}}{d_{n,in}}$$

where d_{out} is the number of distinct IP addresses that node n queries, and d_{in} is the number of distinct IP addresses that issue a query for node n.

When $d_{n,in}$ is zero (which is commonly the case), we can simply consider λ_n to be a very large number. This metric is most effective when hosts performing reconnaissance are disjoint from hosts that are actually used to spam, which appears to the case today.However, as reconnaissance techniques become increasingly more sophisticated (as we describe in Section 2.2), this metric may become less useful. Still, we find that this metric proves to be quite useful in detecting many instances of DNSBL-based reconnaissance.

The *temporal arrival pattern* of queries at the DNSBL by hosts performing reconnaissance may differ from temporal characteristics of queries performed by legitimate hosts. We expect this to be the case because, whereas legitimate DNSBL lookups are driven by the arrival of actual email, reconnaissance queries will not reflect any realistic arrival patterns of actual email.

Property 2 (Temporal relationships). A legitimate mail server's DNSBL lookups reflect actual arrival patterns of real email messages: legitimate lookups are typically driven automatically when emails arrive at the mail server and will thus arrive at a rate that mirrors the arrival rates of emails. Reconnaissance-based lookups, on the other hand, will not mirror the arrival patterns of legitimate email.

We may be able to exploit the fact that email traffic tends to be diurnal [10] to tease apart DNSBL lookups that are driven by actual mail arrival from those that are driven by reconnaissance. Discovering reconnaissance activity using this method is a topic for future work.

2.2 Reconnaissance Techniques

In this section, we describe three classes of DNSBL reconnaissance techniques that may be performed by botmasters: *single-host, or third-party, reconnaissance*; *self-reconnaissance*; and *reconnaissance using other bots*. For each case, we describe the basic mechanism, the heuristics that we can use to detect reconnaissance in each of these cases, and how each technique may complicate detection.

Third-party Reconnaissance

In *third-party reconnaissance*, a botmaster performs DNSBL lookups from a single host for a list of spamming bots; this host may be the command-and-control of the botnet, or it might be some other dedicated machine. In any case, we hypothesize that the machine performing the lookups in these cases is not likely to be a mail server. Single-host reconnaissance, if performed by a machine other than a mail server, is easily detected, because the node performing reconnaissance will have a high value of λ_n.

Once detected, single-host reconnaissance may provide useful information to aid us in revealing botnet membership. First, once we have identified a single host performing such lookups, the operator of the DNSBL can monitor the lookups issued by that host over time to track the identity of hosts that are likely bots. If the identity of this querying host is relatively static (*i.e.*, if its IP address does not change over time, or if it changes slowly enough so that its movements can be tracked in real-time), the DNSBL operator could take active countermeasures, such as intentionally returning incorrect information about bots' status in the blacklist, a possibility we discuss in more detail in Section 5.

Self-Reconnaissance

Single-host reconnaissance is simple, but it is susceptible to detection. To remain more stealthy, and to distribute the workload of performing DNSBL reconnaissance, botmasters may begin to distribute these lookups *across the botnet itself*. A simple (albeit sub-optimal) way to distribute these queries is to have a bot perform reconnaissance on its own behalf ("self-reconnaissance"); in other words, each bot could issue a DNSBL query to itself (*i.e.*, to determine whether it was listed) before sending spam to the victim.

In this case, identifying a reconnaissance-based DNSBL query is fairly straightforward, because, except in cases of misconfiguration, a legitimate mail server is unlikely to issue a DNSBL lookup for itself. Even though this technique has the advantage of distributing the load of reconnaissance across the botnet, we did not observe this technique being used in practice, likely because a self-query is a dead giveaway.

Distributed Reconnaissance

A more stealthy way to distribute the operation across the botnet is to have each bot perform reconnaissance on behalf of other bots either in the same botnet or in other botnets. For instance, note that Property 1 is unlikely to hold: in this case, the nodes performing reconnaissance will also be queried by other mail servers to which they send spam. As a result, these nodes are likely to have a high $d_{n,in}$, unlike nodes performing single-host reconnaissance. Ultimately, detecting this type of reconnaissance activity may require mining temporal properties (*e.g.*, Property 2).

Although using the botnet itself for DNSBL reconnaissance is more discreet than performing this reconnaissance from a single host, a network operator who positively identifies a small number of bots (*e.g.*, starting with a small hit-list of known bots, probably by using a honeynet with known infected machines). As discussed in Section 4, if this *seed list* of bots performs queries for other hosts, it is likely that these machines are also bots.

We suspected that this mode of reconnaissance would be uncommon, possibly because of the complexity involved in implementing and operating such a system (*e.g.*, keeping track of nodes in the looked-up botnet, disseminating this information to the querying nodes etc.). Much to our surprise, we did witness this behavior; we present these results in Section 4.

3 Data and Analysis

This section describes our data collection and analysis. We first describe our DNSBL dataset and its limitations. Then, we describe how this dataset is used to construct the DNSBL query graph described in Section 2.

3.1 Data Collection and Processing

Our study primarily involves two datasets collected from the same time period (November 17, 2005 to December 31, 2005): (1) the DNSBL query logs to a mirror of a large DNSBL, and (2) the logs of bot connections to a sinkhole for a Bobax botnet [3]. Unlike most botnets, the Bobax bot is designed solely for spamming [2], increasing the likelihood that a query for known Bobax host is the consequence of the querying mail server having received spam from that host.

To verify whether the scheme we propose is indeed able to discover *additional* bots, we compared the IP addresses in the DNSBL query graph against the IP addresses of spammers in a large spam corpus collected at a spam honeypot (the setup of this honeypot is described in our earlier work [18]).

3.2 Analysis and Detection

In this section, we describe how the DNSBL query graph is constructed. Definitions for the terminology used in our algorithm follow: (1) B, the set of IP addresses that attempted to connect to the Bobax sinkhole during the observation period (November 17, 2005–December 31, 2005); (2) *querier*, the IP address of the host that performs a given DNSBL query; (3) *queried*, the IP address of the host that is looked up in a DNSBL query; and (4) G, the DNSBL query graph constructed as a result of the algorithm.

The graph construction algorithm takes as input a set of DNSBL query logs (we use tcpdump for packet captures) and the set B and outputs a directed graph G. The algorithm, summarized in Figure 2, consists of two main steps: *parsing* and *pruning*. As the algorithm suggests, we prune DNSBL queries to only include edges which have at least one end (either *querier* or *queried*) present in the set B. Pruning is performed for efficiency reasons: the full DNSBL query logs mostly contain queries from legitimate mail servers. Using B to prune the complete query graph allows us to concentrate on a subgraph which has a higher percentage of reconnaissance lookups than the unpruned graph. We recognize that our analysis will overlook reconnaissance activity where both the *querier* or *queried* nodes are not members of B. To address this shortcoming, we perform a *query graph extrapolation* after the algorithm is run. In this step, we make a second pass over the DNSBL query logs and add edges if at least one of the endpoints of the edge (*i.e.*, either *querier* or *queried*) is already present in the graph. Query graph extrapolation is repeated until no new edges are added to G.

```
CONSTRUCTGRAPH()
create empty directed graph G

/* Parsing */
for each DNSBL query:
    Identify querier and queried

    /* Pruning */
    if querier ∈ B or queried ∈ B then
        add querier and queried to G if they
            are not already members of G
        if there exists an edge E(querier, queried) ∈ G then
            increment the weight of E(querier, queried)
    else
        add E(querier, queried) to G with weight 1
```

Fig. 2. Algorithm to construct a DNSBL query graph

We then compute λ_n for each node in the graph (Property 1), which allows us to identify nodes involved in reconnaissance techniques described in Section 2. Although the results in Section 4 suggest that some bots have large values of λ_n, techniques that use a large number bots to look each other up may be undetectable with this metric. We are developing techniques based on Property 2 to further improve our detection.

4 Results

This section presents preliminary results using Property 1 to identify DNSBL reconnaissance activity on the observed DNSBL query graph. We emphasize that the reconnaissance being performed by bots is distinctly under the radar as far as total DNSBL traffic is concerned: the pruned traffic amounts to less than 1% of the total DNSBL traffic. In this section, we present two surprising results: First, botnets are being used to perform DNSBL reconnaissance on behalf of bots in other botnets, which has implications for botnet detection. Second, the distribution of these queries

Node #	ASN of Node	Out-degree	known spammers
1	Everyone's Internet (AS 13749)	36,875	12
2	IQuest (AS 7332)	32,159	7
3	UUNet (AS 701)	31,682	5
4	UPC Broadband (AS 6830)	26,502	8
5	E-xpedient (AS 17054)	19,530	4

Table 1. AS numbers of hosts which have the highest out-degrees. The last column shows the number of hosts queried by this node that are known spammers (verified using logs from our spam sinkhole).

across bots suggests that some DNSBL reconnaissance activities may be detectable in real-time, which has implications for early detection and mitigation.

Attempts to validate our hypotheses from Section 2 resulted in some interesting discoveries, including the discovery of new bots. We initially expected that most DNSBL lookups would be third-party lookups, as described in Section 2.2, and that we would be able to validate the queried nodes as being known bots. Instead, we discovered the opposite: the nodes with the highest values of λ_n in the pruned graph were *known* bots, while *the queried nodes in the graph were new, previously unknown bots*. Further, using data from our spam sinkhole [18], we found that some of these nodes were Windows machines and confirmed spam originators. This finding suggests that, in general, it may be possible to start with a set of known bots and use the DNSBL graph to "bootstrap" the discovery of new bots.

Table 1 shows five of the top queriers (*i.e.*, high out-degree nodes), *all* of which are known bots from our Bobax trace. Even more interesting is the fact that a few IP addresses queried by these nodes actually sent spam to our spam honeypot. Moreover, nearly all of IP addresses that sent spam to our honeypot were *not* present in our list of known bots. Due to the fact that our honeypot only captures a small portion of the Internet's spam, the fraction of total reconnaissance queries that we can confirm as spamming bots is small. Still, we believe it strongly suggests evidence of a known bot performing DNSBL reconnaissance on a distinct (and possibly newly compromised) botnet.

Figure 3 shows the distribution of out-degrees for all querying nodes present in the pruned DNSBL query graph. The long tail also confirms that bots already have the capability to distribute these queries, which is cause for concern. Our view of DNSBL queries is narrow (most querying nodes are geographically close to the DNSBL mirror), so we expect that more vantage points of DNSBL lookups would reveal other prominent "players". The fact that the prominent players in our analysis were also bots suggests that these nodes may also be obvious candidates for the mitigation techniques described in Section 5.

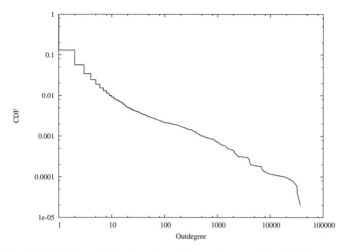

Fig. 3. CDF of the distribution of out-degrees for querying IP addresses.

5 Countermeasures

In Section 4, we found that the known bots in our Bobax trace were not the targets of lookups, but instead were issuing lookups for other, possibly newly compromised bots. This finding suggests a possible technique that could be used for the discovery of new bots, even without an initial list of suspects: an initial set of suspect IP addresses could be constructed by establishing a spam trap, which according to both previous work [18] and the observations in this paper, appear to be largely bots. Alternatively, a suspect node could be detected simply by identifying nodes in the DNSBL query graph with a high value of λ_n. Beginning with this initial suspect list, an operator may be able to conclude that, not only are the nodes that this node is querying likely bots, but also the node itself is likely a bot. If there are other high-degree nodes also querying the same bots, a detection algorithm might be able to "walk" the DNSBL graph (*e.g.*, from parent to parent) to discover multiple distinct botnets.

We believe that using such techniques to aggressively monitor botnet-based DNSBL reconnaissance may prove to be useful for mitigating spam: as noted in our previous work [18], most bots send a very low volume of spam to any single domain; thus, reporting a bot to blacklists *after* the spam is received may not be effective.

With the ability to distinguish reconnaissance queries from legitimate queries, a DNSBL operator might be able to mitigate spam more effectively. We speculate one possibility as follows: an operator could tune the behavior of the blackhole list server to mislead a botmaster, using a class of techniques we call *reconnaissance poisoning*. On one hand, the DNSBL could trick the botmaster into thinking that a particular bot was "clean" (*i.e.*, unlisted) when in fact it was listed, which would induce the botmaster to unwittingly send spam from blacklisted machines. On the other hand, the DNSBL could also reply to a reconnaissance query with an indication that a host was listed, even though it was not listed, thereby discouraging a botmaster from using a machine that would likely be capable of successfully sending spam.

Of course, active countermeasures such as reconnaissance poisoning do run the risk of false positives: if we mistakenly attribute a legitimate DNSBL query to a reconnaissance-based query, we could mislead a legitimate mail server into either mistakenly accepting spam that would have otherwise been rejected or, more regrettably, rejecting legitimate email. Such techniques could also be defeated if the botmaster queries multiple blacklist providers that maintain independent lists. Investigating the extent to which our detection metrics are subject to false positives, as well as the extent to which these false positives interfere with a legitimate mail server's filtering techniques, is part of our ongoing work.

6 Related Work

Botnets have been in use as vehicles of cybercrime for quite some time, but studies on how they spread, and techniques to counter them, are relatively scarce. Previous research has traced the history of botnets [19, 22, 23] and common modes of botnet operation [6]. This section briefly discusses previous botnet detection techniques and previous research on DNSBL traffic analysis.

Previous work has identified bots by examining the communication protocols used by botnets (*e.g.*, for "rallying"), most notably Internet Relay Chat (IRC) [8, 24]. Some have suggested the use of such protocols to identify and remediate botnets. For example, researchers have joined IRC-based botnets and enumerated victims using IRC commands [9]; others have used network traffic to identify IRC zombies [17]. Some researchers have identified bot victims by observing the unwanted traffic they generate, *e.g.*, the RST storms or backscatter generated by DDoS attacks using forged source addresses [16].

Studies show that many botnets are IRC-based [6, 23], though other protocols are being used [15]. Attempts have been made to detect such botnets using misuse-detection or basic intrusion detection analysis [4, 11]. Dagon *et al.* used DNS redirection to monitor botnets [7]. In contrast, the detection techniques described in this paper are more discreet because they do not require direct communication with any component of the botnet.

Jung *et al.* found that 80% of spam sources in their analysis were listed in at least one of seven popular blacklists [12], which correlates well with our independent previous study [18]. To the best of our knowledge, this paper presents the first study that uses direct analysis of DNSBL logs to infer other types of network behavior.

7 Conclusion

This paper has developed techniques and heuristics for detecting DNSBL reconnaissance activity, whereby botmasters perform lookups against the DNSBL to determine whether their spamming bots have been blacklisted. We first developed heuristics for counter-intelligence based on several possible ways we figured reconnaissance was being performed. We then studied the prevalence of each of these reconnaissance techniques. Much to our surprise, we found that bots were in fact performing reconnaissance on IP addresses for bots in other botnets. Based on this finding, we have outlined possibilities for new botnet detection techniques using a traversal of the DNSBL query graph, and we have suggested techniques that DNSBL operators might use to more effectively stem the spam originating from botnets. We are investigating the effectiveness of these detection and mitigation techniques as part of our ongoing work.

References

1. Taormina, Sicily, Italy, October 2004.
2. Bobax trojan analysis. http://www.lurhq.com/bobax.html, March 2005.
3. Symantec Security Alert–W32.Bobax.D worm. http://www.sarc.com/avcenter/venc/data/w32.bobax.d.html.
4. David Brumley. Tracking hackers on IRC. http://www.doomdead.com/texts/ircmirc/TrackingHackersonIRC.htm, 2003.
5. CNN Technology News. Expert: Botnets No. 1 emerging Internet threat. http://www.cnn.com/2006/TECH/internet/01/31/furst/, January 2006.
6. Evan Cooke, Farnam Jahanian, and Danny McPherson. The Zombie Roundup: Understanding, Detecting and Disrupting Botnets. In *Usenix Workshop on Steps to Reducing Unwanted Traffic on the Internet (SRUTI)*, June 2005.
7. David Dagon, Cliff Zou, and Wenke Lee. Modeling botnet propagation using time zones. In *Proceedings of the 13th Annual Network and Distributed System Security Symposium (NDSS '06)*, 2006.
8. S. Dietrich, N. Long, and D. Dittrich. Analyzing distributed denial of service attack tools: The shaft case. In *Proceedings of the LISA 2000 System Administration Conference*, December 2000.
9. Felix C. Freiling, Thorsten Holz, and Georg Wicherski. Botnet tracking: Exploring a root-cause methodology to prevent distributed denial-of-service attacks. Technical Report ISSN-0935-3232, RWTH Aachen, April 2005.
10. Luis H. Gomes, Cristiano Cazita, Jussara Almeida, Virgilio Almeida, and Wagner Meira. Characterizing a Spam Traffic. In *Proc. ACM SIGCOMM Internet Measurement Conference* [1].
11. Christopher Hanna. Using snort to detect rogue IRC bot programs. Technical report, October 2004.
12. Jaeyeon Jung and Emil Sit. An Empirical Study of Spam Traffic and the Use of DNS Black Lists. In *Proc. ACM SIGCOMM Internet Measurement Conference* [1], pages 370–375.
13. Srikanth Kandula, Dina Katabi, Matthias Jacob, and Arthur Berger. Botz-4-Sale: Surviving Organized DDoS Attacks That Mimic Flash Crowds. In *Proc. 2nd Symposium on Networked Systems Design and Implementation (NSDI)*, Boston, MA, May 2005.
14. Sven Krasser, Gregory Conti, Julian Grizzard, Jeff Gribschaw, and Henry Owen. Real-time and forensic network data analysis using animated and coordinated visualization. In *Proceedings of the 6th IEEE Information Assurance Workshop*, 2005.

15. Brian Krebs. Bringing botnets out of the shadows. `http://www.washingtonpost.com/wp-dyn/content/article/2006/03/21/AR20060%32100279.html`, 2006.
16. D. Moore, Geoffrey M. Voelker, and Stefan Savage. Inferring internet denial-of-service activity. In *Proceedings of the 2001 USENIX Security Symposium*, 2001.
17. Stephan Racine. Analysis of internet relay chat usage by ddos zombies. `ftp://www.tik.ee.ethz.ch/pub/students/2003-2004-Wi/MA-2004-01.pdf`, 2004.
18. Anirudh Ramachandran and Nick Feamster. Understanding the Network-Level Behavior of Spammers. In *Proc. ACM SIGCOMM*, Pisa, Italy, September 2006.
19. Puri Ramneek.   Bots & Botnets: An Overview.   `http://www.giac.com/practical/GSEC/Ramneek_Puri_GSEC.pdf`, 2003.
20. S.E. Schechter and M.D. Smith. Access for sale. In *2003 ACM Workshop on Rapid Malcode (WORM'03)*. ACM SIGSAC, October 2003.
21. SpamAssassin, 2005. `http://www.spamassassin.org/`.
22. SwatIt. Bots, drones, zombies, worms and other things that go bump in the night. `http://swatit.org/bots/`, 2004.
23. Virus Bulletin 2005 Paper on 'Bots and Botnets'. `http://arachnid.homeip.net/papers/VB2005-Bots_and_Botnets-1.0.2.pdf`.
24. Y. Zhang and V. Paxson. Detecting stepping stones. In *Proceedings of the 9th USENIX Security Symposium*, August 2000.

A Taxonomy of Botnet Structures

David Dagon[1], Guofei Gu[1], and Christopher P. Lee[2]

[1] School of Computer Science, Georgia Institute of Technology, Atlanta GA 30332
`{dagon,guofei}@cc.gatech.edu`
[2] School of Electrical and Computer Engineering, Georgia Institute of Technology, Atlanta, GA 30332
`chrislee@gatech.edu`

1 Introduction

Malware authors routinely harness the resources of their victims, creating networks of compromised machines called botnets. The attackers' ability to coordinate the victim computers presents novel challenges for researchers. To fully understand the threat posed by such networks, we must identify classes of botnet topologies, their potential uses, and the challenges each class presents for detection and remediation.

We believe that it is inadequate to simply enumerate the botnets we have seen to date in the wild. Botnets have proven to be very dynamic. For example, researchers have observed changes in botnet sizes, which have trended from large networks (100K+ victims) to numerous smaller botnets (1-5K+ victims) [53]. Likewise, we have seen a rapid transition from centralized botnets (e.g., IRC) to distributed organizational structures (e.g., P2P) [64]. We expect that botnets will continue to be a dynamic, evolving threat.

We must therefore consider the structural and organizational *potential* of botnets. Similar to how previous work detailed key aspects of individual classes of worms [57], this paper provides a taxonomy of botnet organization, and their utility for various malicious activity. We believe that future botnet research will share a common goal of reducing the utility of botnets for botmasters. This raises important questions: How are botnets utilized? What metrics should be used to measure the effectiveness of remediation on such networks?

Recent work by Rajab, et al. [47] noted the need for the botnet research community to better define metrics. Their study examined problems in estimating botnet populations. This paper argues that other metrics (bandwidth, communications efficiency, robustness) require a similar thoughtful examination.

This paper therefore proposes a taxonomy of botnet topologies, based on the utility of the communication structure and their corresponding metrics. Section 2 details metrics for measuring botnet uses, and describes the structural organization of botnets. In Section 3, we demonstrate how to perform measurement of selected metrics, and analyze experimental response techniques designed to address particular classes of botnets. We note how our work relates to other areas of inquiry in Section 4. Since this area of research is new and rapidly changing, we conclude with suggestions for future work in Section 5.

Our contribution is the following: we identify a small number of likely structural forms for botnets, based on a utilitarian analysis. We propose metrics for measuring a botnet's effectiveness, efficiency, and robustness. Our analysis of models and real world observations suggests that some botnet structures are more resilient than others to different types of remediation efforts. This analysis can guide future inquiry into how to best address the botnet problem.

2 Botnet Taxonomy

The evolving and evasive nature of botnets requires researchers to anticipate possible topologies. An interesting early contribution in this area is [13], which listed three topologies (centralized, peer-to-peer, and random) for botnets, and roughly evaluated performance metrics in terms of high, medium and low performance.

To more fully understand the threat, we expand on [13] and propose a taxonomy of possible botnet topologies and how to measure their utilization in various malicious activities.

2.1 Purpose and Goals

Taxonomies are most useful when they classify threats in dimensions that correspond to potential defenses [30, 31]. As [29] noted: "[a]n important and sensible goal for an attack taxonomy ... should be to help the defender."

Our botnet taxonomy will help researchers identify what types of responses are most effective against botnets. Our design goals are similar to [57]: (a) assist the defender in identifying possible types of botnets, (b) describe key properties of botnet classes, so researchers may focus their efforts on beneficial response technologies.

Our taxonomy is driven by possible responses, and not detection. There is some initial work in botnet detection [13–15, 17, 18, 20]. Further, the considerable body of literature on worm detection has identified detection techniques that can be adapted to botnet detection [9, 21, 26, 44, 58, 60, 61, 63]. We therefore leave for future work a classification of botnet detection techniques.

2.2 Key Metrics for Botnet Structures

Naively, one could suppose that bots will organize according to various regular network topologies such as star, mesh, or bus networks. These topologies are useful for formal analysis of discrete network properties, but do not let us describe the utility of large complex botnets.

Instead, we need to pay attention to key *discriminators* that let one compare important attributes of botnets. We identify three important measures of botnets: effectiveness, efficiency, and robustness. We acknowledge there are other characteristics the botmaster may desire, but these are not easily designed into the topology of a victim network. For example, botmasters may desire anonymity from their botnet (e.g., to carry out anonymous attacks); however, this property is not inherently obtained from any single topology, and depends more on the application-layer design of a botnet's messaging system.

Table 1 lists a few botnet uses, and key relevant metrics. More than one metric can be relevant to a botnet use, and botnets certainly have multiple uses. However, the table lists key metrics critical to the botnet's specified function.

Major Botnet Utilities	Key Metrics	Suggested Variables	Comment
Effectiveness	Giant portion	S	Large numbers of victims increases the likelihood of high-bandwidth bots. Diurnal behavior favors S over total population.
	Ave. Avail. Bandwidth	B	Average bandwidth available at any time, because of variations in total victim bandwidth, use by victims, and diurnal changes.
Efficiency	Diameter	l^{-1}	Bots sending messages to each other and coordinating activities require efficient communications.
Robustness	Local transitivity	γ	Bots maintaining state (e.g., keycracking or mirroring files) require redundancy to guard against random loss. Highly transitive networks are more robust.

Table 1. Botnet Uses and Relevant Metrics

2.3 Measuring Botnet Effectiveness

The *effectiveness* of a botnet is an estimate of overall utility, to accomplish a given purpose. While botmasters may innovate new uses of botnets, the ability of a botnet to meet existing uses such as spam, DDoS, warez distribution and phishing is roughly approximated by size and bandwidth. Both of these terms require elaboration.

We agree with [47], that "botnet size" must be a qualified term. Here, we do not use size to mean the total population count, such as that usually used in worm epidemiology studies [37–39, 50]. Instead, we mean the "giant" component of the botnet, or largest connected (or online) portion of the graph [10, 42]. Botnets are of course more powerful if they have large infected population, but the giant component lets us directly measure the damage potentially caused by certain botnet functions.

In the case of DDoS, the giant component, S, lets us measure the largest number of bots that can receive instructions and participate in an attack. This contrasts with the total population of all infected victims, which may not always be reachable by the botmaster, e.g., because of diurnal variations. [16].

A related measure is the average amount of bandwidth that a bot can contribute, denoted as B. Estimating bandwidth along a single link is a complex problem, and the subject of numerous investigations in the networking community [6, 25]. To estimate the cumulative bandwidth of an entire botnet presents an even more challenging task. For example, one could measure the bandwidth between bots, between a bot and the botmaster, or between any bot and a third party (e.g., a DDoS victim). By average bandwidth, B, we mean the cumulative available bandwidth in a bot that a botmaster could generate from the various bots (e.g., for DDoS) under ideal circumstances. Such a measurement of course varies with the distribution of bandwidth available to each member of the botnet, the probability that any victim is "on-line" at any given time, and the amount of bandwidth already being consumed by the victims themselves (e.g., for normal use).

We roughly classify three types of bots according to their transit categories: those using modems (type 1), those using DSL/cable (type 2), and those using 'high-speed' networks (type 3). While bandwidth within each class is highly variable in itself, we believe this grouping is a reasonable first approximation because they are standard in industry–e.g., many commodity databases already map connection classes according to these categories [34]. The probability of a bot belonging to type i is denoted as P_i. According to [24], a reasonable distribution for US-based bots could be estimated as $P_1 = 0.3, P_2 = 0.6, P_3 = 0.1$. Similar distributions could be inferred for a global population.

Let us denote the average maximum network bandwidth within each type as M_i, the average normal usage of bandwidth within each type is A_i. Thus, the average available bandwidth could be used by a botmaster on a bot is $M_i - A_i$. We simplify our measurement by assuming a botmaster would not use even more bandwidth, since this would interfere with the victims existing use, and the disruption might alert them to the infection.

We also need to consider the diurnal sensitivity of these networks. More complete diurnal models of bot behavior were presented in [16]. However, to avoid modeling diurnal changes in numerous time zones, we can use a simplified metric based on the estimated number of hours a victim is online per day (and therefore capable of participating in the botnet). We assign different weights (denoting the distribution of time hosts are online each day) to each class of bots. For example, if we assume average online hours per day for a bot using modem is 2, for a bot with DSL/cable is 6, and for a bot with high-speed is 24, then we have the probability vector $\mathbf{W} = [2/32, 6/32, 24/32] = [0.0625, 0.1875, 0.75]$. We selected these numbers based on [43]; however, our analysis considers other ranges of values.

Using the simplified bandwidth estimation for each bot, and a simplified diurnal model, we can express the average available bandwidth of a bot as:

$$B = \sum_{i=1}^{3}(M_i - A_i)P_i W_i \qquad (1)$$

In Section 3, we suggest the utility of this metric by comparing different botnets. The weights and distribution of hosts in each class are of course variable. To understand their sensitivity, we evaluated the weighted bandwidth for different ranges of estimates.

Figure 1 shows the weighted bandwidth, with different variations in diurnal sensitivity. We can see in Figure 1(a), that the final average weighted bandwidth is around 20Kbps for a single bot, for the values fixed in that plot. With approximately 50,000 such bots in a botnet, the botmaster can utilize about 1Gbps bandwidth on average at any time.[3] The parameters for the plots in Figure 1 are drawn from data measurements described in Section 3.

The plots reveal the sensitivity of this metric to the diurnal variation in users. Compare for example Figure 1(a), where low bandwidth users are presumed on-line for only two hours, to Figure 1(c), where six hours is fixed instead. For diurnal weighing above 6 hours/day, variation in the online hours for the medium and high-bandwidth users does not result in much variation in the overall bandwidth, as shown in Figure 1(a). However, in Figure 1(c), the online variation of the other classes has a significant impact on bandwidth particularly when higher-speed users are "always on" and have a diurnal weight of 1. This suggests that botnets with many low-speed connections experience less variation when the lower-speed connections minimize their time online. In Section 3, we further compare estimated bandwidth of two bot-nets.

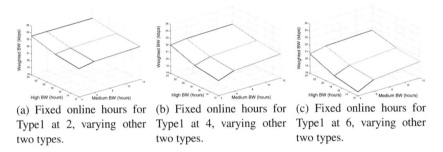

(a) Fixed online hours for Type1 at 2, varying other two types.

(b) Fixed online hours for Type1 at 4, varying other two types.

(c) Fixed online hours for Type1 at 6, varying other two types.

Fig. 1. Weighted bandwidth and diurnal sensitivity. Low-bandwidth bots have a significant effect on average bandwidth when they are online for more than $\approx$ 4 hours. Figures (a) through (c) fix the diurnal weight of low-bandwidth bots at 2, 4 and 6 hours. Only at the extreme, plot (c), does average bandwidth change significantly. This impact is seen when high- and medium bandwidths bots have less than 24-hour/day connectivity.

2.4 Measuring Botnet Efficiency

Botmasters and security researchers may also be concerned about the *efficiency* of a botnet . Whether used to forward command-and-control messages, update bot executable code, or gather host-based information (e.g., keylogging and data ex-filtration), a botnet may be evaluated by its communication *efficiency*.

We propose *network diameter* as one means of expressing this efficiency. By net-work diameter, we mean the average geodesic length of a network, l. This measures

---

[3] We repeat again the caution noted above: our *available bandwidth* metric does not mea-sure the bandwidth between any two points. Rather it measures the amount of traffic the botmaster may reasonably generate using his network.

the average length of the shortest edge connecting any two nodes in the network. If l is large, the dynamics of the network (communications, information, epidemics) is slow. The reader may recall that in Milgram's famous paper, social networks were shown to have short average geodesic lengths, approximately log N, or $l \approx 6$ ("six degrees of separation") for general society [36], while the web has a larger estimated length, $l \approx 17$ [3].

As in [23], we use the inverse geodesic length, l^{-1}, instead of l, defined as:

$$l^{-1} = \left\langle \frac{1}{d(v,w)} \right\rangle = \frac{1}{N(N-1)} \sum_{v \in \mathcal{V}} \sum_{w \neq v \in \mathcal{W}} \frac{1}{d(v,w)'} \tag{2}$$

This way, if bots v and w are disconnected, the distance d is zero. Further, the inverse length is normalized, ranging from 0 (no edges) to 1 (fully connected). In the context of botnets, l^{-1} refers to the overlay network of bot-to-bot connections created by the malware, instead of the physical topology of the Internet. Thus, bot victims on the same local network (one hop away) may be several edges apart or even unconnected in the overlay bot network created by the malware.

This metric is relevant because with each message passed through a botnet, there is a probability of detection or failure. Some researchers have already investigated zombie detection via stepping stone analysis, or the detection of messages being relayed through victim proxies [59]. It is difficult to express this chance of detection precisely, since botnet identification is a new, developing field. But at a high level, botnet detection techniques will generally rely on the chance of intercepting (i.e., detecting and corrupting or halting) a message between two bots in a network. Assume that bots u and v are connected through n possible paths, $P_1, \ldots P_n$, and that each node in the path can be recovered (cleaned) with probability α. If ϵ_i is the chance that path P_i is corrupted, quarantined or blocked, then all paths between u and v are blocked with probability:

$$\prod_{i=1}^{n} \epsilon_i \leq (1-\alpha)^n \tag{3}$$

While bots u and v are connected through *some* path with probability $1 - (1 - \alpha)^n$, the chance of failure increases with α (i.e., as detection technologies improve). Section 3 characterizes the performance of l^{-1} under increasing link decay.

We expect that in the future, botnet researchers will propose many techniques to detect, disrupt, or interfere with botnet messaging. Network diameter, l^{-1} is therefore a basic, relevant metric to determine how many opportunities network administrators have to observe, disrupt or measure messaging.

The incentive of the botmaster is to increase l^{-1}, which yields a more efficient botnet, at least for selected uses noted in Table 1. Under an ideal $l^{-1} = 1$, every bot can talk directly to every other bot. Since a botnet with more interconnections has more short paths, it passes messages quickly, and provides fewer detection opportunities.

2.5 Measuring Botnet Robustness

A final category of botnet use can be expressed in the *robustness* of such networks . Bots routinely lose and gain new members over time. If victim machines are performing state-sensitive tasks (e.g., storing files for download, or sending spam messages from a queue), a higher-degree of connection between bots provides fault tolerance and recovery.

To some degree this metric correlates with an improved redundancy. But we more precisely capture the robustness of networks using local transitivity to measure *redundancy*. Local transitivity measures the likelihood that nodes appear in "triad" groups. That is, given two node pairs, $\{u, v\}$ and $\{u, w\}$, that share a common node, u, local transitivity measures the chance that the other two, v and w, also share an edge. A clustering coefficient γ, measures the average degree of local transitivity [56], in a neighborhood of vertices around node v, Γ_v. If E_v represents the number of edges in Γ_v, then γ_v is the clustering coefficient of node v. Where k_v represents the number of vertices in Γ_v, then we have:

$$\gamma_v = \frac{E_v}{\binom{k_v}{2}}, \gamma = \langle \gamma \rangle = \frac{1}{N} \sum_{v \in V} \gamma_v. \tag{4}$$

The average clustering coefficient $\langle \gamma \rangle$ measures the number of triads divided by the maximal number of possible triads. Just like l^{-1}, γ ranges from $[0, 1]$, with 1 representing a complete mesh.

Local transitivity is an important measure for certain botnet uses. Warez (stolen programs) and key cracking require reliable, redundant storage, particularly since botnets exhibit strongly diurnal properties. To ensure uninterrupted key cracking, or that file resources are always available, botmasters routinely designate multiple victims to store identical files. (For examples, consult [12].) Botmasters could use quorum systems in addition to simple backups. However, the transitivity measure γ index generally captures the robustness of a botnet.

2.6 Botnet Network Models

To measure the robustness of different botnet architectures, we must further specify the types of response actions available to network administrators. In a general sense, botnets can suffer random and targeted responses. Random failures correspond to patching by normal users, diurnal properties of computers being powered off at night, and other random failures in a network. Targeted responses are those that select "high value" machines to recover or patch. These response types all correspond to actions directed at botnet vertices. Edge-oriented responses (e.g., quarantine, null routing) have been considered elsewhere, e.g., [62].

Expanding on the general categories of botnets noted in [13], we consider different types of graphs studied in the extensive literature on complex networks. Our taxonomy uses the major models from that field . For a comprehensive overview of complex network mechanics, see [4].

Erdös-Rényi Random Graph Models

To avoid creating predictable flows, botnets can be structured as random graphs. In a random graph, each node is connected with equal probability to the other $N - 1$ nodes. Such networks have a logarithmically increasing l^{-1}. The chance a bot has a degree of k is the binomial distribution:

$$Pr(k) = \binom{N-1}{k} p^k (1-p)^{N-1-k} \tag{5}$$

Particularly for large networks like botnets, it makes sense to limit the degree k to a maximum number of edges, L. For our analysis below, we select an average $\langle k \rangle$ appropriate to botnets, instead of $\langle k \rangle \approx 2L/N$ used by others studying general network complexity problems [23]. Without such a limitation, a pure Erdös-Rényi random botnet would potentially create individual bots with hundreds of edges, even for small (5K victim) botnets. Large numbers of connections on a client host are highly unusual, even for P2P software [33, 49]. So, unless the victim is a rare high-capacity server, botmasters would keep $\langle k \rangle$ small, say $\langle k \rangle \approx 10$. In Section 3, we measure the degree of connection in an unstructured P2P botnet, to confirm that $\langle k \rangle$ will have fairly low values.

One difficulty in random graphs is easily overcome by certain types of botnets. Since each node has a probability $Pr(k)$ of being connected to each vertex, the creation of the graph requires some central collection (or record) of vertices. That is, each bot must either know or learn the address of all the other bots, in order to have a chance of sharing an edge. Because such a list may be discovered by honeypot operators, botmasters have an incentive to not create such a centralized master list, and some bots, e.g., those created by the Zindos worm [32], take explicit steps to limit the number of victim addresses stored in one place.

This creates a technical problem for botnets that propagate through traditional (e.g., scanning, mass-mailing) techniques. The first victims will not know the address of subsequent victims, and have a $Pr(k)$ biased towards zero. One solution is for the attacker to keep track of victims joining their botnet, generate a desired topology overlay, and transmit the edge sets to each bot.

Bot masters can easily select a desired $\langle k \rangle$ to generate such a network. For example, they may select $\langle k \rangle \le 10$, so that bots appear to have flow behavior similar to many peer-to-peer applications [33, 49]. A botmaster could of course select a higher $\langle k \rangle$, even one close to N to create a mesh, but such structures quickly exhaust bot resources, and may be easily detected by network administrators.

If existing botnets are not available to generate a random graph, one solution was proposed by [13], where bots could randomly scan the Internet to find fellow bots. Although noisy, this approach provides a last-resort technique for botnet creation. Assuming random scanning up to L connections, the resulting botnet would have a Poisson k distribution, and both the clustering and diameter properties of a random graph.

Watts-Strogatz Small World Models

Another topology botnets can use is a Watts-Strogatz network. In such a network, a regional network of local connections is created in a ring, within a range r. Each bot is further connected with probability P to nodes on the opposite side of the ring through a "shortcut". Typically, P is quite low, and the resulting network has a length $l \approx \log N$. See [4] for further discussion of small world networks.

Intuitively, we can imagine a botnet that spreads by passing along a list of r prior victims, so that each new bot can connect to the previous r victims. To create shortcuts in the small world, bots could also append their address to a growing list of victims, and with probability P connect back to a prior bot. As noted in Section 3, we have witnessed only a few anecdotal botnets that create prior victim lists, e.g., Zindos [32]. To frustrate remediation and recovery, the lists are typically small $r \approx 5$. In the case of propagation-created botnets, botmasters may prudently use $P = 0$, to avoiding transmitting a lengthy list of prior victims. Otherwise, a bot would have to append its address to a growing list of IPs forwarded to each new victim. As noted above, if a botmaster desired to have shortcuts in a small world botnet, they could instead just use an existing botnet.

Barabási-Albert Scale Free Models

The previous botnet structures are characterized by variations in clustering, and each node exhibits a similar degree, $k \approx \langle k \rangle$. In contrast, a Barabási-Albert network is distinguished by degree distribution, and the distribution of k decays as a power law. Many real-world networks have an observed power-law distribution of degrees, creating a so-called scale free structure.

Scale-free networks contain a small number of central, highly connected "hubs" nodes, and many leaf nodes with fewer connections. This has a significant impact on the operation of the network. As discussed in Section 3, random node failures tend to strike low-degree bots, making the network resistant to random patching and loss. Targeted responses, however, can select the high degree nodes, leading to dramatic decay in the operation of the network. This phenomenon is explored in many articles, e.g., [5].

Researchers have noted that bots tend to organize in scale free structures, or even star topologies [11, 15, 17]. For example, botnets might use IRCd [27] for coordination, which explicitly uses a hub architecture.

P2P Models

In a P2P model, there are structured and unstructured topologies [45, 48]. For example, a structured P2P network might use CHORD [52], or CAN [48], while an unstructured P2P might use the hub-and-spoke networks created under gnutella or kazaa [45].

The unstructured P2P networks tend to have power-law link distributions [45]. We therefore treat this type of P2P network as a Barabási-Albert (scale free) model in our analysis. Similarly, structured P2P networks are similar to random networks, in the sense that every node has almost the same degree.

In Section 3, observe new P2P-based botnets, and perform some measurements on their structures. Since our selected metrics concern only basic botnet properties (length, giant, and local transitivity), we can treat these networks as random or scale free in our analysis. We encourage others to refine these models to identify distinct P2P botnet features that distinguish them from random and scale free networks. For the metrics proposed in this work, however, we will address P2P botnets as special cases of the previous categories.

3 Taxonomy-Driven Botnet Response Strategies

The previous discussion of botnet organization suggests the need for diverse response strategies. To guide future research in this developing area, we model different responses to each botnet category. Our analysis confirms the prevailing wisdom [13] that command-and-control is often the weak link of a botnet. We confirm our model with an empirical analysis of a real-world botnet response. Significantly, our analysis also shows that targeting the botnet C&C is not always an effective response. Some botnets will require new response strategies that research must provide.

3.1 Erdös-Rényi and P2P Models

For ranges appropriate to botnets, we evaluate the relationship between node degree, k, and the diameter of the botnet, expressed as l^{-1}. We assume that, to evade trivial detection, botnets will attempt to limit $\langle k \rangle$ to some value similar to P2P. Empirical studies of P2P systems reveal very low median link scores (e.g., $k \approx 5.5$) [33, 49]. Figure 2(a) plots $\langle k \rangle$ against l^{-1} for realistic values, $k \leq 20$. Others have noted that for increasing average degrees, $\langle k \rangle$, random Erdos-Renyi models have logarithmically increasing diameters [23]. However, in Figure 2(a), realistic values of k show a *linear* relationship to l^{-1}.

We also note that giant, s, improves significantly with increases in k, enabling connections with most of the botnet when $k \approx 10$ for a 5K botnet. This agrees with the general principle noted in Eqn. (3), where logarithmically connected networks enjoy nearly universal broadcasting.

Local transitivity, γ, also increases logarithmically with k. But for a range of small values of k, typical of botnets, it shows a linear increase. This means that each additional value of k equally improves the general robustness of the botnet. We also note a slight flare at the base of the γ plot for Figure 2(a), for very low values of k. Intuitively, this means botnets with a very low average degree have difficulty forming triads, but this is quickly overcome as k increases. Botmasters therefore have incentives to increase k.

Our current analysis, however, shows that for botnets using a random topology, random loss (e.g., infrequent user patching or anecdotal cleanup) will not diminish the number of triads in the botnet. We also omit plotting the performance of random

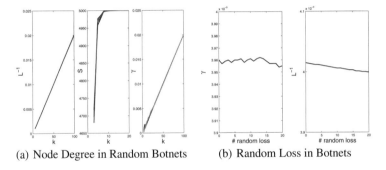

(a) Node Degree in Random Botnets   (b) Random Loss in Botnets

Fig. 2. (a) Changes in length l^{-1}, giant (s), and local transitivity (γ) in response to changes in critical values of k, for 5K victim botnet. (b) Effect of loss on random networks.

networks under targeted responses. Targeting nodes can at best remove a few nodes with k slightly higher than $\langle k \rangle$. The result is asymptotically the same as random loss.

The work in [55] is a good example of a hybrid botnet with a random graph structure formed using a technique similar to Erdös-Rényi graph, through the use of a peer list. They also confirm the robustness of such networks against targeted and random attacks. The work in [54] is also a good example of botnets created using a random graph structure.

In section 2 we noted that structured P2P networks are very similar to random networks, at least in terms of the metrics we care about: length, giant and transitivity. Structured P2P networks in fact have a constant k (often set equal to the log N size of the network), so they are slightly more stable than purely random networks. Thus, changes in γ and s, and l^{-1} are constant with the loss of random nodes.

Clearly botnets with random topologies (including structured P2P networks) are therefore extremely resilient, and deserve further study. We speculate that the most effective response strategies will include technologies to remove large numbers of nodes at once. Detecting and cleaning up large numbers of victims (perhaps at the host level) appears to be the most viable strategy. Likewise, strategies that disrupt the ability of the network to maintain indices may be fruitful, as suggested by the P2P index poisoning research in [51].

3.2 Watts-Strogatz Models

There are some experimental botnets [32] that use small world structures, but overall they do not appear to have a high utility value, using the metrics we've proposed. The average degree in a small world is $\langle k \rangle \approx r$, or the number of local links in a graph. Thus, random and targeted responses to a small world botnet produce the same result: the loss of r links with each removed node. Thus, the key metrics for botnets, s, γ, l^{-1} all decay at a constant rate in a small world.

We presumed that shortcut links in a small world botnet are not used ($P = 0$), but even if present, they would not affect γ with $r \geq 4$. That is, if the number of local links is large enough to form triads, the absence of shortcuts does not significantly increase the number of triads (which are already formed by r local neighbors).

There may be other benefits (e.g., propagation stealth or anonymity), for which we have not proposed a utility metric. But overall, small world botnets do not have benefits different from random networks. In other domains, researchers have noted that small world graphs are essentially random [23].

Our investigation of experimental of botnet structures only reveals only one representative of the Watts-Strogatz model: the Zindos [32] worm. We speculate that the poor utility scores in the face of targeted and random loss may explain this phenomena. An equally likely explanation is hinted at by Zou, et al., in [64], where the authors noted the desire of botmasters to avoid revealing a lists of confederate botnet members to honeypot operators.

3.3 Barabási-Albert and P2P Models

While random networks present a challenge, at least scale free networks provide some good news for researchers. Figure 3(a) plots the change in diameter and transitivity against changes in the "core" size of the botnet, C. The "core" of a scale free botnet is the number of high-degree central nodes–the routers and hubs used to coordinate the soldier bots. As more core nodes are added, the diameter of the scale free botnet stays nearly constant for small regions of C. Intuitively, splitting a hub into smaller hubs does not significantly increase the length of the overall network.

The local minima in Figure 3(a) has an intuitive explanation. If we have a single hub in a scale free network, $C = 1$, many of the added leaf nodes have a good chance of forming triads. The scale-free generation algorithm we chose prefers high degree nodes, and tends to form many triads when there are few hubs.

As we increase C, we create several high degree hubs that attract distinct groups of leaf nodes. This creates many "squares", where hubs are connected to each other, and leaves are connected to each other. But transitivity is only measured locally (in triads, and not other polygon paths). Thus, increasing C diminishes γ slightly. As we increase C more, we observe a tendency for the hubs themselves to form triads, so γ grows logarithmically.

Can botmasters avoid this drop in transitivity? We suspect not, if they wish to maintain a "normal" degree count, relative to other applications. In Figure 3(c), we compare changes in γ against core size using different link counts for leaf nodes. If nodes have more links, $m \approx 16$, the loss in γ shallows out. But increasing the link count of nodes can help anomaly detection algorithms that examine link degrees (e.g., flow log analysis). This reveals a curious mix of incentives. On the one hand botmasters would like to have $C >> 1$, since a single core node is too easily removed. But increasing C just a little drops local transitivity. To recover the loss in transitivity, botmasters would have to increase link counts to rates far in excess of average P2P degree counts.

Responses to scale free botnets are more effective. As expected, random losses in scale free botnets are easily absorbed. Figure 3(b) shows that random patching has almost no affect on a botnet diameter or the frequency of triad clusters. Intuitively,

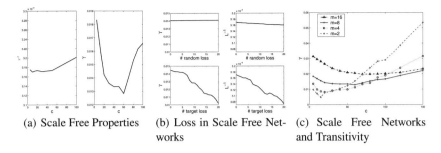

Fig. 3. (a) Changes in diameter and transitivity vs. core size, for a 5K scale free botnet. (b) Loss in scale free networks. (c) Changes in link count for leaves in a scale free network.

because of the power law distribution of node degrees, random losses tend to affect low-degree nodes (e.g., the leaves), and not important nodes (e.g., hubs).

Targeted responses, however, can select key nodes for response. This results in a dramatic increase in diameter, and loss of transitivity. This suggests that researchers should focus on technologies that allow targeted responses to high-degree nodes in botnets. Figure 3(b) validates the intuitive idea that by removing a botnet C&C, the network quickly disintegrates into a collection of discrete, uncoordinated infections.

As noted in [47], measuring aspects of botnets presents a challenge to researchers. To demonstrate the practicality of our proposed metrics, we measured the average link degree in an unstructured P2P botnet. We selected the nugache worm [41], and measured the degree of connections between neighbors in the network mesh. Nugache uses a link encrypted, peer-to-peer filesharing protocol, WASTE [1], and uses several hard-coded IP addresses to request a list of peers to from [41]. After connecting to peers, the bot discovers more peers and continue to form new connections. The resulting botnet is an unstructured P2P network, which tends to create a scale-free form. Thus, although nugache spreads by P2P systems, the resulting mesh is a scale-free network.

Since we believe our data collection technique is somewhat unusual, we describe it in some detail. We note that obtaining precise measurements is, of course, nearly impossible given the distributed nature of nugache. We therefore ran multiple instances of the nugache worm in a modified version of WINE [2], which guaranteed that each copy would obtain a unique IP when a network socket is allocated under bind() system calls. Thus, using a single multi-homed machine, we "controlled" hundreds of nugache nodes and were able to observe their connections to the rest of the victims in the wild. (This is similar to the use of numerous heavy-weight honeypots to track botnets, noted in [13].) We ran two such "batch WINE runs" for several weeks, creating hundreds of nodes, and measured the connections degree among our subsample of the overall population.

Figure 4(a) shows the distribution of link degrees found in the Nugache sample. The vast majority of victims maintained less than 6 links to other victims. There are a few nodes with a very high degree, ≈ 30. This suggests a scale-free network typical of unstructured P2P networks. Our sampling technique unfortunately could not inject nodes into the inner ring of the nugache network (created from the hard-coded peers), where we would expect to observe a very high link degree.

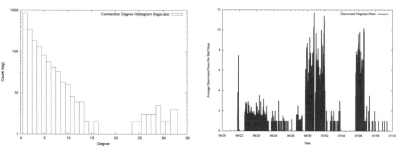

(a) Nugache Worm Link Distribution   (b) Nugache Victim Joins over Time

Fig. 4. Measurements of (a) link degree in Nugache and (b) joins observed over time.

If we had contacted the owners of the low-degree nugache nodes we observed, or otherwise caused their remediation and cleanup, our impact on the network's utility would have been negligible, according to our analysis. Our model above shows that random losses in scale free networks (and unstructured P2P networks) do not significantly degrade the network. Figure 3(b) shows that random losses fail to significantly reduce either the diameter or transitivity values.

Of course, we were unable to measure the entire population, s, of the nugache network using our data collection technique. Figure 4(b) illustrates the problem. This figure plots the rate of new SYN+ACK connections observed by our batch WINE nodes. This is therefore a rough measure of the rate of new link creation, which may or may not correspond to the rate of new victims being recruited. (That is, a new SYN+ACK may represent an old nugache victim we've just discovered, or a new victim joining for the first time.) Since we did not catch nugache in its early formation, or successfully inject our honeypots into the inner ring of high-degree nodes, we saw only a small number of potentially new victims over the study period.

As the authors in [47] noted, measuring population values is a complex undertaking. We believe our analysis shows that our proposed metrics are both practical and useful. However, we leave for future work the design of effective data collection techniques for P2P networks (whether structured or unstructured). Given the often stealthy creation of such networks, we expect this may remain a challenging problem for researchers.

3.4 Empirical Analysis

Our taxonomy also suggested that available bandwidth B is a useful metric for botnet utility. We again note that bandwidth estimation for end-to-end hosts is a complex task. Nonetheless, to show the utility of our proposed metric, we estimated the available average bandwidth in two botnets.

Using techniques described in [16], we measured one botnet of approximately 50,000 unique members in February 2005, and estimated the bandwidth of 7,326 bots chosen in a uniformly random manner. Likewise, we measured the bandwidth of a 3,391 member subsample from a 48,000 member botnet in January of 2006.

We used the `tmetric` [7] tool to perform the bandwidth estimation. `tmetric` essentially uses successively larger probes to estimate the bandwidth to a host. We used a high-capacity link (OC-48) close to our network's core routers, so that we were more likely to measure the end host's available bandwidth, rather than any limitations in our internal network. Dozens of probes sent over minutes were used to obtain an average. Again, we note that the networking community has developed far more sophisticated techniques to estimate bandwidth *end-to-end*. We believe our simple measurements were useful to quickly obtain a first order approximation of the average bandwidth in an entire distributed *network*.

Figure 5(a) and (b) show the distribution of bandwidth, with min/max and average bandwidth values observed during the probes. Table 2 shows the average available bandwidth (that the botmaster can utilize) from a single bot. Using Eq(1) and without considering the diurnal sensitivity, we can calculate the average available bandwidth for botmaster to use on one bot is around 53.3004 Kbps. For data set 2, the average is 34.8164 Kbps, a few less than the first case.

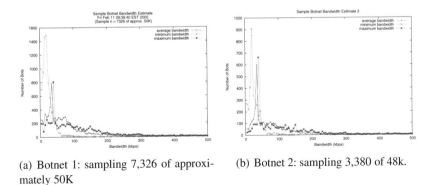

(a) Botnet 1: sampling 7,326 of approximately 50K

(b) Botnet 2: sampling 3,380 of 48k.

Fig. 5. An estimate of bandwidth usage in two sampled botnets. Just examining the maximum bandwidth, the botnets appear to have roughly the same distribution of high, medium and low-speed bots, and therefore appear to pose the same DDoS threat potential. The analysis below, however, shows how diurnal changes significantly reduce the average available bandwidth of (b), compared to (a).

But when accounting for diurnal sensitivity, and assuming the average online times for each class of bots is [2, 4, 24] hours, then the final average bandwidth for botmaster on one bot is 22.7164 Kbps. If a botnet has a size of 50K, then on average

Bot Bandwidth Type	Low (std)	Medium (std)	High (std)
Dataset 1: Average Max BW	28.2356 (11.9612)	119.1708 (54.2837)	601.7158 (989.2654)
Average usage BW	19.2395 (8.5739)	74.3089 (34.4838)	364.8714 (636.2601)
Average available BW	8.9961	44.8619	236.8444
Dataset 2: Average Max BW	33.9266 (9.3649)	116.0036 (51.0478)	432.4184 (354.3628)
Average usage BW	27.9144 (8.8397)	86.2721 (33.3334)	280.6805 (229.9276)
Average available BW	6.0122	29.7315	151.7379

Table 2. Average and standard deviation of bandwidth observed in two botnets, plotted in Figure 5

the botmaster consistently has more than 1Gbps bandwidth on average at anytime. This suggests the botnet could easily launch a successful denial of service attack on almost any web site. (Indeed, during our period of observation, the 50K member botnet did DDoS several websites that only had 100Mbs transit.) For data set 2, the weighted bandwidth is 14.6378 Kbps– comparatively lower.

The metric therefore reveals something counter-intuitive about botnets. Just looking at the sampled bandwidth in Figure 5(a) and (b), it seems that the botnets have roughly the same maximum bandwidth, and the same number of bots, and therefore have the same general utility from a DDoS perspective. When accounting for diurnal changes in populations, however, the second botnet (plotted in Figure 5(b)) has approximately half the average available bandwidth, despite having only 2,000 less members than the other network. If network administrators had to select between these two botnets and prioritize a single response effort, the simple bandwidth estimate B shows a higher utility in the botnet in Figure 5(a).

Our bandwidth estimate metric may have other uses besides priority ranking botnets. This exercise suggests that diurnal changes in botnet membership can significantly affect a botnet's utility as a DDoS vehicle. We leave for future work an analysis of how this metric can be leveraged in a targeted attack on a botnet. That is, we speculate that responders might significantly reduce a botnet's DDoS potential by targeting the "high-speed" members of a botnet. The bandwidth B metric should let researchers measure their progress in such a response, and tell them how many more high-speed members must be removed, relative to the mix of low-speed members, for a given estimated diurnal usage pattern.

4 Related Work

Our work fits into the larger body of literature addressing the statistical mechanics of complex networks [4]. Others have studied the brittle nature of scale-free networks and resilience of random networks in other contexts [5,23,40]. Our work adapts these findings to the particular domain of botnets.

The topology of networks under active decay was analyzed in [40]. Many of the results in [40] anticipate our own. The authors took a fascinating look at all domains of network structures (e.g., including terror cells, and global history), and not just computer networks. By restricting our analysis to botnets, we identified several unique and interesting phenomena not considered in [40]. For example, the authors in [40] suggest a strategy of splitting high-degree nodes to avoid targeted responses. This is analogous to increasing C in scale free networks, discussed in 3. Since we focused on the botnet domain, we were able to further observe that this results in a degraded transitivity.

Botnet research is still maturing. The work in [13] anticipated many of the general categories of botnets analyzed in Section 2, including the difficulty in responding to different type of botnet taxonomies. The models and empirical data we presented in Section 2 flesh out and formalize the intuitive discussion in [13].

Recently, advanced botnets with complex network structures have been studied. Vogt, et al. [54] presented a super-botnet, the network of many independent, small botnet, which is a special case of a random graph botnet. Wang, et al. [55] introduced an advanced hybrid peer-to-peer botnet. Grizzard, et al. [19] provided an overview of P2P botnet and a case study of a specific bot.

There have been several works on botnet measurement. In [17, 46], the authors used honeynets to track existing IRC-based botnets and report a few simple statistics about botnets. Rajab, et al., [47], argue that the estimation of botnet size is actually hard in practice, and call for further research on the measurement of botnets. We believe our analysis in Sections 2 and 3 help with this problem.

Wang, et al. [55], propose two metrics, connection ratio and degree ratio, to measure the resilience of removing mostly-connected bots from a botnet. In this paper, we propose more metrics, and not only measure the robustness, but also the effectiveness and efficiency of a botnet for the botmaster.

Researchers have attempted to study the botnet problem in a systematic way. Barford and Yegneswaran [8] codify the capabilities of malware by dissecting four widely-used Internet Relay Chat (IRC) botnet codebases. Each codebase is classified along seven dimensions including botnet control mechanisms, host control mechanisms, propagation mechanisms, exploits, delivery mechanisms, obfuscation and deception mechanisms. Trend Micro [35] also proposed a taxonomy of botnet threats, along dimensions such as attacking behavior, command and control model, rally mechanism, communication protocol, evasion technique, and other observable activities. Our taxonomy is different from this existing work. It is a use-driven taxonomy focused on the botnet structure. We study the problem from specific aspects such as the structure and the utility metrics of the botnets.

Our taxonomy and discussion of general response options presumes a sensitive detection system. We have not considered detection of botnets, and urge further research. We note preliminary detection work in misuse systems [22], and IRC traces [11]. Significantly, this early work focuses on tracking *individual* bots (e.g., to obtain a binary) and not the *network* cloud of coordinated attackers addressed in our study. In [13, 17], researchers focused on countering bot*nets* (as opposed to individual bots), which used honeypots and broad sensors to track and infiltrate botnets.

Recently, there are several works on the botnet detection problem. BotHunter [20] is a bot detection system using IDS-Driven Dialog Correlation according to defined bot infection dialog model. Rishi [18] uses the similarity of nick name to detect bot-net channel. Karasaridis, et al. [28], proposed to detect botnet command and control through passive network flow record analysis.

5 Conclusion

Botnets present significant new challenges for researchers. The fluid nature of this problem requires researchers anticipate future botnet strategies and design effective response techniques. To assist in this effort, we presented a taxonomy of botnets based on topological structure.

Our analysis shows that random network models (either direct Erdös-Rényi models or structured P2P systems) give botnets considerable resilience. Such formations resist both random and targeted responses. Our analysis also showed that targeted removals on scale free botnets offer the best response.

We have demonstrated the utility of this taxonomy by selecting a class of botnets to remediate. Our analysis suggested that by removing command and control nodes, targeted removal was an effective response to scale-free botnets. We measured the impact of such responses in simulations, and using a real botnet.

5.1 Future Work

Our response strategies considered only targeted and random responses to botnets. Byzantine failures in a botnet, where administrators infiltrate a network, e.g., [17], may present a third response option. To some extent, [40] anticipates some issues in such failures. Future work should assess the impact of such failures on key metrics, and identify metrics for evasion and detection.

Because of the difficulty in measuring botnets, our empirical analysis necessarily considered only changes in giant, s, in scale free botnets. Future work will investigate the potential of honeypots to measure local transitivity in botnets, including P2P botnets. The botnets we captured were very large (100K+ members), and proved difficult to manage using current honeypot technologies.

Acknowledgments

This material is based upon work supported by the National Science Foundation under Grant No. CCR-0133629 and CNS-0627477, and by the U.S. Army Research Office under Grant No. W911NF0610042. Any opinions, findings, and conclusions or recommendations expressed in this material are those of the author(s) and do not necessarily reflect the views of the National Science Foundation and the U.S. Army Research Office.

References

1. Waste: Anonymous, secure, encrypted sharing. `http://waste.sourceforge.net/index.php?id=projects`, 2007.
2. WineHQ: Windows API Implementation for Li5Dnux. `http://www.winehq.com/`, 2007.
3. A.-L. Barabási and R. Albert. *Science*, 286(509), 1999.
4. Réka Albert and Alert-László Barabási. Statistical mechanics of complex networks. *Reviews of Modern Physics*, 74(1), 2002.
5. Réka Albert, Hawoong Jeong, and Alert-Lászloó Barabási. Error and attack tolerance of complex networks. *Nature*, 406:378=382, 2000.
6. Mark Allman and Vern Paxson. On estimating end-to-end network path properties. In *ACM Special Interest Group on Data Communication (SIGCOMM '99)*, volume 29, 1999.
7. Michael Bacarella. TMetric bandwidth estimation tool. `http://michael.bacarella.com/projects/tmetric/`, 2007.
8. Paul Barford and Vinod Yegneswaran. An inside look at botnets. In *In Series: Advances in Information Security*. Springer Verlag, 2006.
9. V.H. Berk, R.S. Gray, and G. Bakos. Using sensor networks and data fusion for early detection of active worms. In *Proceedings of the SPIE AeroSense*, 2003.
10. B. Bollobás. *Random Graphs*. Academic Press, 1985.
11. David Brumley. Tracking hackers on IRC. `http://www.doomdead.com/texts/ircmirc/TrackingHackersonIRC.htm`, 2003.
12. Edwin Calimbo. Packetnews: The ultimate irc search engine. `http://www.packetnews.com/`, 2007.
13. Evan Cooke and Farnam Jahanian. The zombie roundup: Understanding, detecting, and disrupting botnets. In *Steps to Reducing Unwanted Traffic on the Internet Workshop (SRUTI '05)*, 2005.
14. David Dagon. The network is the infection. `http://www.caida.org/projects/oarc/200507/slides/oarc0507-D\agon.pdf`, 2005.
15. David Dagon, Amar Takar, Guofei Gu, Xinzhou Qin, and Wenke Lee. Worm population control through periodic response. Technical report, Georgia Institute of Technology, June 2004.
16. David Dagon, Cliff Zou, and Wenke Lee. Modeling botnet propagation using time zones. In *Proceedings of the 13th Annual Network and Distributed System Security Symposium (NDSS'06)*, 2006.
17. Felix C. Freiling, Thorsten Holz, and Georg Wicherski. Botnet tracking: Exploring a root-cause methodology to prevent distributed denial-of-service attacks. Technical Report ISSN-0935-3232, RWTH Aachen, April 2005.
18. Jan Goebel and Thorsten Holz. Rishi: Identify bot contaminated hosts by irc nickname evaluation. In *USENIX Workshop on Hot Topics in Understanding Botnets (HotBots'07)*, 2007.
19. Julian B. Grizzard, Vikram Sharma, Chris Nunnery, Brent ByungHoon Kang, and David Dagon. Peer-to-peer botnets: Overview and case study. In *USENIX Workshop on Hot Topics in Understanding Botnets (HotBots'07)*, 2007.
20. Guofei Gu, Phillip Porras, Vinod Yegneswaran, Martin Fong, and Wenke Lee. Bothunter: Detecting malware infection through ids-driven dialog correlation. In *16th USENIX Security Symposium (Security'07)*, 2007.
21. Guofei Gu, Monirul Sharif, Xinzhou Qin, David Dagon, Wenke Lee, and George Riley. Worm detection, early warning and response based on local victim information. In *20th Annual Computer Security Applications Conference (ACSAC)*, 2004.

22. Christopher Hanna. Using snort to detect rogue IRC bot programs. Technical report, October 2004.
23. Petter Holme, Beom Jun Kim, Chang No Yoon, and Seung Kee Han. Attack vulnerability of complex networks. *Phys. Rev.*, E65(056109), 2002.
24. John Horrigan. Broadband adoption at home in the united states: Growing but slowing. http://web.si.umich.edu/tprc/papers/2005/501/TPRC%20Horrigan%20Broadband.2005b.pdf, 2005.
25. Manish Jain and Constantinos Dovrolis. End-to-end available bandwidth: Measurement. methodology, dynamics, and relation with tcp. In *Special Interest Group on Data Communication (SIGCOMM '02)*, 2002.
26. Xuxian Jiang, Dongyan Xu, Helen J. Wang, and Eugene H. Spafford. Virtual playgrounds for worm behavior investigation. Technical Report CERIAS Technical Report (2005-24), Purdue University, February 2005.
27. C. Kalt. Internet relay chat: Architecture. http://www.faqs.org/rfcs/rfc2810.html, 2000.
28. Anestis Karasaridis, Brian Rexroad, and David Hoeflin. Wide-scale botnet detection and characterization. In *USENIX Workshop on Hot Topics in Understanding Botnets (Hot-Bots'07)*, 2007.
29. Kevin Killourhy, Roy Maxion, and Kymie Tan. A defense-centric taxonomy based on attack manifestations. In *International Conference on Dependable Systems and Networks (ICDS'04)*, 2004.
30. Carl E. Landwehr, Alan R. Bull, John P. McDermott, and William S. Choi. A taxonomy of computer program security flaws, September 1994.
31. Ulf Lindqvist and Erland Jonsson. How to systematically classify computer security intrusions. In *Proceedings of the 1997 IEEE Symposium on Security and Privacy*, pages 154–163, 1997.
32. LURHQ. Zindos worm analysis. `http://www.lurhq.com/zindos.html`, 2004.
33. Qin Lv, Pei Cao, Edith Cohen, Kai Li, and Scott Shenker. Search and replication in unstructured peer-to-peer networks. In *ICS '02: Proceedings of the 16th international conference on Supercomputing*, pages 84–95, New York, NY, USA, 2002. ACM Press.
34. MaxMind LLC. Maxmind - ip geolocation and online fraud prevention. http://www.maxmind.com/, 2007.
35. Trend Micro. Taxonomy of botnet threats. Technical report, Trend Micro White Paper, November 2006.
36. S. Milgram. The small world problem. *Psychology Today*, 2(60), 1967.
37. D. Moore. Code-red: A case study on the spread and victims of an internet worm. http://www.icir.org/vern/imw-2002/imw2002-papers/209.ps.gz, 2002.
38. D. Moore, V. Paxson, S. Savage, C. Shannon, S. Staniford, and N. Weaver. Inside the slammer worm. *IEEE Magazine on Security and Privacy*, 1(4), July 2003.
39. D. Moore, C. Shannon, G. M. Voelker, and S. Savage. Internet quarantine: Requirements for containing self-propagating code. In *Proceedings of the IEEE INFOCOM 2003*, March 2003.
40. Shishir Nagarja and Ross Anderson. The topology of covert conflict. Technical Report UCAM-CL-TR-637, University of Cambridge, July 2005.
41. Jose Nazario. Botnet tracking: Tools, techniques, and lessons learned. In *Black Hat*, 2007.
42. M.E.J. Newman, S.H. Strogatz, and D.J. Watts. Random graphs with arbitrary degree distributions and their applications. *Phys. Rev.*, E64(026118), 2001.
43. Nielsen NetRatings. Average web usage. `http://www.nielsen-netratings.com/reports.jsp?section=pub_reports&repor%t=usage&period=weekly`, 2007.

44. Janak J Parekh. Columbia ids worminator project. http://worminator.cs.columbia.edu/, 2004.
45. L. Qin, C. Pei, E. Cohen, L. Kai, and S. Scott. Search and replication in unstructured peer-to-peer networks. In *16th ACM International Conference on Supercomputing*, 2002.
46. Moheeb Rajab, Jay Zarfoss, Fabian Monrose, and Andreas Terzis. A multifaceted approach to understanding the botnet phenomenon. In *Proceedings of the 6th ACM SIG-COMM on Internet Measurement (IMC)*, pages 41–52, 2006.
47. Moheeb Rajab, Jay Zarfoss, Fabian Monrose, and Andreas Terzis. My botnet is bigger than yours (maybe, better than yours): Why size estimates remain challenging. In *USENIX Workshop on Hot Topics in Understanding Botnets (HotBots'07)*, 2007.
48. S. Ratnasamy, P. Francis, M. Handley, R. Karp, and S. Shenker. A scalable content-addressable network. In *Proceedings of the ACM Conference of the Special Interest Group on Data Communication (SIGCOMM)*, pages 161–172, August 2001.
49. M. Ripeanu, I. Foster, and A. Iamnitchi. Mapping the gnutella network: Properties of large-scale peer-to-peer systems and implications for system design. *IEEE Internet Computing Journal*, 6(1), 2002.
50. Colleen Shannon and David Moore. The spread of the witty worm. *Security & Privacy Magazine*, 2(4):46–50, 2004.
51. Atul Singh, Tsuen-Wan Ngan, Peter Druschel, and Dan Wallach. Eclipse attacks on overlay networks: Threats and defenses. In *Proceedings of INFOCOM'06*, April 2006.
52. Ion Stoica, Robert Morris, David Karger, M. Frans Kaashoek, and Hari Balakrishnan. Chord: A scalable peer-to-peer lookup service for internet applications. In *Proceedings of the ACM SIGCOMM '01 Conference*, San Diego, California, August 2001.
53. Ryan Vogt and John Aycock. Attack of the 50 foot botnet. Technical report, Department of Computer Science, University of Calgary, August 2006.
54. Ryan Vogt, John Aycock, and Michael Jacobson. Army of botnets. In *Proceedings of NDSS'07*, 2007.
55. Ping Wang, Sherri Sparks, and Cliff C. Zou. An advanced hybrid peer-to-peer botnet. In *USENIX Workshop on Hot Topics in Understanding Botnets (HotBots'07)*, 2007.
56. D.J. Watts and S.H. Strogatz. *Nature*, 393(440), 1998.
57. N. Weaver, V. Paxson, S. Staniford, and R. Cunningham. A taxonomy of computer worms. In *2003 ACM Workshop on Rapid Malcode (WORM'03)*. ACM SIGSAC, October 2003.
58. Yinglian Xie, Hyang-Ah Kim, David R. O'Hallaron, Michael K. Reiter, and Hui Zhang. Seurat: A pointillist approach to network security, 2004.
59. Y. Zhang and V. Paxson. Detecting stepping stones. In *Proceedings of the 9th USENIX Security Symposium*, August 2000.
60. C. C. Zou, L. Gao, W. Gong, and D. Towsley. Monitoring and early warning for internet worms. In *Proceedings of 10th ACM Conference on Computer and Communications Security (CCS'03)*, October 2003.
61. C. C. Zou, W. Gong, and D. Towsley. Code red worm propagation modeling and analysis. In *Proceedings of 9th ACM Conference on Computer and Communications Security (CCS'02)*, October 2002.
62. C. C. Zou, W. Gong, and D. Towsley. Worm propagation modeling and analysis under dynamic quarantine defense. In *Proceedings of ACM CCS Workshop on Rapid Malcode (WORM'03)*, October 2003.
63. C.C. Zou, D. Towsley, W. Gong, and S. Cai. Routing worm: A fast, selective attack worm based on ip address information. Technical Report TR-03-CSE-06, Umass ECE Dept., November 2003.

64. Cliff Zou and Ryan Cunningham. Honeypot-aware advanced botnet construction and maintenance. In *International Conference on Dependable Systems and Networks (DSN)*, pages 199–208, June 2006.

Index

Printed in the United States of America

The Berenstain Bears
GET STAGE FRIGHT

Playbill

Most little bears like to play,
To show off, read aloud, and to sing.
But on a stage in the spotlight,
For some — the play's not the thing.

A FIRST TIME BOOK®

FRIGHT

Random House 🏠 New York

Published in the United States by Random House Children's Books,
a division of Random House, Inc., New York.
Random House and the colophon are registered trademarks of Random House, Inc.
First Time Books and the colophon are registered trademarks of Berenstain Enterprises, Inc.
randomhouse.com/kids
BerenstainBears.com
Library of Congress Cataloging-in-Publication Data
Berenstain, Stan. The Berenstain bears get stage fright. Summary: Sister Bear worries
about her lines in the school play while Brother Bear has no fear. Guess who forgets
the lines during the performance?
ISBN 978-0-394-87337-4 (trade) [1. Bears—Fiction. 2. Plays—Fiction.]
I. Berenstain, Jan. II. Title.
PZ7.B4483Beof 1986 [E] 85-25716
Printed in the United States of America
48 47 46 45 44 43 42 41 40

On the way to school one day Sister
Bear, Brother Bear, and Cousin Freddie
got to talking about an important
subject: their teachers.

"Teacher Bob is tough but fair,"
said Freddie, who was in the same class
as Brother.

Brother agreed. "How about your teacher?"
he asked Sister. "Is she easy or hard?"

"Teacher Jane isn't easy *or* hard,"
Sister said. "She's *good.*"

Then the bell rang and
the cubs were ready for
the school day.

The reason Sister thought Teacher Jane was good was that she made things interesting. When they were learning to add and subtract, Teacher Jane set up a pretend store with play money and a toy cash register. It helped the cubs learn, and it was fun.

When the class was studying words and ideas, they made posters. That helped them learn too.

And sometimes in reading class, instead of just reading from their books, they acted out the stories.

That's what they were doing with *Grizzlystiltskin*, the story of the funny old elf-bear who was sure that nobody could ever guess his name. Sister Bear was acting out the part of the miller's daughter who becomes a princess and has to spin straw into gold. They had come to the part where the princess has one last chance to guess the elf-bear's name:

"'Ah, good sir,'" read Sister in a loud, clear voice.

"'We've come to the end of our guessing game, because I say...*Grizzlystiltskin* is your name!'"

That's when Grizzlystiltskin flies into a rage and disappears in a puff of smoke—and the princess lives happily ever after.

"That was very good, class," said Teacher Jane. "So good, in fact, that I have a surprise for you. I'm in charge of the school play this year, and guess what—the play is going to be *Grizzlystiltskin*, and some of you will have parts in it!"

Then she gave out the parts. One of them had Sister's name on it. What fun! What excitement! Sister was going to be in the school play on the auditorium stage with scenery and costumes and makeup and everything!

It turned out that Brother and Freddie had gotten
parts too. Brother was going to be the woodsbear
who finds out the elf-bear's name, and Freddie was
going to play the part of Grizzlystiltskin himself.

"Who are you going to be?" Freddie asked Sister.

When Sister, who hadn't even thought to look,
turned to her part, it said THE PRINCESS.

"Wow!" said Brother and Freddie. "That's the main
part!"

"Well, how about that!" said Papa Bear when he heard the news. "My little princess is going to play the part of the princess! Say, we'd better tell Grizzly Gramps and Gran! And Uncle Willie and Aunt Min!"

"Calm yourself, dear!" said Mama, taking Papa aside. "Sister has a lot of work ahead of her and she doesn't need a lot of fuss and excitement."

"Hmm," said Papa. "You're absolutely right, my dear."

"Yeah, why all the fuss?" said
Brother. "It's just a dopey school
play. I already know my whole part...

      "'Hear me, oh, Princess!
I was deep in the forest
and this is what I heard:
The princess's firstborn
shall be mine!
If she had guesses
nine times nine,
she could not win
this guessing game,
'cause *Grizzlystiltskin*
is my name!'

   "See?" he said.
"Nothing to it!"

   But Sister wasn't so sure.
She was beginning to feel
a little nervous about the
whole thing.

The next day, when Teacher Jane asked Sister to take a message to the office, Sister decided to take a shortcut through the auditorium. She had been in the auditorium many times, of course, but she had never been on the stage. She climbed the steps and looked out over the rows of seats. It looked enormous.

Then she imagined all the seats filled with everybody in the school *and* Grizzly Gramps and Gran and Uncle Willie and Aunt Min. It looked even more enormous.

"Why the long face?" asked Brother on the way home from school. Sister told him she was worried about the play.

"Relax," he said. "There's nothing to it. It's a piece of cake.

"Why, I can do my part standing on my head...

HEAR ME, OH, PRINCESS...

"...hanging from a branch...

and from inside a hollow log!"

Cousin Freddie and the gang
thought Brother was pretty
funny. But Sister didn't
even smile.

That evening Sister's worries all came out.

"Reading a part in class just isn't the same as getting up in front of the whole school! And I have to learn it all by heart!" she wailed. "How am I ever going to do it?"

"The same way you learn anything else," said Mama. "Line by line, page by page. Papa and I will help you.

"Besides, you already know lots of things by heart—the alphabet, dozens of songs and rhymes, the Pledge of Allegiance. Why, I bet you know enough things by heart to fill a book.

"You already know the story. All you have to do is learn your part and practice."

That's what Sister did. She learned her part line by line, page by page.

And she practiced.

She practiced in her room in front of her toys.

OH, GOOD SIR...

She practiced in the field in front of her forest friends.

WE'VE COME TO THE END OF OUR GUESSING GAME...

She practiced in front
of Mama and Papa.

BECAUSE GRIZZLYSTILTSKIN
IS YOUR NAME !...

"That was wonderful, Sweetie!"
said Papa, applauding.
"Letter perfect!"

"Yes," sighed Sister, "but practicing in front
of my toys and forest friends and you and Mama
just isn't the same as getting up on the stage
in front of the whole school. How do I
practice for that?"

"Sweetie," said Mama, "there are some things
in life you can't practice—you've just got
to *do* them."

"But what if I get nervous and scared?" she asked.

"Oh, but you *will*," said Mama.

"I will?" she said.

"Of course!" said Mama. "Everybody gets nervous when they have to perform in front of an audience—even famous opera singers and star athletes. But if you know it's natural and you expect to be a little nervous, it won't really bother you that much—and you'll do yourself proud!

"And besides," she added, "you'll be
having a big rehearsal in the auditorium.
That'll help. Now, where's that brother
of yours? I've got to finish his costume.
I do wish he'd take this thing a little
more seriously."

"Don't worry about him, Mama," said
Sister. "He can do his part standing
on his head."

The rehearsal did help, but an empty
auditorium still wasn't the same as
a real live audience.

And now, at last, the moment had come! The curtain was opening on the Bear Country School's production of *Grizzlystiltskin*!

And there was Sister all alone on the
big stage looking out at the whole school
and Grizzly Gramps and Gran and Uncle
Willie and Aunt Min. It *was* a little
scary. But it was also very exciting.
Then she heard a loud, clear voice saying,
"I am the miller's daughter and woe is me,
for my father has told the king I can spin
straw into gold and, in truth, I cannot!"

It took her a split second
to realize that the voice
was *hers*!

From there on everything went beautifully. There was one little rough spot near the end when it was time for Brother to do his part. He came on stage in his handsome woodsbear costume, looked out at the hundreds of eyes staring at him...
and completely forgot what he was supposed to say!

"I can't remember my lines!" he whispered.

"Why don't you try standing on your head?" whispered Sister. But then she took pity on him and helped him with his lines.

The play ended magnificently
with Grizzlystiltskin flying into
a fury and disappearing in
a puff of smoke.

The applause was long
and loud.

After the show Mama and Papa came backstage.
"Terrific show!" said Papa. "Terrific!"
"Congratulations," said Mama, "on a job well done!"
"A piece of cake," said Princess Sister.